TRANSFORMING LEADERSHIP

Jesus' Way
of Creating Vision,
Shaping Values
& Empowering
Change

Leighton Ford

INTERVARSITY PRESS
DOWNERS GROVE, ILLINOIS 60515

©1991 by Leighton Ford

InterVarsity Press is the book-publishing division of Inter-Varsity Christian Fellowship, a student movement active on campus at hundreds of universities, colleges and schools of nursing in the United States of America, and a member movement of the International Fellowship of Evangelical Students. For information about local and regional activities, write Public Relations Dept., InterVarsity Christian Fellowship, 6400 Schroeder Rd., P.O. Box 7895, Madison, WI 53707-7895.

Published in England by Hodder & Stoughton under the title Jesus: The Transforming Leader.

ISBN 0-8308-1831-6
Printed in the United States of America ∞

Library of Congress Cataloging-in-Publication Data
Ford, Leighton.
    Transforming leadership: Jesus' way of creating vision, shaping
values, and empowering change/Leighton Ford.
        p.   cm.
    Includes bibliographical references.
    ISBN 0-8308-1831-6
    1. Christian leadership.   2. Jesus Christ—Person and offices.
    I. Title.
    BV652.1.F59   1991
253—dc20
                                                                            91-34428
                                                                            CIP

14	13	12	11	10	9	8	7	6	5	4	3	2	1
02	01	00	99	98	97	96	95	94	93	92	91		

*To Jack Dain, Billy Graham, and Tom Zimmerman,
from whom I have learned
so much about leadership in Christ,
and to the younger leaders
who will follow in His steps
and theirs.*

ACKNOWLEDGMENTS

I wish to thank my friend Michael Green, whom I have long admired, for inviting me to write this book, and encouraging me in the process, and being patient with the time constraints on my schedule.

Todd Hahn and Cindy Bunch graciously supplied some research material at certain points, and Dr. Scott Hafemann was kind enough to comment helpfully on some of the early chapters.

Jo Boynton typed and retyped the drafts of the manuscript with her usual skill and dedication. Leola Linkous, my longtime, tireless secretary, typed some of the early lectures and proofread the manuscript most helpfully.

My friends, Michael and Nancy Timmis, made their lovely home in Florida available at two different periods for my use while writing, which offered both needed quietness and the tempting distractions of the nearby ocean.

The staff of Leighton Ford Ministries have put up with my absences with patience and support. Those who are a part of our Numbers 11:17

prayer support group have lifted me up regularly in their prayers during the whole period of completing this manuscript. I wish especially to thank my friends and brothers who are also the board members of Leighton Ford Ministries for insisting that I take the time to do this kind of writing, and seeing it as part of our ministry.

I want to express the gratitude in my heart for the love and interest shown as always by my wife Jeanie, our daughter Debbie, our son-in-law Craig, and our son Kevin, in believing that this book has been an important piece of work, even while wondering why it has taken so long to complete!

FOREWORD

Jesus of Nazareth was the greatest leader in the history of the world. But there was something which set him apart from all other leaders. Charles Lamb put it well when chatting with a group of friends one night: "If Alexander the Great or Charlemagne or Napoleon were to come into the room, we would all stand up out of respect. If Jesus Christ walked in, we would fall on our faces in adoration." That is the difference.

But that is not the difference which this book is designed to explore. Dr. Leighton Ford is looking at Jesus from the point of view of what he shared with the very greatest leaders of mankind, and exemplified more than any of them. He wants to discover and to pass on to us some of the quintessential marks of leadership to be found in Jesus. For Jesus is not only our Lord but our example. And in leadership, as in all else, he is the supreme pattern for human life.

This was a very difficult book to write, and I know Leighton has toiled long and hard over it. But the key to its success, if he will forgive my saying so, is the author. It is no good asking someone who is not himself a dislinguished leader to write about Jesus the leader of humanity who can transform others into his mold. To write about Jesus the leader, you must yourself be an outstanding Christian leader. There are only a very few names in the world to whom one could turn for such a book, and Leighton was one of the foremost of them. He is well-known as Billy Graham's brother-in-law, well-known for his chairmanship of the Lausanne movement and his worldwide ministry as a preacher, and a much-sought-after speaker at large crusades.

It is not so widely known that he is an immensely warm and attractive human being, with no sniff of the platform presence about him as he engages in personal conversation, no suggestion of having all the answers. But he is every inch a leader—and he is a tall man! This man who, like his Master, has spoken to hundreds of thousands in the open air, is now, like his Master, training the next generation of evangelists, and he is doing it among the young, emerging Christian leadership worldwide.

Can you see why I was grateful that he wrote this book? You too will be grateful, as you get into it, and see the different aspects of leadership which Jesus modeled. Nobody in Christian leadership can afford to neglect the model of Jesus the leader. Many of the scandals in Christian leadership have occurred precisely because church leaders have not made Jesus their example in this matter. This book will concentrate the gaze unfalteringly on the greatest of all leaders, and I cannot believe that some of the charisma of that leadership will not rub off on the humble, open-minded reader who longs to be the best in the service of others.

Michael Green

PREFACE

When Michael Green suggested that I write this book, I felt very honored. Yet I was also hesitant. What a subject and what a topic he was asking me to tackle! To describe adequately the leadership of Jesus is certainly beyond anyone's grasp.

Nevertheless, I was most intrigued. After all, I have sought to follow Jesus Christ as my own Savior, Lord and Leader for many years. My life has also been deeply influenced by a number of leaders who follow Christ—like Billy Graham and Bishop A. Jack Dain, my predecessor as chairman of the Lausanne Committee, and the late Tom Zimmerman, for many years general superintendent of the Assemblies of God in the United States.

Further, I have gone through a major transition in my own life and ministry. After thirty-one years of being closely associated with my brother-in-law, Billy Graham, in the work of evangelism, I felt led several years ago to launch out into a new direction which, while continuing my preaching ministry, would concentrate on the development of younger leaders for Christ's global cause. In part this sprang from the death of our older son,

Sandy, at the age of twenty-one, a grievous loss which nevertheless gave me a strong desire to help other young men and women run their race for Christ. It came also from the need to return some of the encouragement which senior mentors offered me as a young man.

There was also a growing realization that the world is undergoing a major leadership shift (which I discuss in the opening chapters of this book) in which a generation of older leaders is close to retirement and a generation of younger leaders is now emerging. While this older generation has provided many excellent models of integrity and ability, it is also true that some of the younger generation have been disillusioned by the tragedies of failed leadership: political, business and religious leaders who have been seriously flawed. So a fresh look at the leadership qualities of Jesus seemed very timely.

On a broader scale the need for a new kind of leadership—often called transformational leadership—seems critical for two fundamental reasons.

The first is the enormous acceleration of change in our so-called post-modern world. Until roughly a century ago civilization in its many aspects grew at a relatively modest and steady pace, and whole cultures remained at a fairly primitive level. But in our lifetime everything has speeded up. Within the century we have gone from the horse and buggy to spacecraft, from the printing press to computers that rival the human brain in their capacity, from a largely rural world to a largely urban world, from growing populations to populations growing exponentially, from a world centered on the nuclear family to a world haunted by the nuclear bomb.

Yet, as the irresistible flow of change and information engulfs us, a sense of direction eludes us. The Eastern European philosopher Michael Polanyi has pointed out in his most famous book, *Personal Knowledge* (Chicago: Univ. of Chicago Press, 1974), that since the Enlightenment doubt has been elevated over dogma as the fundamental principle of life. Quite properly, scientists have learned to call into question that which cannot be reasonably investigated and confirmed. The results have been unmistakably positive in many areas. Even the stoutest critic of modern trends would hardly want to roll back the achievements of modern medicine—especially if that critic has clogged arteries and may need heart by-pass surgery! Nevertheless,

Polanyi contends that in elevating doubt, we have created a skepticism that may well undo us. The rocket of our modern progress, says Polanyi, has been fueled by a sense of purpose inherited from Christian sources and the power of reason emerging from Greek thought. Yet "progress" itself has consumed and exhausted the fuel which empowered it!

One might compare postmodern civilization to a gigantic spacecraft, thrust into orbit by twin rockets—faith in divine providence and confidence in intelligent order. Yet the blast of lift-off has exhausted the fuel of the booster rockets and destroyed the guidance system. The result is that we hurtle at incredible speed into the future while lacking instruments that can track our course and tell us where we have been, where we are, or where we are going.

Such a situation calls for more than competence. We need commanders for spaceship earth who can not only keep the atmosphere of the spaceship livable, but, more urgently, can also bring to the crew the belief that there is a future and a hope—a star to steer by.

At such a time it may seem futile or downright naive to point to the leadership of Jesus as a model, except in the most sentimental or narrowly religious sense. Can we possibly believe that the one who led ancient Galilean fishermen can be relevant to modern astronauts or cosmonauts, or to those who send them on their journeys into space?

It is my deep conviction that the understanding of Jesus' leadership is not only important, but essential to our time. He was able to create, articulate and communicate a compelling vision; to change what people talk about and dream of; to make his followers transcend self-interest; to enable us to see ourselves and our world in a new way; to provide prophetic insight into the very heart of things; and to bring about the highest order of change. Because of the great paradigm shifts which our world is undergoing at the end of a millennium, we need both a supreme model and the source which Jesus provides for transforming leaders—leaders who can enable us to see beyond our narrow and often selfish horizons, who can empower us to be more than we have been. Transforming leaders are those who are able to divest themselves of their power and invest it in their followers in such a way that others are empowered, while the leaders themselves end with the greatest power of all, the power of seeing themselves reproduced in others.

Is this not something parents desire in healthy human families? There can be a morbid and unhealthy drive to have our children compensate for our own failures. But parents who, for all their imperfections, have a strong sense of their own selfhood, and who implant their own best values and dreams in their children without stunting their children's individuality, then have the joy of seeing their dreams outgrow themselves in their children.

If we can take such healthy pride in our children, then how much more does our heavenly Father? This kind of leadership is Godlike. When God created, the high point of his work was the appearance on the scene of human beings made in his image. Jesus, the exact representation of God's being (so the writer of the letter to the Hebrews says), was sent by the Father into the world that he might bring many sons and daughters to show forth God's glory (Heb 1:3; 2:10). True faith and devotion, according to Jesus, lies not merely in following certain prescribed rules, but in being Godlike. "I tell you: Love your enemies and pray for those who persecute you, that you may be sons of your Father in heaven. . . . Be perfect, therefore, as your heavenly Father is perfect" (Mt 5:44, 48). As Paul put it, the followers of Christ are like people who with unveiled faces reflect the Lord's glory and are being "transformed into his likeness" (2 Cor 3:18). Godlike leadership follows this pattern: the divesting of one's power (that is, putting it aside for a while as Jesus did when he took on human form and veiled his glory in the flesh), in order to invest it in others, so that the end result is the returning of that glory and power to the author.

If Jesus' venture in leadership was to invest and reproduce himself (and his Father) in those he chose at that time, then his leadership is more than a historical curiosity. It is an ongoing reality. It is his continuing reproduction of himself in human beings in every generation until the consummation of all history. He is fully as able to live out his life again in the crew of spaceship earth, hurtling toward the twenty-first century, as he was able to put himself into a band of first-century fishermen, to become their companion and ride out the night storms with them in their little boat on the lake of Galilee.

With this conviction I have entered into this study. While I am neither a biblical scholar nor a leadership theorist, I have sought, using material from the Gospels, to provide a credible portrait of Jesus as a leader, and to interact at a number of points with certain aspects of transformational leadership as put forward by the specialists. I have tried to illustrate and apply this in a way which will be of interest not only to full-time religious workers, but also to informed lay people, to women as well as men, and to people in many different areas of leadership responsibility. It would give me great joy if there were those not yet believers or followers of Jesus who might read this book and be brought to recognize Jesus Christ not only as the Supreme Leader, but as their own personal Lord and Savior.

I myself have been humbled, challenged and inspired in the preparation and writing of this book. I understand more profoundly than ever why the early Christians believed that Jesus was the fulfillment of Isaiah's prophecy that one would come, greater than David, who would be "a leader and commander of the peoples" (Is 55:4). I can see why Paul, himself no mean leader, could write: "I consider everything a loss compared to the surpassing greatness of knowing Christ Jesus my Lord" (Phil 3:1). I wish to dedicate myself in a new way to Jesus as Savior and Sovereign, in the hope that others who read this book will themselves be led to explore even further the unsearchable riches of Jesus, the transforming leader.

1

LEADERSHIP: WHY NOW?

•

*T*wenty-five hundred years ago the philosopher Aristotle wrote these words:

> Young men have strong passions. . . . They would rather do noble deeds than useful ones. . . . They think they know everything and are always quite sure about it; this, in fact, is why they overdo everything.
>
> [Old men] have lived many years: They often have been taken in. . . . The result is that they are sure about nothing and *under-do* everything. They "think" but they never "know." . . . They always add "possibly" or a "perhaps." . . . They guide their lives too much by considerations of what is useful and too little by what is noble. . . . They lack confidence in the future . . . for most things go wrong, or anyway worse than one expects.[1]

Citing the philosopher's words, a commentator on contemporary students writes: "Like Aristotle's *old men—not* his young men—'today's students live in a time when dreams and heroes have died.' "[2]

Whether or not the dreams and heroes have all died, it is clear that our world is going through both a tremendous *leadership challenge* and a major *leadership transition.*

Early this century the missionary statesman and student leader John R. Mott published his book *The Future Leadership of the Church,* based on hundreds of interviews he had held around the world. He called for spiritual leaders who should "have a message and be conscious of a mission," who should be able "effectively to express their passion for Christ and people," and who above all should be "great in character."[3]

As we face the final years of the twentieth century, the challenge of developing future leaders is an even greater one.

A Changing World

The emerging younger leaders face a world going through vast shifts.

About a billion minutes have passed since Jesus walked the earth; in the next twelve years, one and a half billion babies will be born. The world population will be not only larger but will be tilted toward the Pacific rim, with 60 per cent of the world's population living within two thousand miles of Singapore. It will also be an urban world, with some twenty-two mega-cities of ten million plus by the year 2000. It will become both an older and a younger world. In the first quarter of the twenty-first century there will be a billion people over sixty. And yet, 60 per cent of the world's population is now under twenty-four. Mexico City alone has a population under fourteen years of age that is equal to the total population of New York City!

We can expect it to be a world of continuing conflict between ideologies, races and classes. Fifty per cent of the world's scientific minds, it is estimated, are now engaged in so-called defense activities. The possibility of a nuclear terrorist incident by the end of this century is far from improbable.

Paradoxically, as conflict divides our world, communication is drawing it closer because of the information implosion. The information era is tending to divide people between the "know and know-nots" and not just the "have and have-nots." A text the size of the *Encyclopedia Britannica* can be flashed across the ocean six times a minute. One major corporation has a system which links nineteen countries and sends out a hundred thousand messages a day at a cost of eight cents each and at an average time lapse of ten seconds. Yet, as Jean Pierre Dupuy, an information specialist, has said somewhere: "The more we 'communicate' the way we do, the more we create a hellish world." Ours is a world about which we pretend to have more and more information, yet one that is increasingly void of meaning.

Because of meaninglessness, loneliness and isolation, ours is also a world of religious searching. Despite secular lifestyles and the various nonreligious philosophies which have attracted large parts of today's postindustrial society, religious movements are growing—Islam's adherents are increasing at the rate of 16 per cent a year, Hinduism's at 13 per cent, Buddhism's at 10 per cent and Christianity's at 9 per cent. The followers of Christ are growing more rapidly than at any time in history, particularly in Africa, Latin America and parts of Asia. In the 1980s, for the first time in two thousand years, there were in Asia, Africa and Latin America more who claimed to follow Christ than in the West. Yet it must be noted that the surge of Christianity has not kept pace with the worldwide population increase, and its growth has been uneven, particularly in urban settings.

Ours is also a world hungry for hope; yet, curiously, it is increasingly bleak, if not cynical. After a television interview in Australia I was talking about nuclear war to the young woman who was taking off my make-up. I told her I had been to Hiroshima, had seen the devastation of the atomic bomb dropped there, and had prayed, "God, don't let this happen again." She shrugged her shoulders and said nonchalantly, "Oh, it will." Living for today, she believed that tomorrow might never come. I wanted to take her by the shoulders and look her in the eyes and say, "Don't say that. There is hope. We can make a difference."

A Leadership Vacuum?

No wonder, then, that there is today a widespread call not just for leadership, but for a new kind of leadership—a transformational leadership, if you will.

For half a century leadership studies have focused on leadership as an "exchange process," a transactional relationship which promises rewards to followers in exchange for performance.

Now leadership theorists are saying that leadership as a transaction must give way to a higher order of change—to leading-edge leadership. James

21

McGregor Burns, the leadership scholar, was perhaps the first to speak in terms of transformational leaders.[4]

Bernard Bass characterizes transformational leadership as that kind of motivation which raises the consciousness of people about what they want.[5] Exchange theories, he believes, fail to account for the symbolic and almost mystical leadership of a Pope John Paul in religion, a Charles De Gaulle in politics, or a Lee Iacocca in the automobile industry.

Transactional leaders, says Bass, work within the situation; transformational leaders *change* the situation.

Transactional leaders accept what can be talked about; transformational leaders *change* what can be talked about.

Transactional leaders accept the rules and values; transformational leaders *change* them.

Transactional leaders talk about payoffs; transformational leaders talk about *goals*.

Transactional leaders bargain; transformational leaders *symbolize*.

In short, says Bass, the transformational leader motivates us to do more than we expected to do, by raising our awareness of different values, by getting us to transcend our self-interests for the cause and by expanding our portfolio of needs and wants.

Transformational leadership is, however, a double-edged sword. When we look for leaders who can transform, we need to be aware that people can be transformed *down* in destructive ways as well as *up* to lift their level of achievement. Mother Teresa is a transformational leader, elevating the aspirations of people. So was Jim Jones, only he led nine hundred followers into a downward spiral, a blind obedience which ended in a mass suicide at a jungle camp in Guyana. The same dynamics which can lead people to better things can also be used by leaders in ways that bring great social disorder, as the historian Barbara Tuchman has shown so vividly in *The March of Folly.*

Where Are the Leaders?
But where are our transformational leaders today? And if they are not here, where are they coming from?

22

Looking at the American scene, John Gardner in his Leadership Papers has pointed out that at the time the United States was formed it had a population of around three million. Out of that emerged perhaps six world-class leaders—Washington, Adams, Jefferson, Franklin, Madison and Hamilton. Today, with a population of around 240 million, the U.S.A. might expect to have eighty times as many world-class leaders. But, he asks, where are they?[6]

There seems to be an adequate supply of leaders aged over fifty-five, with many emerging under forty, but there are not so many in between. Ray Bakke, a specialist in urban trends, has pointed out (in personal conversation) that in many of the world's largest cities there is a gap in leadership in the Christian church, a gap roughly between the ages of forty and fifty-five. When I asked an Australian church leader to name those who might become the future bishops in his diocese, he paused and said, "I can think of several under forty, but no one over that age." After I pointed out this phenomenon to a gathering of business leaders, one of them said, "That's interesting. When I look at potential future presidents in my company, everyone that comes to mind is under forty."

If there is a gap in the line of leaders, what are some of the causes?

Part of the reason may simply be a cycle covering four generations. Leadership specialist James Crupi notes that we are now in a transition between a generation of leaders that emerged after the Second World War—people now in their sixties and seventies—and a third generation of leaders who are in their thirties and forties. A second postwar generation of those largely in their fifties has almost been passed over, creating a partial leadership vacuum.

How did this happen? The *first-generation* leaders who emerged after the Second World War were movers and shakers, people of large dreams who exhibited strong and forceful leadership. On the business scene they built the great corporations. On the religious scene they pioneered organizations like the Billy Graham Association, Campus Crusade and World Vision.

The *second generation,* those now in their fifties, were born during the Great Depression and grew up during the conservative years after the Second World War. The older leaders did not give them many opportunities for leadership, and the second-generation leaders were by and large not prepared to take risks and be adventurous. So they tended to become the managers of their elders' visions. Perhaps some of the first-generation leaders saw the second-generation leaders as unwelcome competitors and consequently did not set out to develop them. An Indian proverb says, "Nothing grows under a banyan tree." Often the shadow of these strong leaders was so large that the little seedlings were not nurtured under them.

Today a *third generation* is moving into leadership. Born in the 1940s and 1950s, they are part of the newer world, the first truly postmodern generation. They want to lead, are tired of waiting, and are willing to take risks. Having grown up in the television age, they are information-oriented and more concerned with people than with products. As James Crupi of Leadership Concepts has said, "They understand they will be leading in a post-industrial global society where information is the new wealth and people are the new products." Often cut off from traditional family, community and spiritual roots, they are, says Crupi, "absorbed with a search for values."

A *fourth generation* is also on the way, those who are presently in their twenties, some of whom are still in college and university. The question arises: Will the same fate befall this *fourth* generation as did the *second*? Will they be overlooked? Undernurtured? Underprepared for leadership?

According to John W. Gardner a number of other factors may also have contributed to the leadership vacuum.

Large and complex organizations can inhibit the development of leaders. Impersonal societies can create a sense of powerlessness. Overspecialized training can drain off the potential leaders. An "antileadership vaccine" may persuade young people that society needs experts, not leaders. The contemporary skepticism toward authority and the withering criticism heaped on public figures, compounded by the well-publicized moral and ethical failings of some well-known personalities—religious, corporate and political—could all combine to choke off the kind of leadership that is called for in the closing years of this century.[7]

However, it often takes a crisis to produce great leaders. As Abigail Adams wrote in a letter to Thomas Jefferson in 1790, "Great necessities call forth great leaders." Perhaps the creeping crises of our world will yet produce a new wave of leadership.

What Is Leadership?

"I would follow him." We had just finished interviewing a candidate for a major post, and as we left a colleague made that comment. My mind flashed back to a time a few years earlier, when another friend made almost exactly the same comment about the same individual. "I was willing to direct that project," he said, "because he was going to be the chairman, and I knew I could count on him to lead."

Why are we prepared to follow certain people? What is it that makes them leaders?

Early studies of leadership and what makes a good leader began by examining qualities of the so-called great men, and then moved on to consider leadership "traits." After many years the researchers in effect threw up their hands and said they could not satisfactorily define the traits that make one person rather than another a leader. Their attention then focused on the situations in which leaders operate and on the question, What do people called leaders do to change those situations?

Two factors began to emerge. First, leaders *take the lead*. That is, they initiate ideas and plans. Second, leaders *move people to follow them* by showing them consideration!

It also became clear that different leaders behave in different ways, that there is no one set style of leading, that leadership is contingent on circumstances, and that what works in one situation may not work in another.

Much thought has also gone into considering the kind of leadership that results from occupying certain positions. Most leadership is exercised from day to day by virtue of the position one holds in a school, an organization, a family or a church: Position provides power.

Eventually, coming full circle, leadership theorists have returned to the study of the qualities that characterize leaders. Current thinking, however, is not simply a recycling of the old view that "leaders are born, not made." Rather, it seeks to understand what makes a leader effective in a given situation. If a leader is a person who helps followers to change, to move from where they are to where they should be or where they want to be, how does that happen?

At the risk of being thought overly simplistic, one can say, therefore, that a consideration of leadership must pay attention to the position which the leader holds, the person that the leader is, and the process which the leader employs.

Empowering Leadership

One of the most fascinating recent leadership studies has been done by Warren Benniss of the University of Southern California. In his book *Leaders: The Strategies for Taking Charge,* which he coauthored with Burt Nanus, he describes a style of "empowering" leadership.[8] Benniss interviewed ninety leaders who had outstanding records in the fields of education, business, government, sports or the arts. He tried to get them to identify their strategies for taking charge. Four common elements emerged: vision, communication, trust and empowerment.

These leaders get *attention through vision.* Benniss describes vision as "the commodity of leaders." Managers are people who concentrate on *doing things right,* but leaders are concerned to *do the right things.* They catch their followers' attention by the vision they cast. They also bring *meaning through communication,* although their communication styles may be very different. Bill Moog, a manufacturer who trained as an engineer, is not very verbal, but he gets his thoughts across to his staff by the models he draws. Ronald Reagan, a great verbal communicator, uses word pictures, for example, enabling people to see a stack of one trillion dollar bills by comparing it to the height of the Empire State Building.

Trust through taking a clear, committed stance is another key strategy, for trust is the lubrication that helps relationships and organizations work smoothly. "Leadership is heading into the wind . . . to move others to wish to follow," says Theodore Friend III, past president of Swarthmore College. "The angle into the wind is less important than choosing one and sticking reasonably to it."[9] Believability over the long haul is vital.

And, finally, says Benniss, these leaders know how to *deploy themselves through a positive self-regard.* Here he is speaking not of narcissism or self-centeredness, but of leaders who know their worth, their strengths and weaknesses, where they fit and where they don't. Because of this inner security they are able to free others to give their best.

The Ultimate Leader

I happened to have Benniss' book beside me as I ate breakfast at a hotel in Australia. A young bearded man carrying a guitar, obviously some kind of entertainer, sat down beside me. Curious, he asked about the book I was reading. I asked him what qualities he thought made a good leader.

After a moment's thought he ticked off three—"Patience, determination and faith."

His was an interesting answer, so I pursued it further. "Who do you think is the greatest leader?" I asked.

Without a moment's hesitation he answered, "I would say Jesus."

Later I thought of his answer in terms of Benniss' key strategies. Who had greater visions than Jesus? Who knew better how to communicate with his followers through everyday stories? Who was more trustworthy, credibly positioned and believable than Jesus in carrying through his mission? And who has ever been able to empower others more than he, through his own wonderful self-knowledge and the total positive giving of himself?

2

JESUS AND LEADERSHIP

•

*N*ot long ago a friend of mine was invited to serve as the chairman of a large national conference of younger leaders. My friend was in his thirties, and he had already established an impressive track record as a youth worker and an effective executive in a large Christian organization. He also happens to be Black, and etched into his soul and bones are the memories of all the struggles and pain that came from growing up in a low-income, urban Black family.

When he was asked to take on the job as chairman of such a significant and highly visible event, he was very moved. He said that he was honored, but that he needed some time to make his decision.

He was one of the first younger Black leaders asked to take a national leadership role. As such, he knew he would be very vulnerable to criticism if he failed. So before he gave his answer he took the train home to have time to think and pray.

"I wept on that train ride," he told me later. "I searched my heart. I felt deeply my responsibility and inadequacy. I really was afraid I wouldn't measure up. The scars of being made to feel inferior from the past caught up with me and I almost decided I couldn't do it."

After hours of struggle he decided to say yes to the challenge, and gave outstanding leadership. But that same struggle he went through, the feeling of inadequacy, is almost always present in the woman or man who is asked to move into a position of key leadership. As with Moses, when asked to lead ancient Israel out of Egypt, the heart cry comes, "Why me, God?"

Jesus the Model Leader?

Given our all-too-human feelings of inadequacy, in what sense can Jesus be taken as our leadership model? If he is unique, if he is the Son of God, does that not put him in a category light years beyond us? And what relevance can a leader like that have for us? How can the leadership of Jesus be good news for us? If _we_ are not what _he_ is, then is his leadership model not a model of despair?

Several lines of thought can carry us beyond this dilemma.

First, though fully divine, Jesus was also truly human. He was not 99 per cent God and 1 per cent man, but fully both. As the writer of Hebrews put it, "Since the children have flesh and blood, he too shared in their humanity" (Heb 2:14). His was a genuinely human existence, but it was human nature restored to what it was originally meant to be.

Second, Jesus plainly said his model is for us. When toward the end of his ministry he washed the grimy feet of his disciples, he said to them, "Now that I, your Lord and Teacher, have washed your feet, you also should wash one another's feet. I have set you an example that you should do as I have done for you" (Jn 13:14-15). Of course, he is far more than our example, but he is no less than that.

Third, the kingdom which he proclaimed and embodied is for now as well as for the future. He himself said that the kingdom had drawn near (Mk 1:15). Once, when being asked when the kingdom of God would come, he replied, "The kingdom of God does not come with your careful observation, nor [when] people say, 'Here it is,' or 'There it is,' because the kingdom of God is within [or among] you" (Lk 17:20-21).

Fourth, Jesus has clearly influenced leadership in a very practical way. Mahatma Gandhi, the Indian civil rights leader, though not a believer in

Jesus, nevertheless admired and modeled himself on Jesus in many ways. One of the highest compliments that can be paid to someone in India, even to a Hindu, is to say, "That is a Christlike person."

Fifth, Jesus' leadership was both culturally relevant to his time (he was born and brought up in a Jewish home under Roman occupation in Palestine) and transcultural (all authority, in heaven and on earth, being given to him). So to follow him we need be neither literalists (assuming that we too, for example, must make our living as carpenters) nor idealists (making Jesus into a larger-than-life figure above this world).

Sixth, Jesus' leadership was not *value-neutral,* a set of tools to be used for any cause at all. Rather his leadership was kingdom leadership, value-driven, as we will see later. Jesus' leadership is not a "how-to" program for achieving secular goals; it is uniquely a leadership related to the dynamic of God's purposes.

Seventh, the knowledge that Jesus is a perfect leader may keep us from holding unrealistic expectations of ourselves and others. Some years ago I asked a friendly Christian psychologist to help me see whether I might fit a position that I had been offered. One of the things he deduced was that I tended to have unrealistic expectations concerning those in positions of leadership. In my early years as an adopted child I did not have a strong father-figure to look up to. Reacting to that, I had formed a picture of anyone in leadership as having to be almost superhuman. As a result, I tended to be disappointed in the leadership of others and to shrink back from responsibility myself. The unrealistic expectations that we place on ourselves or others can paralyze us. But the reality which is in Christ is a far different model. It not only challenges our pretensions, but also frees us to see ourselves as God intends and wills us to be. His is the model not only of the great example but also of the great enabler. When I have false ideas of my strength, Jesus Christ exposes my incompetence. When I feel totally beyond my depth, he provides for me God's enabling power.

Eighth, Jesus gave his followers responsibilities, but he also promised them the gift and leadership of his Holy Spirit. Meeting with them privately after his resurrection, he said: "As the Father has sent me, I am sending you." Then he breathed on them and said, "Receive the Holy Spirit" (Jn

20:21-22). That bit of prophetic drama was fulfilled some days later when the promised Spirit was given to the leaders of the early church on the day of Pentecost (Acts 2:1-4). As Peter explained, Jesus had been exalted to God's presence and had "received from the Father the promised Holy Spirit and has poured out what you now see and hear" (Acts 2:33). The leadership of Jesus was to be continued by the leadership of his Holy Spirit. The Spirit was to give special gifts of leadership to chosen people who would carry out God's purposes. As Paul later put it, having ascended to heaven, Jesus "gave gifts to men . . . some to be apostles, some to be prophets, some to be evangelists, some to be pastors and teachers, to prepare God's people for works of service" (Eph 4:8, 11-12).

So the study of Jesus does not provide us with a "how-to" recipe—"How to be a leader like Jesus." Rather, we learn that Jesus in us continues to lead through us: "Those who are led by the Spirit of God are sons of God" (Rom 8:14).

Perhaps it is clearer why the presentation of Jesus the leader is good news. Here is a leader who is one with us; in Jesus, God has totally identified himself with us. A chaplain who went through the Second World War invasion of Normandy told me: "Before the invasion, the men respected me. After I had been with them on the beaches, I was one with them." Jesus "hit the beaches" with his people. He did not recruit angels to be his leaders, but flesh-and-blood humans who would take this world as a theater in which to show forth his power. He planned to build a new world through transformed sinners, so at his baptism he chose to be one with sinners and to offer them forgiveness and sonship with the Father. He wanted leaders who would lead from the experience of real-life testings, so he himself was tested. He wanted men and women whose hearts would be set on serving God, so he came as a servant who trembled at God's word.

This total identification was at the heart of Jesus' leadership style, as it must be at the heart of all who will lead in Christ.

The most spectacular cross-cultural leadership in the history of humanity took place when the Son of God became a first-century Galilean Jew. In that identification he renounced the status and the rights that he enjoyed as God's Son. Among them, Jesus gave up any right to independence; he was born in a borrowed manger, preached from a borrowed boat, entered Jerusalem on a borrowed donkey, ate the Last Supper in a borrowed upper room, died on a borrowed cross and was buried in a borrowed tomb. In renouncing entitlement he exposed himself to temptation, sorrow, limitation and pain, and yet, "although Jesus identified himself completely with us, he did not lose his own identity. He remained himself." And so his incarnation taught "identification without loss of identity."[1]

What Does This Mean for Our Leadership?

In Christ we find the answers to two great ego problems of leadership. The first is fear, the sense of inadequacy, "I'm not good enough or strong enough to be a leader!" Sinful pride can make us shrink back from responsibility.

The second and opposite temptation is the power-hungry self wanting to lord it over others. Sinful pride can, in fact, make us want to be puffed up and to exalt ourselves.

All of us may be driven to minister from a variety of motives, including the deep longings and disappointments of our own ego needs. The antidote is to realize more and more fully what it means to be in Christ.

In Christ we too can be sons and daughters, accepted by God's beloved Son despite our imperfections and inadequacies. In the first chapter of his letter to the Ephesians Paul piles phrase upon phrase to remind us that we are blessed with every spiritual blessing in Christ, chosen in Christ, redeemed in Christ, sealed in Christ (Eph 1:3-14). Those who hear the word of truth, the gospel of salvation, are accepted by Christ's Father (Eph 1:5) and included among Christ's people (Eph 1:13). If all that is true, then whatever fears and inadequacies we have, what more do we need? What more could we ask?

Several years ago Dr. Richard Halverson left his long-term pastorate at the Fourth Presbyterian Church in Bethesda, Maryland, to become chaplain of the United States Senate. In a talk I heard him give he described his first day at the powerful institution: "I felt like a non-person, a mascot to one of the most powerful political bodies in the world. I wondered what I was doing there." That evening he read the words of Jesus: "All authority in heaven and on earth has been given to me. . . . And surely I am with you

33

always" (Mt 28:18-20). As he meditated on those words he realized, "I am a garment which Jesus Christ wears every day to do what he wants to do in the United States Senate. I don't need power; my weakness is an asset. If Christ is in me, what more do I need?"

But in Christ we are servants too. Paul sets out this paradox of privilege and responsibility: "All things are yours, whether . . . the world or life or death or the present or the future—all are yours, and you are of Christ, and Christ is of God" (1 Cor 3:21-23). But the conclusion he draws is not that we should feel entitled, but that "men ought to regard us as servants of Christ and as those entrusted with the . . . things of God" (1 Cor 4:1).

For this reason we cannot simply baptize secular leadership models and import them into our work for Christ without subjecting them to critical examination. When the pagan Goth soldiers of Europe went through a form of conversion, it was reported that those who were baptized lifted up their swords to keep them out of the water! They wanted the benefits of Christ's name without the demands of Christ's kingdom.

In *Kingdoms in Conflict,* Charles Colson has given a powerful dramatic presentation of the roots of the Second World War in Germany. German youth responded to Hitler's so-called leadership principle, the idea of a Führer who would bring purpose and unity back to their nation. He imagines the Confessing Church pastor Dietrich Bonhoeffer talking to a young official of a German broadcasting company just before a scheduled speech. The young man excitedly welcomes Bonhoeffer's announced topic— the younger generation's concept of a leader—and says they are inspired by the chord Hitler has struck in their hearts, a leader who will transform the nation.

In his talk Bonhoeffer says he knows the powerful attraction of the leadership principle to young Germans who knew only chaos as they grew up. It seems he is embracing the Führer concept. Then at the end he warns: "Should the leader allow self to succumb to the wishes of those he leads, who will also seek to turn him into an idol, then the leader will gradually become the 'mis-leader.' . . . This is the leader who makes an idol of himself and his office, thus mocking God."

At the end of the talk the young broadcaster hurries over to explain that it has run overtime, and that, of course, Dr. Bonhoeffer will understand that the director had to cut off those last sentences of his address.[2]

But those sentences are the very ones that are most relevant to us today in every area of life. For we can trust ourselves as leaders only after we have stood with Jesus to hear God's word, to worship him and to await his time.

3

THE LEADER
AS SON

●

Jesus knew who he was—
he had a quiet sense of confidence
that grew from his relationship
with his Father.

●

"He was made what we are
that he might make us what he is himself."
IRENAEUS

"Whatever the Father does the Son also does."
JESUS CHRIST

"Those who are led by the Spirit of God are sons of God."
PAUL

Calling

*G*enuine leaders operate out of a sense of calling, not a sense of driven-
ness. The writer George MacDonald has said somewhere that real Christian
leaders are people who are moved at God's pace and in God's time to God's
place, not because they fancy themselves there, but because they are drawn.
The strongest leaders are those who have received a strong affirmation of
their personhood, in a way which frees them not only to lead a cause but
also to serve others. A sense of identity, a security that comes from knowing
who one is, lies at the very heart of leadership.

Leadership is first of all not something one does but something one is. This comes out clearly in the story of Jesus when his Father affirms him as his special son (Mt 3:17; Mk 1:11; Lk 3:22). Jesus operated out of a sense of quiet confidence that came from knowing who he was in his everlasting relationship with his Father.

The first act in God's affirmation of Jesus' leadership was the arrival on the scene of his cousin. John came calling the people to turn from their evil and sin and to begin living God's way. As a sign of cleansing, he urged them to be baptized in the Jordan River, so he was called John the Baptist. He was sent to "prepare the way for the Lord," a direct quotation from the prophecy about God's servant in Isaiah 40. John's message was about one who was yet to come, who would be far more powerful than he, "the thongs of whose sandals I am not worthy to stoop down and untie." He contrasted his own effectiveness with that of the new leader. "I baptize you with water," that is, with an outward symbol. "But he will baptize you with the Holy Spirit," that is, with an inner change of heart (Mk 1:2-8).

When Jesus came from Nazareth he asked John to baptize him in the Jordan. As he was coming up out of the water, "he saw heaven being torn open and the Spirit descending on him" in the form of a dove. A voice came from heaven: "You are my Son, whom I love; with you I am well pleased" (Mk 1:11).

So far as the record shows, only Jesus and John saw the dove and heard the voice. The onlookers may have sensed that something deep and mysterious was happening as this young man went under the waters and came out looking up to heaven with his ear cocked as if he were hearing another voice.

Like the patriarchs and prophets in the old days, he was hearing a call. Yet Jesus' call was completely different because it was the affirmation of a special intimacy and identity with God. He and his Father were one—one in nature, in love and in purpose.

"The sonship of Jesus," it has been said, "is not something which he achieved through his mission; rather it is itself the very basis of the mission. It is as the Son that Jesus proclaimed the Kingdom."[1]

Over and over again, the Gospels repeat this theme of Jesus' sonship. It is a key thought throughout Mark's account. Later there came a crucial point when his disciples confessed that he was God's chosen Messiah. After that he led three of them—Peter, James and John—to a mountaintop where a cloud appeared. A voice then repeated almost exactly the words spoken at his baptism: "This is my Son, whom I love. Listen to him!" (Mk 9:7). Even a centurion standing at the cross heard Jesus' final death cry and exclaimed, "Surely this man was the Son of God!" (Mk 15:39).

What others discovered later, Jesus heard deep in his soul at his baptism in the muddy waters of the Jordan.

What did that vision and that voice mean to Jesus? We know from other parts of Scripture that Jesus was the pre-existent Son of God. That is, he did not *become* God's Son when he was born on earth; he was his Son from all eternity. On one occasion Jesus said, "Before Abraham was born, I am!" (Jn 8:58). And Psalm 2 gives us a hint of the divine dialog that might have taken place in eternity when the Father said, "You are my Son" (Ps 2:7). But now on earth, at a specific time and place in the warm waters by the muddy banks of the Jordan, Jesus hears again what he heard long before in eternity, "You are my Son, whom I love; with you I am well pleased" (Mk 1:11).

The Gospel accounts make it clear that at his baptism Jesus did not suddenly realize that he was God's Son. Luke tells the story of how, as a boy, Jesus enthralled the teachers in the temple, and how, when his parents found him, he talked about his "Father's house" (Lk 2:41-50).

Throughout the years leading to his baptism, there had no doubt been "a deepening appreciation of his own filial responsibility, of growing insight into his mission and the world's need, of meditation on the meaning of the scriptures and their application to himself."[2] And now, at the Jordan, he hears his Father's voice, "You are my Son. . . ." What pictures might have been in his mind?

It happens that I am involved in three father/son relationships: one by natural birth, one by adoption, one by spiritual relationship. Suppose I introduced you to someone saying, "I would like you to meet my father." Would you gather that I was introducing you to my natural father? My adopted father? Or my heavenly Father? You would need to know the context of my words and the pictures in my mind.

J. Ramsey Michaels, in his book _Servant and Son,_ suggests two things that would have come into Jesus' mind when he heard those words, "You are my Son, whom I love": scriptural passages about sonship and parabolic stories about sonship (the latter perhaps even deriving from his eternal relationship with his Father).[3] Certainly Jesus would have read and reread that wonderful prophecy from Isaiah 42, "Here is my servant . . . my chosen one in whom I delight" (Is 42:1). And as a boy growing up in a Jewish home he would have delighted in the story of Isaac, Abraham's one and only beloved son, whom his father had been willing to sacrifice, if necessary, to please God (Gen 22:1-19). So the words he heard at his baptism would have come to Jesus as a tremendous affirmation.

When I was discussing the story of Jesus' baptism with a group of businessmen, one of them raised some questions, "Did Jesus need that affirmation? Didn't he already know he was God's Son? Did he need to have it reinforced?" A fascinating conversation followed. One man suggested that in his humanness, Jesus may have found that affirmation important to him. Another suggested that the voice came not for Jesus' sake but for the onlookers. But then we noted that the record does not indicate that anyone other than Jesus and John actually heard the voice.

As the discussion went back and forth, a thought came to me. "Suppose," I said, "that it wasn't the Son who needed to hear it. Suppose it was the Father who needed to say it? Or who wanted to say it?" The other day I saw my thirty-three-year-old daughter and she looked as beautiful as a movie star. I think she gets more attractive every year. One of our friends said she must take pretty pills. I couldn't help saying to her, "Deb, you are absolutely gorgeous! I am so glad you are my daughter." Now maybe she needed to hear that to build her up, because not all pretty girls think they are. But as a father I simply wanted to affirm, "I love you, I am glad I am your father, I am glad you are my daughter, I think you are absolutely wonderful."

At Jesus' baptism, perhaps the great Heavenly Father's heart just over-flowed and he had to say, "My Son, I love you. I am so thankful you are my Son. I am so pleased with all that you are and all that you say and do.

We are one in our spirit and our love and our purpose. And don't forget this as you go, because there will be some tough days ahead in your human life as you carry out our mission."

I like to think that it might have been something like that. And I am impressed that before Jesus had done a single thing to start his ministry God said he was pleased with who he was. It says to us that God is far more interested in our *being* than our *doing,* in what we are than in our actions.

If we lack leaders who operate out of a strong sense of affirmation and confidence or if we have mis-leaders who lead people in wrong directions because of their own insecurities, perhaps the reason is that there has been a lack of affirmation. Senior leaders, parents, employers and others need to learn the art of affirmation. Affirmation is not flattery. Flattery encourages manipulation, not growth. Affirmation, on the other hand, means pointing out and being grateful for the strengths that we see in others and encouraging them to build on them. Affirmation involves nothing but paying attention, caring, and expressing our care. Think of the multiplied dividends it would pay in raising up future leaders.

A Leader Tested

A study of great leaders suggests that leaders may be formed not only out of affirmation, but also out of deprivation. Paul Tournier, the Swiss doctor, has written a fascinating book called *Creative Suffering.*[4] He was moved to write it after reading about a study done by another physician, Dr. Pierre Rentchnick. Rentchnick had been studying how disease affected political leaders. When he read the life stories of leaders who had had a great influence on world history, he was struck by the astonishing coincidence that so many of them had been orphans. Some had lost parents in infancy; some had lost theirs later through separation; others had simply been abandoned. Rentchnick compiled a list of almost three hundred of the greatest names in history, including Alexander the Great, Julius Caesar, George Washington, Napoleon, Golda Meir, Adolf Hitler and Fidel Castro. He published his findings in a book with the striking title *Do Orphans Lead the World?* He concluded that emotional deprivation may arouse an exceptional will to power.

Intrigued by Rentchnick's discovery, Tournier, who was himself an orphan, took up the study. Soon he realized that many of the greatest religious leaders were also virtual orphans. Moses' parents had to give him up because of the Jewish persecution in Egypt, and he later became the son of the princess. Muhammad's parents died before he was one year old. Confucius lost his father at the age of one, and Pascal lost his mother at three.

Tournier extended his research to include leaders who have suffered other deprivations, and his conclusions suggested a close link between the experience of deprivation and creativity. For the leader, creativity is essential. Life is constantly changing, but people always fear change. The leader is responsible to help them adapt and do something new. So, by increasing creativity, suffering or deprivation may feed the springs of leadership in a young soul.

And so it was with Jesus, as we see in Mark's Gospel. The theme of his story is that a privileged Son was also an obedient servant. Jesus' public leadership was preceded by the call of personal affirmation and by a conflict which involved private struggle. The conflict emerges immediately after his baptism: "At once the Spirit sent him out into the desert, and he was in the desert for forty days being tempted by Satan. He was with the wild animals, and angels attended him" (Mk 1:12-13).

In the baptism he has heard the Father saying, "You are my Son." Now in the temptation he has the opportunity to answer back, "I am your servant."

For forty days Jesus was alone in the desert, going through the "wilderness experience" of the leader. One wonders whether the desert has some special psychological and spiritual significance in the forming of great spiritual visionaries. Moses spent forty years in the desert before he became the leader who rescued the Jewish people from Egypt. Muhammad was a desert figure, and it was in the desert that he was reported to have received the Koran. Paul, the persecutor of Christians, went to the desert for several years to be alone before undertaking his role as a public apostle of Christ. Perhaps there is something about desert scenery that creates a sense of awe and a sense of proportion in the mind and heart. In any case, during those forty days, Jesus experienced true aloneness.

The desert experience dramatically illustrates the leader's need not just for affirmation, but also for testing during which he or she stands alone before God. Leadership can be a very lonely thing. In one sense leaders are seldom alone, for people are always pressing in on them, as the crowds did on Jesus. But those in leadership have to be prepared for aloneness, for burdens they have to carry, for decisions they must make and for issues they have to wrestle with that no one else can share.

Richard Foster, in his book *Money, Sex and Power,* cites the example of Moses, who tried to bring justice by killing an Egyptian. As a result, "he has to go into the desert for forty years to learn the difference between human manipulation and divine power. By the time Moses stood before God at the burning bush, he was a different man."

As Foster comments, "If we expect to engage in the ministry of power, we must understand the hidden preparation through which God puts his ministers."[5]

So, like Moses, Jesus now spends time in the desert, all alone. The Son of God was able to fulfill his leadership and to identify with ours only by going through the same testing that all leaders face. The writer of Hebrews describes this call enigmatically: "Although he was a son, he learned obedience from what he suffered" (Heb 5:8). As sinners, we learn to be obedient because of the unpleasant results that follow wrongdoing. Jesus, by contrast, was without sin and obedient to God from the start. He learned, by the sufferings which came his way, what obedience to God involved in living a human life on earth.

In *The Way of the Heart,* Henri Nouwen relates the story of the Desert Fathers who lived in the Egyptian desert in the fourth and fifth centuries. Their spirituality offers an important perspective on our leadership today. The idea of living for many years alone in the desert strikes most modern people as strange, but for these Desert Fathers the desert was a place of solitude, silence and prayer. We are such busy people, says Nouwen, that "compulsive" may be the best adjective to describe our work in this world of domination and manipulation, where it is easy to lose our souls. Solitude, he says, is "the furnace of transformation," the place of the great struggle and the great encounter, where we learn to deal with the compulsions of the world. In solitude we get rid of the scaffolding, those artificial supports which keep us from being real. In our own "desert time" we learn the experience of Jesus, who "affirmed God as the only source of his identity."[6]

My friend Lloyd Ogilvie, the well-known writer and pastor, had a serious accident in Scotland while on study leave. Walking on a deserted beach late one afternoon, he fell between some rocks and snapped a leg bone. No help was near. Almost fainting from the pain, he pulled himself along with his arms for several miles until a doctor who happened to be nearby came across him and took him to the hospital. The break was a major injury, and his recuperation meant months of time away from work. Reflecting on those inactive months, Ogilvie told me how, during that time, he had learned of the "seduction of the secondary." Alone with his pain, away from the compulsions of work, he was reminded of the pre-eminent need to have a heart for God. With the scaffolding put aside, solitude became his "furnace of transformation."

What are the compulsions of the world? Nouwen describes them as the pressures to be relevant, spectacular and powerful. Jesus faced those same compulsions. The Gospel accounts of the epic story of his temptations are among the most moving in literature (Mt 4:1-11; Mk 1:12-13; Lk 4:1-13). They make it clear that Jesus was led into the desert. He did not stumble there by accident, or go as a result of his own prior decision. This was part of his Father's plan for his training.

In the desert, when Jesus was most hungry, the tempter came to him. The first line of temptation was a ploy to persuade him to use magical powers to turn stones into bread to feed himself. The second involved a trip, whether imaginary or literal, to Jerusalem. There Jesus was made to stand at the very pinnacle of the temple. Satan suggested that if he were indeed the Son of God he should prove it by jumping off, for surely the angels would save him from harm and the crowds below would gasp in awe when they realized who he was. The final temptation took place at the top of a high mountain where the devil showed Jesus a vision of the whole world and promised him power over all of it if he would bow his knee and recognize another power than his Father's.

Pressures

Here, then, Jesus faced the same compulsions that Nouwen says we face today. First came the pressure to be relevant: "Tell these stones to become bread" (Mt 4:3). This was not merely an attack on a hungry man; it was an attempt to get him to take a shortcut and create a utopia where all physical needs would be met. Next came the pressure to be spectacular: "Throw yourself down from the top of the temple." Here the temptation to do something spectacular was allied to the subtle invitation to play to the gallery. Finally came the pressure to be powerful: From a high mountain the devil promised, "All this I will give you, if you will bow down and worship me" (Mt 4:9). Probing for a weakness, he tried to get Jesus to hitch God's purposes to the forces and powers of this world.

Twenty centuries later those same testings face every leader. Today the devil might take a leader, show him the misery and poverty of the world, and whisper, "Be merely a humanitarian." Or he might hand him a contract for TV time and promise, "Be a great entertainer and people will get your message on the side." In his book *Christ and the Media,* British wit and writer Malcolm Muggeridge seriously questions whether Jesus would take an offer of prime time on network television if it were offered to him. This, says Muggeridge, might be the "fourth temptation"![7] Or the tempter might turn the head of the Christian leader by having her courted by politicians (and the ultranationalistic ones at that) and put into her head the thought, "You are as smart as they are, and you can communicate better. Why not go into politics?"

This is not to say that those who feed the hungry, or entertain, or lead a political cause are doing less than God's best. The issue is: What is God's call? Most temptations promise that some good will result from them; otherwise they would not be attractive. Indeed, if we are to believe that Jesus was tempted in all the ways others are, he must have felt the pull of the devil's suggestions. But the appeal of the good can be the enemy not only of the best, but of the call of God's kingdom.

Following the First World War, the great missionary statesman and church leader John R. Mott was asked by President Woodrow Wilson to serve as the United States ambassador in China. As a result of his extensive travels and his evangelistic work among students, Mott knew China as few other Americans did and was, therefore, well-qualified for the job. He thought about it carefully and eventually replied to Wilson that, although he was honored to have been asked, he could not accept. He had to be free to continue his work of evangelism and leadership in the cause of Christian unity. Having heard that unique and personal call of Christ, he had to turn a deaf ear to other calls. What someone else could have done was not for him.

Reflections on a Leader's Preparation

After I drafted this chapter, the contrast between the Father's words at Jesus' baptism and Jesus' words during his testings caught my attention. At his baptism in the Jordan, Jesus heard the voice of God saying, "You are my Son." Yet when he was tested, Jesus did not once refer to God as his "Father." He spoke of him simply as "God." "Every word that comes from the mouth of *God*," and "Do not put the Lord your *God* to the test," and "Worship the Lord your *God*." And always he quoted from the Scripture, "It is written. . . ." as one who is under authority. When he was in the river of baptism the Father had affirmed him and said, "I am so pleased with you, my Son." In the loneliness of the desert he was going through the experience of deprivation, being tested as a servant, and firmly committing himself to hear God, worship God, and wait for God. God's leader/Son was learning his priorities as leader/servant.

Before he speaks, he must listen. When he announces that "the kingdom of God is near," he has himself first listened to "every word that comes from the mouth of God."

When the devil says, "Worship me," he replies, "Worship the Lord your God," learning in the harshness of the desert furnace that God alone is his authority and power. Later he would say, "All authority in heaven and on earth has been given to me" (Mt 28:18). Like Daniel, who went through a fiery furnace before him, he was learning commitment to "the Most High [who] is sovereign over the kingdoms of men and gives them to anyone he wishes" (Dan 4:25).

And when the devil tries to force the issue, to get him to jump off the pinnacle of the temple, he responds that he will not put God "to the test."

46

He will eventually confront the chief city of Jerusalem, but it will be in God's time and in God's way.

So the leader rises out of the water of Jordan and walks out of the desert, knowing that his priorities are to hear God's word, worship God's greatness, await God's time.

4

THE LEADER
AS STRATEGIST

●

*Jesus knew where he
was going—he had a great purpose.*

●

*"Managers want to do things right—
leaders want to do the right thing."*
WARREN BENNIS

*"The Spirit of the Lord is on me,
because he has anointed me
to preach good news to the poor.
He has sent me to proclaim freedom for the prisoners
and recovery of sight for the blind,
to release the oppressed,
to proclaim the year of the Lord's favor."*
JESUS CHRIST

---

*T*he prisoner sat hunched over, brooding, in the grim confines of his cell.
A plate of rancid food sat untouched nearby. Neither insects crawling on
the floor nor the mocking insults of the guards down the corridor could
interrupt the dark train of his thoughts.

Shifting painfully on the cold floor, John the Baptist looked up at the
two men who stood silently outside his cell door.

"Tell me again," he demanded. "Tell me exactly what you saw him do."

The first spoke up, "I saw him heal the servant of the centurion at

Capernaum. He was at the point of death. The centurion sent to Jesus and asked him to heal him. He told him he wasn't worthy to have him come under his roof, but he was sure Jesus knew how to give orders just as a centurion would. Would he please just command the disease to leave? When the messengers got back, they found the servant well."

"At Nain there was a widow," added the second. "Her only son had died, and they were actually on the way to bury him when Jesus stopped the funeral procession and touched the coffin, and the boy sat up and began to talk!"

"All the people are saying that a great prophet has appeared," said the first, "that God has come to help his people."

"Has he now!" snorted John. "Then what am I doing here? What is Herod doing still living with that woman who is not his wife?"

The two men stood silently. For many years they had followed John, but they had never seen him so depressed. They had admired his courage when he dared to tell King Herod that it was not lawful for him to be living with his brother Philip's wife, Herodias. They knew how badly Herod wanted to kill him. John sat lost in thought, swept by memories. It seemed as if it were just the other day he was a little boy. He could hear the voice of his father, Zechariah, telling him that God would send a leader—the Messiah—to deliver them. All Jewish fathers told their boys that, but John's father told him that he had been chosen to prepare the way for that leader.

It was hard for John to remember his youthful enthusiasm in those days . . . the bitter cold nights, the blazing hot days he had endured in the desert . . . the locusts and honey that were his sole rations . . . the crowds who had come to hear him preach.

Had it been worth it?

He glanced up at his disciples. "You have been with me from the beginning," he said. "Do you remember the day by the Jordan River when my cousin Jesus showed up? There was something about the look in his eyes. I was surprised when he asked me to baptize him. But I knew he was the one God had chosen. I just knew it. When I heard the voice 'This is my Son,' I knew he was the one.

"I didn't mind when the crowds stopped following me and started after him. Do you remember? I wasn't jealous, was I? I was content just to prepare the way for him.

"But for what? For these?" He held up the chains fastened to his wrists, and his sunken eyes blazed. "If he is God's Chosen One, why doesn't he act like it? Why doesn't he get rid of Herod and those damned Romans? Why am I sitting here in this rat-infested hole, wondering every night if I will die the next dawn?"

Painfully, he struggled to his feet and limped over to the barred door. His men stared at him in distress. "Look," he said, "I want you to find Jesus, wherever he is. I want you to go to him and ask this one question: 'Are you the one that is to come or should we expect someone else?' "

Shaken, they quickly left the prison. After some hours they learned where Jesus had last been seen, and, eventually, they located him in the middle of a crowd. Pushing through to him, they said, "John the Baptist sent us to you to ask, 'Are you the one that was to come, or should we expect someone else?' "

Jesus looked at them thoughtfully, but he made no immediate reply. Instead, he kept on walking through the crowd, touching the sick, praying for them. John's men watched as many were cured, especially those who had lost their sight because of the blazing Middle Eastern sun. When he was finished, Jesus walked back to John's men.

"Go back," he said compassionately, "and report to John what you have seen and heard: The blind receive sight, the lame walk, those who have leprosy are cured, the deaf hear, the dead are raised, and the good news is preached to the poor." As they turned to go, Jesus reached out and touched one of them on the shoulder and added, "Blessed is the man who does not fall away on account of me. Tell John that."

He watched them leave, then turned back to the crowd and said with admiration, "I tell you, among those born of women there is no one greater than John; yet the one who is least in the kingdom of God is greater than he."

Charisma—for What?

Like John the Baptist, people in every part of today's world look to their

51

leaders and ask, "Are you the one? Who is that charismatic leader, that woman or man with the magic touch, the ideas and the strength to untangle our existence and weave the pattern of a new world?"

But how important a criterion is charisma? Some of the most charismatic leaders of this century—Hitler, Stalin, Mao—have brought about the greatest evil.

In his book _Modern Times_, historian Paul Johnson has described how the disciples of the Left in Russia and of the Right in Germany looked for a leader, a modern messiah, to emerge.[1] A central tragedy of modern history is that both groups found their leaders: Lenin and Hitler. According to their own principles, both were revolutionaries. And both were corrupted by absolute power and violent revolution leading to tyranny.

So the question remains, disturbingly, probingly: charisma, for what purpose? For it is the mission that makes the difference between leadership and mis-leadership.

Two vivid street scenes illustrate the difference for me.

One is a ride through the streets of Bucharest, the capital of Romania, on a wet June afternoon. At a traffic circle, police suddenly appear, stopping all vehicles.

Our driver turns to us and says, "I think you are going to see our president come by; they are clearing the way."

We peer out, trying to see this infamous character, Nicolae Ceausescu, the ruthless dictator who had executed thousands of his enemies and ruined Romania's economy. Half a block away a motorcycle escort appears, followed by an official black limousine. And in the back of the car we can see a mass of black hair. Is it the president's wife, with an enormous hairdo?

Our driver begins to laugh. "It's his dog!"

The president's dog, with a chauffeur, a limousine and a motorcycle escort? In a city where the people cannot buy meat and get a ration of two-thirds a tank of petrol per month? In the uprising of 1989, the Romanian dictator and his wife ended their lives before a firing squad, summarily executed by a people's court for their mis-leadership.

The contrasting scene is a dirty, trashy street in Calcutta, littered with piles of garbage and crowds of beggars. Down a narrow side street is a brown door with a small sign, "Sisters of Mercy." We ring a bell and are admitted. In a few minutes a woman appears, less than five feet tall, dressed in a blue habit, with deep wrinkles and a bunion on her bare foot. For many years I had wanted to meet Mother Teresa. She sits down and chats with no sense of hurry, although she has to leave shortly for New Delhi to talk to some rich people about how they can help the poor. We ask her about her ministry of caring for the dying poor and what we can pray for. Instead of asking for staff or money, she responds, "Pray that I might be humble like Mary, and holy like Jesus."

Mother Teresa grew up in Albania, the country next door to Romania, where the president's dog rated a chauffeur. But the kind of leadership they represent is—both literally and figuratively—worlds apart.

How, then, are we to understand Jesus' leadership? What were his aims? To understand the elements of his leadership, which we will examine later in this book, we must first grasp his strategy. To understand his strategy, we must see how it grew out of his mission.

A Strategy of Fulfillment: Jesus' Sense of Destiny

Centered in any great leader's soul is a sense of transcendent purpose. "To be a man," wrote Saint-Exupery, the French aviator, "is to feel that by one's own contribution one has helped to build the world." To explore the Amazon. To find a cure for polio. To understand energy. To walk on the moon. To eliminate poverty and disease. To build a commercial empire. To . . . to . . . to . . . whatever the goal, the leader senses a restless vocation.

A sense of messianic mission coursed strongly through the arteries of Jesus' forebears. Abraham was called to go into the unknown and father a new nation. Joseph had a dream in which the sun and moon bowed down to him, foreshadowing his destiny to become the delegated ruler of Egypt. Moses at a burning bush discovered his life purpose to lead the Jews from slavery. Joshua led them into the promised land; David subdued it; Solomon built a temple there. All lived and died with a belief that through them God was working out a purpose greater than themselves. Only a few saw beyond the boundaries of their own time and kin, to a day when "the earth [would] be full of the knowledge of the Lord as the waters cover the sea" (Is 11:9).

The boy Jesus inherited that same sense of destiny. The man Jesus lived it out. At the age of twelve Jesus told his anxious parents, who had lost him and then found him in the temple, "Didn't you know I had to be in my Father's house?" (Lk 2:49). At the midpoint of his ministry he exclaimed, "I have come to bring fire on the earth, and how I wish it were already kindled! But I have a baptism to undergo, and how distressed I am until it is completed!" (Lk 12:49-50). Later, when he was told that King Herod wanted to kill him, he was not the least disconcerted, but calmly replied, "Go tell that fox, 'I will drive out demons and heal people today and tomorrow, and on the third day I will reach my goal' " (Lk 13:12).

Our words reveal our character, and in Jesus' case that inner sense of destiny emerges from his frequent use of the phrases "I was sent" and "I came." John's Gospel especially picks up that idea of *sending*. "My food is to do the will of him who sent me and to finish his work"; "The work of God is this: to believe in the one he has sent"; "As long as it is day, we must do the work of him who sent me"; "As the Father has sent me, I am sending you" (Jn 4:34; 6:29; 9:4; 20:21). These are the words of one who is pursuing a vision, not simply passing through life.

Jesus frequently asserted that he had "come" for specific purposes: "to call . . . sinners to repentance" (Lk 5:32); "not . . . to be served, but to serve, and to give his life as a ransom" (Mk 10:45); "to preach the good news of the kingdom" (Lk 4:43); "to seek and to save what was lost" (Lk 19:10); "that they may have life, and have it to the full" (Jn 10:10); "to testify to the truth" (Jn 18:37). He had been sent not to condemn, but to save the world (Jn 3:17), to lay down his life for the sheep, so they would have life to the full and there would be "one flock and one shepherd" (Jn 10:16).

Yet, while the purpose of his mission was to save, there was also a down side. Shortly after his birth the elderly Simeon had told Mary, his mother, "This child is destined to cause the falling and rising of many in Israel" (Lk 2:34). Jesus sensed that his mission would not be welcomed by all. "Do not suppose that I have come to bring peace to the earth," he told his followers. "I did not come to bring peace, but a sword" (Mt 10:34). He repeats this again: "I have come to bring fire on the earth. . . . Do you think I came to bring peace on earth? No, I tell you, but division" (Lk 12:49, 51). As a result,

54

families will be divided against each other, three against two and two against three (Lk 12:52). For those who respond it will be life; for the others there will be doom. So he could say about those who thought they could see but were really spiritually blind, "For judgment I have come into this world, so that the blind will see and those who see will become blind" (Jn 9:39). Yet he could truthfully say that while judgment was a consequence, it was not his purpose: "For I did not come to judge the world, but to save it" (Jn 12:47).

The Fulfiller

When at the beginning of his career Jesus went down to the Jordan River and asked John to baptize him, John protested, "I need to be baptized by you." Jesus replied, "Let it be so now; it is proper for us to do this to fulfill all righteousness" (Mt 3:14-15). In many ways his teaching was new and radical, yet he saw himself as fulfilling rather than replacing what was there before: "Do not think that I have come to abolish the Law or the Prophets," he told his disciples when he was teaching them on the mountain, "I have not come to abolish them but to fulfill them" (Mt 5:17).

Often the events of his life were seen as the fulfillment of the old prophecies. When he left Nazareth and moved his headquarters to Capernaum, he was fulfilling Isaiah's prophecy that the people living in Galilee of the Gentiles would see that "a light has dawned" (Mt 4:15-16). Clearly Jesus had immersed himself in the Jewish Scriptures and saw them as a clue to the mystery of his mission. When he ate the Last Supper with his disciples he warned them of his betrayal, but also that "the Son of Man will go just as it is written about him" (Mk 14:21). After his resurrection he patiently explained to them, "This is what I told you while I was still with you: Everything must be fulfilled that is written about me in the Law of Moses, the Prophets and the Psalms" (Lk 24:44). And he opened their minds so they could understand that the Scriptures had said that the Christ would suffer and rise from the dead (Lk 24:45-46).

This sense of destiny especially gripped him with a consciousness that he had come to fulfill a purpose which had only been hinted at in previous times.

Sometimes he spoke of this as fulfilling a task. Facing impending arrest, he reviewed his life in prayer with his Father, and said, "I have brought you glory on earth by completing the work you gave me to do" (Jn 17:4).

He saw himself as the Son of Man, fulfilling history. Once the Pharisees asked him when the kingdom of God would come. He replied, "The kingdom of God does not come with your careful observation, nor will people say, 'Here it is' or 'There it is,' because the kingdom of God is within you" (Lk 17:27-28), and he pictured the time when "the Son of Man in his day will be like the lightning, which flashes and lights up the sky from one end to the other" (Lk 17:24). At that very time, nations filled with anguish and perplexity "will see the Son of Man coming in a cloud with power and great glory. When these things begin to take place, stand up and lift up your heads, because your redemption is drawing near" (Lk 21:27-28).

Some teachers and philosophers have seen life as "a tale told by an idiot, full of sound and fury, signifying nothing."[2] Some have seen it as an illusion. Others have interpreted it as an endless cycle of futility. Jesus saw history as an arrow shot toward a target, a fire cast on the earth, a lightning-flash across the sky, a door opened to fulfillment, a task that would be completed. A new time had arrived. A new reality had come. He himself embodied that new reality, and he called people to seize it and to follow him. This was his sense of destiny, and this determined his strategy.

A Kingdom Strategy: Jesus' Master Thought

Jesus' very first message was, "The time has come. The kingdom of God is near. Repent and believe the good news!" (Mk 1:15). This was his compelling passion. Once, when people tried to keep him from moving on, he said, "I must preach the good news of the kingdom of God to the other towns also, because that is why I was sent" (Lk 4:43). So he "traveled about from one town and village to another, proclaiming the good news of the kingdom of God" (Lk 8:1). When he sent out seventy-two followers on an initial mission, he told them to eat what was set before them, to heal the sick, and to say, "The kingdom of God is near you" (Lk 10:8-9). This concept of "the kingdom of God" was absolutely central to Jesus, and it is explicitly mentioned 121 times in the accounts of Matthew, Mark and Luke. Indeed the kingdom has been described as "his master thought."

Did Jesus have a grand design? An all-embracing plan? Yes, but it was not his own design or his own plan. He had come to do his Father's work, to announce his Father's kingdom which he fully shared. To understand Jesus' leadership we must understand his mission and his message, and at its heart was the kingdom of God.

To call Jesus' leadership a "kingdom leadership" may seem out of date and irrelevant in our modern world. Presidents and chief executive officers we understand; their constituents can vote them out of office. Dictators have been many, and we have gladly gotten rid of them. But kings and queens seem like fanciful figures from our remote past, who, if they still exist, are figureheads without power.

But in Jesus' day there were plenty of powerful kings who could be dangerous. When Jesus spoke about God's "kingdom," he was talking not about a place, but about a powerful reality. The reality was God at work to bring out into the open a people who would voluntarily live their lives under his guidance. Hence the late Clarence Jordan, founder of the Koinonia community, described the "kingdom of God" as the "God movement." It was real, down-to-earth, present and powerful. In fact, when he declared that the kingdom of God was near, Jesus was saying that God has invaded this world in a new way. Rather like the way soldiers invade an island during a war, God has established a beachhead and will not stop until the whole world is taken.

David Wenham catches this dynamic thought when he paraphrases the "kingdom of God" as the "revolution of God." He suggests that the idea of revolution may help us understand the excitement of Jesus' message:

He was announcing a dramatic and forceful change in society to people who—unlike many in our complacent, modern world—really longed for such a change: God was at last intervening to put things right. Not surprisingly Jesus' contemporaries understood Jesus to mean that the Roman imperialists and their unprincipled and unpleasant lackeys such as the Herods were about to be driven out of Palestine: "kingdom" to many of them, like "revolution" to many of us, suggested something primarily political and military. But Jesus had in mind a bigger revolution than that: God's revolution was to be a total revolution overthrowing Satan and evil and bringing earth and heaven back into harmony. This would not be accomplished by force of arms, but—unbelievably so far as the disciples were concerned, and who blames them?—through suffering and death.[3]

This "God movement" or "revolution of God" was far more than an idea or a heavenly dream. It was down-to-earth. Jesus taught his followers to pray, "Your kingdom come, your will be done *on earth* as it is in heaven" (Mt 6:10). As Wenham puts it, "The kingdom which Jesus proclaimed was not just up in heaven; it was more like an invasion of earth by heaven!"[4]

Jesus' leadership was not leadership in a vacuum. It operated in a real world, among real people with real problems, and showed that a *new* reality had come.

The arrival of God's revolutionary kingdom brought history to a decisive moment of challenge. There was a *higher standard* than ever before. The law had said, "Do not murder" and "Do not commit adultery." But for Jesus peace and faithfulness in the heart were the new benchmarks for the new reality (see Mt 5:21-22, 27-28).

If the standards of the revolution were higher, there was also a *wider entrance.* Jesus called sinners (like Matthew the tax collector) to follow him, and when he was criticized he replied, "I have not come to call the righteous, but sinners" (Mt 9:13).

The revolution also brought a *deeper reality*—a new reality in traditional practices such as observing the sabbath. He healed a man on the sabbath day, technically breaking the sabbath rules in the eyes of religious leaders, then went to the root of the tradition: "What is the sabbath for? Is it lawful to do good or to do evil? Was man made for the sabbath or the sabbath for man?" (See Mt 12:12 and Mk 2:27.)

A *stronger power* also marked this revolution. It was a dynamic, liberating charismatic movement, characterized by powerful works. After healing a man who was blind and mute because of demonic possession, Jesus told the amazed crowd, "If I drive out demons by the Spirit of God, then the kingdom of God has come upon you" (Mt 12:28). Then he compared kingdom power to tying up a strong man and ransacking his house.

To sum it up, *greater commandments* were at the heart of the revolution: " 'Love the Lord your God with all your heart and with all your soul and with all your mind.' This is the first and greatest commandment. And the second is like it: 'Love your neighbor as yourself.' All the Law and the Prophets hang on these two commandments" (Mt 22:37-40).

Jesus' entire strategy grew from the reality of this revolution—the dynamic and powerful "God-movement" which brought healing to people's bodies, reconciliation to their relationships, reality to their faith, fresh meaning to their traditions, forgiveness for their sins, and an overwhelming love in their hearts for God and for one another.

A Global Strategy: Jesus' Long-Range Goal

There is a well-known slogan in environmentalist circles: "Think globally, act locally." It could well have originated with Jesus. Matthew's Gospel, a very Jewish book, tells us that he was named Jesus "because he will save his people from their sins" (Mt 1:21). Presumably these were his Jewish people, yet Matthew closes with Jesus' sweeping commission, "All authority in heaven and on earth has been given to me. Therefore go and make disciples of all nations" (Mt 28:18). Luke's account, aimed more toward a Gentile audience, opens with the angels' good news of "great joy that will be for all the people" (Lk 2:10). Luke closes with his version of Jesus' final marching orders, that "repentance and forgiveness of sins will be preached in his name to all nations, beginning at Jerusalem" (Lk 24:47).

True, Jesus deliberately limited himself to Jewish people at the beginning. A Canaanite woman from the region of Tyre and Sidon cried out to him, "Lord, Son of David, have mercy on me! My daughter is suffering terribly from demon-possession." Jesus answered not a word until the disciples intervened. Then he said, "I was sent only to the lost sheep of Israel." Then the woman knelt and again begged him to help. His reply sounds strangely grating on the lips of a person we think of as having universal compassion, "It is not right," he replied, "to take the children's bread and toss it to their dogs." When she persisted, "Even the dogs eat the crumbs that fall from their masters' table," Jesus granted her request and healed her daughter. We can only interpret his harsh words as a stern test of her faith and a refusal to be diverted from his mission to the Jewish people until he was ready (Mt 15:21-28). Any suggestion of racism or hypernationalism on Jesus' part is refuted when we remember that he commended this woman, "You have great faith!" He also said of a Roman centurion, "I have not found such great faith even in Israel" (Lk 7:9).

Jesus was born and brought up in a small town, concentrated his early ministry on Jews in Galilee, and died in Jerusalem. Yet the world was always in his thoughts. His plan was first to concentrate on Israel. But when he healed the centurion's servant and commended his faith, he also commented, "I say to you that many will come from the east and the west and will take their places at the feast with Abraham, Isaac and Jacob in the kingdom of heaven. But the subjects of the kingdom will be thrown outside" (Mt 8:11-12). In his parable of the sower and the seed he explained that "the field is the world" (Mt 13:38). He pictured Israel as a vineyard which received special favor from its owner yet never returned any fruit. He warned that "the kingdom of God will be taken away from you and given to a people who will produce its fruit" (Mt 21:43). His prophetic key to future history was: "This gospel of the kingdom will be preached in the whole world as a testimony to all nations, and then the end will come" (Mt 24:14). He taught that all the nations—Jewish and Gentile—will be gathered before the Son of Man at the final judgment, to be judged according to what they had done with Jesus, who had come to them, perhaps incognito, as the stranger, the sick or the prisoner (Mt 25:31-46). A woman poured expensive perfume on his head at a dinner party, shortly before his arrest. He took this as a preparation for his burial, and said in warm approval, "Wherever this gospel is preached throughout the world, what she has done will also be told, in memory of her" (Mt 26:13). His last thoughts were not of his personal prestige or comfort, but of his global mission.

Evidently, everything Jesus did during his intensive, focused, three-year career was done deliberately to secure the beachhead which would eventually fulfill his long-range strategy to reach the whole world.

I went for a walk in the mountains above San Bernardino, California, with a friend, a layman with a heart for the world. We viewed the lights of the city glittering below us, and my friend said, "Those lights make me think of God throwing a huge luminous net around the entire world. Each of the strands is glowing. I see them growing closer together until that glow will touch the entire world. That's the kind of network Jesus is building!" Then he mused, "My life expectancy is about eighteen years. I want to commit myself for those eighteen years to help raise up in every nation lay people like myself who will be the light of Jesus in their nation and be part of the net he's spreading around the world." Two thousand years later, and two continents away, the global strategy of Jesus was still alive, still catching up another leader in his vision!

A People Strategy: Jesus' Radical Solution

A Soviet journalist said that, as a communist, he could not believe in a god or in pie-in-the-sky. "I believe in people," he said. Jesus would not have argued with him. Power, position and personal magnetism were for him not ends, but tools to be used for God's kingdom, a kingdom not so much cause-oriented as people-oriented. When he gave his inaugural speech at the synagogue in Nazareth, Jesus read from the prophecy of Isaiah:

The Spirit of the Lord is on me,
  because he has anointed me
  to preach good news to the poor.
He has sent me to proclaim freedom
  for the prisoners
  and recovery of sight for the blind,
to release the oppressed,
  to proclaim the year of the Lord's favor. (Is 61:1-2)

Then he said, "Today this scripture is fulfilled in your hearing" (Lk 4:18-21).

When John sent his puzzled question, "Are you the one?" what was Jesus' reply? He told the messengers to go back and tell John about blind people seeing, lame people walking, lepers being cured, deaf people hearing, dead people being raised, poor people hearing the gospel (Lk 7:13).

His choice of a primary target audience was astonishing. He did not go first for the leaders, the influential and the rich, although he welcomed and attracted many of them. Deliberately, he went for the poor. They would have the gospel preached to them. The blind and the oppressed and the prisoners who had no one to champion their cause—he would be their champion. Yet even here he saw the poor in a special way. He reminded the people in the synagogue about Elijah feeding a poor widow, but he also told them about Elisha healing a rich general (Lk 4:25-27). In back-to-back instances, he healed the servant of a powerful, well-off centurion, then he stopped a funeral procession and raised the only son of a poor widow. He seemed to say that poor people could be self-sufficient and Godless, and rich people could be humble and God-hungry. But those who qualified for his kingdom were the poor who were *really* poor, people who, whatever their economic status, were desperately aware of the depth of their need.

When we review Jesus' multimission statements—"to call sinners to repentance," "to give his life a ransom for many," "to seek and to save what was lost," "that they may have life to the full"—the ringing theme is the longing to set people free, to remove the obstacles (sin or suffering or death or poverty), and to supply the resources (forgiveness or purpose or life or Spirit) that would enable people to be all that God wanted them to be. E. Stanley Jones, the writer and evangelist to India, used to describe Jesus' kingdom as "the kingdom of right relations." And so it *was,* a kingdom to reconcile poor lost sinners to their Father, to themselves and to one another.

But if Jesus' strategy was a people strategy, it was also *a radical strategy* that demanded radical transformation. Not only did he come for the "poor" who knew their need, but he was also open to the children and all those who like children were prepared to be changed. He said that his Father had hidden truth from the wise and learned and had revealed it to little children (Mt 11:25). Asked who was the greatest in the kingdom, he called a little child and said, "Unless you change and become like little children, you will never enter the kingdom of heaven. Therefore, whoever humbles himself like this child is the greatest in the kingdom of heaven" (Mt 18:1-4).

Jesus saw the heart of the human problem as the problem of the human heart. A radical change from inside out was at the core of his strategy. Some Pharisees asked why his disciples did not wash their hands in the ceremonial fashion before eating. He replied by quoting Isaiah's words, "These people honor me with their lips, but their hearts are far from me" (Mk 7:6).

Later he told the crowd, "Nothing outside man can make him 'unclean' by going into him. Rather, it is what comes out of a man that makes him 'unclean' " (Mk 7:15). When his disciples asked him to explain, he went on, "What comes out of a man is what makes him 'unclean.' For from within, out of men's hearts, come evil thoughts, sexual immorality, theft, murder, adultery, greed, malice, deceit, lewdness, envy, slander, arrogance and folly. All these evils come from inside and make a man 'unclean' " (Mk 7:20-23).

What Jesus taught about the inner spirit applied to ceremonial ritual, for example, to the food laws. But his principle "not from without but from within" is even more fundamental. Is it the world that is the source of wrong, or the human heart? The environment, or the heart? Pollution, or the heart? Social injustice, or the heart? Ignorance, or the heart? Is the way to "clean up" a matter of laws, ritual, education, political structures, or most fundamentally a change of heart? What Jesus said not only has a religious significance but also has powerful implications for politics, law and order, education, and all our social systems.

These words of Jesus spoken two thousand years ago are profoundly significant today.

Alexander Solzhenitsyn, the Russian novelist, said in his Harvard University address, "A World Split Apart," that the most significant lines of division in our world today are not those which run _between_ nations, but the line which runs _through_ East and West, which separates all of us from our spiritual nature.[5] The mayor of Timisoara, Romania, where the December 1989 Romanian uprising began, spoke after the revolution about the social problems that came from bad working habits and massive alcoholism. "We have accomplished only 20 per cent of the revolution by changing the old system," he said. "Now, the new system has to change the people." On the capitalist side of the world, Michael Maccoby, a management consultant, writes of interviewing many engineers and executives who have "over-developed heads and under-developed hearts."[6]

This need for remade hearts shows the penetrating realism of Jesus' promise that the pure in heart will see God (Mt 5:8) and his incisive warning that "unless you forgive your brother from your heart" you yourself will not be forgiven (Mt 18:35).

The experience of forgiveness was at the heart of Jesus' radical change. "Take heart, son," he said to a paralytic who was brought to him, "your sins are forgiven" (Mt 9:2). He took great delight in mingling with those others called "sinners." When the Pharisees asked his disciples why he did this, Jesus shrewdly replied, "It is not the healthy who need a doctor, but the sick. . . . For I have not come to call the righteous, but sinners" (Mt 9:12-13).

With the forgiveness of sins Jesus also brought an empowering liberation from other forces that crippled and bound people. The blind man received his sight. The woman who was previously bent over and bound now stood tall. The oppressed lost their fear. Those afflicted by demons were set free. A little man, all bound up in the insecurity of his riches, was called by Jesus just as he was. With reckless abandon he told Jesus, "Here and now I give half of my possessions to the poor." To this Jesus responded in jubilation, "This man, too, is a son of Abraham. For the Son of Man came to seek and to save what was lost" (Lk 19:9-10).

In these liberating acts Jesus saw Satan's kingdom divided and falling, for when he drove out demons by the Spirit of God, it meant that "the kingdom of God has come upon you" (Mt 12:28).

Jesus' radical transformation brought a double freedom—liberation from the guilt of sinning and also from the bondage of being sinned against. In David Wenham's words, Jesus "diagnosed the human problem as having to do with Satan on the one hand and with the human heart on the other." And he therefore came with a power "to bring cleanness and renewal to the heart, producing that inward revolution which is the key to any real revolution."

A Minority Strategy: Jesus' Infiltrating Style
A leading fashion magazine once advertised that it was read by "the overwhelming minority"! Jesus understood how to leverage a minority position into an overwhelming force. To touch the whole world, he had to begin by deliberately focusing on a few.

As a young Jew, he had history to back him up. From the beginning, God had worked with a minority. Noah had stood alone in his day and become the vanguard of a new world when he and his family were saved from the flood in an ark. Abraham had become the seed from which came descendants as numerous as the stars of the sky. When the famous judge Gideon had to go out against the Midianite army, facing overwhelming odds, the Lord told him, "You have too many men for me to deliver Midian into their hands" (Judg 7:2). In a series of startling moves Gideon pared his army down from thirty-two thousand to ten thousand and finally to three hundred totally dedicated soldiers. Gideon's band, using their commander's brilliant night-attack tactics, threw terror into the enemy army and routed them.

We can visualize a number of concentric circles surrounding Jesus: an outer circle, made up of crowds (on one occasion five thousand, on another four thousand) whom he taught and fed and healed; another much smaller circle of seventy, whom he sent out two by two, as his first missionary force; a smaller circle of twelve close disciples; and out of that small group, three (Peter, James and John) who became his intimate inner circle.

A time comes when the leader of a movement must focus on a few. He cannot handle everything, so others must be deployed. Opposition that cannot be won over must be countered by a loyal, committed core who will carry on, regardless of what happens to the leader. A leader must also ensure that there are others who are quite clear as to what the mission is, so the movement does not dissipate or deviate through mistaken or incomplete understandings.

Jesus' call to the three and the twelve and the seventy was not complex. He simply said, in the words of his first recruiting call, "Come, follow me, and I will make you fishers of men" (Mk 1:17). Over and over, to all kinds of people in many different situations, he stated those simple words, "Follow me." The core definition of a Christian is one who trusts and follows Jesus.

His followers were to have a single priority (to seek first the kingdom) and a single loyalty (to himself). Jesus was the kingdom personalized. "Follow me, and I will make you . . . ," he said. He called them to be with him and to go for him. Just to be with him hour after hour and day after day was in itself a transforming relationship. He developed them in a living classroom, letting them watch him teach and heal, then sending them out to do the same. To see how deep and real their faith was, he tested them, asking them to find bread to feed five thousand or to cross a storm-tossed lake in a tiny boat. Above all, he wanted them to learn that the secret of his work was not learning routines or imitating his style or doing good things in their own strength. The secret of his work was faith. As he put it, "The work of God is this: _to believe in the one he has sent_" (Jn 6:29). His aim was to pour himself into them, so that they thought his way and operated by his Spirit. If Jesus' minority strategy was to work, it was imperative that there be a deep unity of purpose and mind among his followers. It was an amazingly diverse group of personalities and loyalties he had called. Peter was a man of action; John was a man of thought and quietness; Matthew, a tax collector, had worked for the occupying Roman forces; Simon the Zealot had likely been a guerrilla, fighting against the Romans. Such diverse loyalties could only be kept together by a greater person and a higher cause. It was the mark of Jesus' leadership that he could bring partial loyalties and lesser talents together in a unifying passion which brought out the best in them.

Reconciliation with God and peace among people were keynotes of the kingdom. If his people were to represent that kingdom, they had to model the kingdom peace. He once said to them, "Salt is good, but if it loses its saltiness, how can you make it salty again? Have salt in yourselves, and be at peace with each other" (Mk 9:50).

Jesus had a passion for unity. He was prepared to lay down his life for his sheep, so there would be "one flock and one shepherd" (Jn 10:15-16). He was going to die not only for the Jewish nation, but "also for the scattered children of God, to bring them together and make them one" (Jn 11:52). If he was going to die to make that oneness possible, then his inner core of disciples had to show among themselves a preview of the coming kingdom. His last intimate prayer to the Father before his death revealed concern that this should be so. He had completed the work the Father gave him. He had revealed the Father to his closest followers. His plan was for them to be "little Christs," sent into the world as he had been sent (Jn 17:18). And he had three prayers for them. First, he wanted them not to be taken out of the world, but to be protected from the evil one (Jn 17:15). Then he wanted them to be holy, totally dedicated and set apart for the Father's work, even as he had been: "Sanctify them by the truth; your word is truth" (Jn 17:17). And last he prayed that they might be one, sharing in the same unity he had with the Father: "I pray also for those who will believe in me through their message, that all of them may be one, Father, just as you are in me and I am in you. . . . May they be brought to complete unity to let the world know that you sent me and have loved them even as you have loved me" (Jn 17:20-23).

He fully believed that his minority strategy would work, on four conditions:

First, that his followers showed his love and holiness in their personal lives.

Second, that they showed his love in relationships with one another.

Third, that this love would flow out of their remaining in a vital relation with him. "My command is this," he told them at their last meal. "Love each other as I have loved you. Greater love has no one than this, that he lay down his life for his friends" (Jn 15:12-13).

Fourth, that they would have the same relationship to the world as he did—not withdrawn from it nor compromised by it, but sent into it.

His minority strategy might be called a strategy of penetration or infiltration. The metaphors he used showed this vividly. His followers were to be "salt of the earth," "light of the world," "leaven," entrusted with "the keys of the kingdom." All are metaphors of penetration—salt into food, light into darkness, leaven into loaf, keys into a lock. Not a lot of salt is needed to flavor and preserve, as long as the salt is rubbed into the food. Nor does it take a great deal of light to dispel darkness, as long as the light is not covered. A tiny bit of fermenting yeast can make a whole loaf rise. And a small key can open a great door.

These metaphors suggest Jesus' teaching was not a primer for majorities, but a strategy for minorities. The world was not to be changed by building great institutions, behind whose walls his followers could safely hide; nor by passing legislation to make people conform; nor by the force of arms or coercion; nor by militant majorities of high-powered publicity campaigns.

It was to be moved by a quiet minority, little platoons of men and women who had been with Jesus and whose hearts and minds had been changed. Living by his Spirit as "little Christs," in the highways and byways of everyday life, they would restrain and reshape from the inside, the institutions, the armies, the legislatures, the homes, the temples and the trading-posts of the nations.

Richard Halverson has highlighted the same minority emphasis in Jesus' analogy of the good seed:

In its gathered, visible form in the granary, seed is useless. To serve the purpose for which it exists, it must be scattered, it disappears into the soil and literally dies. When seed is doing the work for which it was intended, it is invisible.

Think of the church in this scattered, invisible form, penetrating the social, economic and political structures of the world between Sundays. Think of the potential of this dispersion, multiplied millions of disciples, scattered throughout the world, planted by the Son of Man in millions of acres of the field which is the world, disappearing like salt and seed into the substance, the soil of the life where they live and labor between Sundays.[8]

Robert Bellah, the renowned sociologist, quite remarkably confirms Jesus' strategy.[9] Bellah believes that if only 2 per cent of any nation has a new vision of what they would like their society to be, they can change that society. As evidence, he cites Japan, a nation which has been influenced by Christ far beyond the small number of those in Japan who profess to be Christians. Public policy issues with regard to the rights of women, labor laws and many other issues have been substantially, though indirectly, impacted by the teachings of Jesus.

"I am sending you out like sheep among wolves," said Jesus the first time he deployed his followers (Mt 10:16). But with Christ in them, and them in the world, who could forecast what would happen!

A Strange Strategy: Jesus' Puzzling Tactics

Jesus' strategy is seen as much in what he chose not to do as in what he did.

Take for example his choice of *text,* or the terms in which he set out his leadership. When modern politicians announce their candidacy, campaign managers carefully think through the symbolism they will use to "sell" their candidate. A candidate may go back to the place where she was born, as if to say, "Yes, I am ready to lead you, but I haven't lost my roots, or the common touch. I am one of you."

Jesus' opening announcement was not staged, but it was significant. He went to the synagogue where he had been brought up, and chose to read the portion of Isaiah's prophecy which begins, "The Spirit of the Lord is on me, because he has anointed me. . . ." He was to proclaim good news for the poor, freedom for the prisoners, sight for the blind (Lk 4:15-21). He deliberately positioned himself by making a revolutionary personal claim to be God's Messiah, his leader, implementing God's revolutionary program.

But what he left out was just as significant. He concluded the scripture reading with Isaiah's sentence about "the year of the Lord's favor," but omitted Isaiah's follow-up statement about "the day of vengeance of our God" (Is 61:2). His point was definite and dramatic: He had come to inaugurate God's favor, not to execute God's wrath. There would be a long year of mercy before a short day of judgment.

This is probably what threw John the Baptist into doubt. He had fully expected Jesus to call down thunderbolts to wipe out wicked King Herod and mobilize the people to roll the Roman armies back into the Mediterranean. John was so disillusioned that he sent his messengers to ask in effect, "Can you really be the Messiah? Herod hasn't repented. He hasn't been overthrown. He has thrown me into prison. Have you missed the mark?"

What Jesus deliberately left out of the text in his inaugural speech pointed to a truth that underlay his strategy. It was time to proclaim the kingdom. It was time to make good news happen. It was not yet time to overthrow evil powers or execute judgment.

The *tactics* Jesus used were also crucial and revealing. A strange reticence marked Jesus' modus operandi. Again and again, just when it seemed he had swept the people off their feet and they were ready to start a popular movement, he would disappear or do something else, seemingly to dampen enthusiasm. When he cast out evil spirits and the demons shouted, "You are the Son of God," he quieted them (Mk 1:24-25, 34). After touching and healing a man with a dreaded skin disease, he ordered him, "See that you don't tell this to anyone" (Mk 1:44). Crowds wanted to make him king, but he withdrew to a lonely place to pray (Jn 6:15). What kind of leader was this?

What a curious mix Jesus was! This strange strategy ran through his speech and actions. He could be so assertive, walking up to a fisherman who had never seen him before and saying, "Follow me," and yet he could be so reticent. He would say things clearly, almost bluntly, then hide the truth in little stories that made people puzzle. He would mingle freely with the crowds, then pull aside to his inner circle. Was it simply a question of keeping a distance?

Many leaders instinctively understand the mystique of leadership, which they maintain by staying a bit beyond ordinary mortals. Charles Colson, once counsel to President Nixon, recalls the night when Nixon, looking across the White House lawn, mused, "The people really want a leader a little bigger than themselves, don't they, Chuck? I mean someone like de Gaulle." He continued, "There's a certain aloofness, a power that's exuded by great men that people feel and want to follow."[10]

Thus, the astute politician, aware of the danger of overexposure, provides occasions for photo opportunities or carefully planned "spontaneous" walks with the crowd. But everything is calculated to preserve the mystique.

With Jesus it has nothing to do with that. His timing was not a public relations stroke; it was the authentic reflection of his mission. He was his Father's Son. He was sent to his Father's people. He bore his Father's good news. This required that he have space and time to be in close and intimate communication with the Father. It also required times when he was available to give himself without reserve to people.

The good news Jesus was bringing had both a present and a future point of reference. Salvation began with the forgiveness of sins. The day would come when finally he would release all of those he saved from every evil, whether social, physical or political. But this salvation was going to come in stages. He did not want people to think of him as being primarily a physician or an exorcist, a bread-provider or a political leader. For this reason there were times when he would walk among the crowds and speak and heal, and times when he would withdraw.

Jesus' practice of "strategic withdrawals" makes an interesting study in itself. The Gospels show him withdrawing from the crowds when he needed personal renewal (Mk 1:35), when there was the danger of being misunderstood as merely a healer or a bread-giver (Mk 1:45; Jn 6:15), when there were other places to preach (Lk 4:43), when he had gone as far as he could against opposition (Mk 3:7), when he wanted time to pray about crucial decisions (Lk 6:12), when he learned of a plot to take his life before he was ready to go (Jn 11:54). Jesus knew when to be assertive and out-going and when to withdraw.

His biographer Matthew caught this characteristic in an apt quotation from Isaiah:

He will not quarrel or cry out;
  no one will hear his voice in the streets.
A bruised reed he will not break,
  and a smoldering wick he will not snuff out,
till he leads justice to victory. (Mt 12:19-20)

Assertive yet withdrawing, tough yet tender, reticent yet not faltering—this was God's leader.

We can only understand Jesus' strategy if we see it as an expression of his underlying mission.

That mission was in two phases; consequently, it demanded a two-stage strategy. He made this point dramatically in a story about wheat and weeds. A man sowed wheat in his field, but while he was sleeping an enemy came and sowed weeds in the same field. When the seed sprouted, the wheat and the weeds were mingled together. The servants wanted to pull up the weeds, but the owner said, "No, because while you are pulling the weeds, you may root up the wheat. Let both grow together until the harvest. At that time I will tell the harvesters: First collect the weeds and tie them in bundles to be burned; then gather the wheat and bring it into my barn" (Mt 13:24-29). This was more than a nice moral tale; it was a view of history. Good and evil, the wheat and the weeds, the sons of the kingdom and the sons of the evil one, these would coexist until the end of history and that final moment of judgment.

The picture of the "God movement" emerges in two stages. From the time the seed (the word of God) is sown, there is a period of growth. At the end there will be harvest time and the final judgment. In between is an overlap, a period of time when God's kingdom and Satan's power will still coexist.

John the Baptist's puzzled query, "Are you the one?" came because John had a very different idea of the kingdom. He saw it like this:

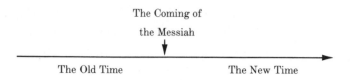

But Jesus taught that the kingdom would come like this:

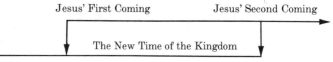

David Wenham aptly describes this two-stage effect:

> Few revolutions are established overnight; there is often a long and fierce struggle with drawn-out resistance from reactionary elements. Jesus' revolution was no exception nor did he suppose that it would be. He . . . established a decisive bridgehead in the occupied territory; but it would be a long struggle with many casualties before Satan was completely ousted and God's legitimate rule restored.[11]

And because there were two phases of the kingdom, it is significant that there were two stages to Jesus' strategy.

A Strategy of Suffering and Glory: Jesus' Saving Role

Jesus' career has two distinct stages.

First, there is the stage in which Jesus is revealing to those who follow him his identity as the Messiah. This is the period when he first announces the kingdom, calls his disciples, does miracles, teaches the crowds—and repeatedly asks that his identity not be spread abroad publicly. This stage takes up roughly the first sixteen chapters of Matthew, the first eight chapters of Mark, the first nine chapters of Luke, and the first twelve chapters of John.

In the second stage, Jesus is showing what kind of Messiah he is—one who will go through suffering to glory. To this point, he has hardly spoken of being arrested and suffering, of dying on the cross and rising again, or of his return. But once his closest followers confess openly that he is the Christ (see Mt 16:16; Mk 8:29; Lk 9:20), he is ready to tell the rest of the story.

Mark makes this point in a most intriguing way. He describes the scene at Caesarea Philippi, when Jesus asked his disciples, "Who do people say I am?" and "Who do you say I am?" Peter answered, "You are the Christ." But Mark prefaces this critical moment with an interesting story that he alone tells:

Some people brought a blind man and begged Jesus to touch him. He took the blind man by the hand and led him outside the village. When he had spat on the man's eyes and put his hands on him, Jesus asked, "Do you see anything?"

He looked up and said, "I see people; they look like trees walking around."

Once more Jesus put his hands on the man's eyes. Then his eyes were opened, his sight was restored, and he saw everything clearly (Mk 8:22-5).

Each of Jesus' other recorded healings took place as a single action. This one alone happened in two parts, for the healing of this blind man was an acted parable of Jesus at work. As he touched the man's blind eyes twice, he also touched his disciples' spiritual eyes twice. Many of those who saw and heard Jesus had closed eyes, seeing him only as another prophet, or even as a devil! His disciples had open eyes and saw that he was the Messiah, the Christ, but still they had to see what kind of Messiah he was—and that is what took a second touch.

So it was, then, that Jesus began to teach them that the Son of Man must suffer many things and be rejected by the elders, chief priests and teachers of the law, and that he must be killed and after three days rise again.

Why "must" God's leader suffer and die? The imperative came not from circumstances but from his Father's will. He must suffer to fulfill the Prophets and be the suffering servant. He must suffer to identify with suffering humanity. He must suffer to procure salvation (Mk 10:45).

Jesus' "must" is not that of a forced necessity or of a fateful inevitability; it is the "must" of a moral imperative. Jesus showed that a true leader does not resist the "must" that God lays on him, but, accepting these moral imperatives, he transforms them into the material of victory.

There are also "musts" for those who will follow in Jesus' steps. Mark (along with the other Gospel writers) tells us that Jesus "called the crowd to him along with his disciples," and said:

If anyone would come after me, he must deny himself and take up his cross and follow me. For whoever wants to save his life will lose it, hut whoever loses his life for me and for the gospel will save it. . . . If anyone is ashamed of me and my words in this adulterous and sinful generation, the Son of Man will he ashamed of him when he comes in his Father's glory with the holy angels. (Mk 8:34-35, 38)

And why "must" those who follow Jesus take up their cross? Because this imperative is the meaning of discipleship: "Follow me." It is the way to life: "Whoever loses his life for me and for the gospel will save it." It is the key to avoiding eternal shame: "If anyone is ashamed of me . . . the Son of Man will be ashamed of him."

John puts the same strategy of suffering and glory into different words. Some Greeks came to Philip, one of the disciples, and asked to see Jesus. When Philip and Andrew reported this, Jesus replied:

The hour has come for the Son of Man to be glorified. I tell you the truth, unless a grain of wheat falls to the ground and dies, it remains only a single seed. But if it dies, it produces many seeds. The man who loves his life will lose it, while the man who hates his life in this world will keep it for eternal life. Whoever serves me must follow me; and where I am, my servant also will he. My Father will honor the one who serves me. (Jn 12:23-26)

And then, to show the kind of death he was going to die, he said, "Now is the time for judgment on this world; now the prince of this world will be driven out. But I, when I am lifted up from the earth, will draw all men to myself" (Jn 12:31-32).

The cross was pivotal to Jesus' strategy. Above all, the Son of Man had come not to be served, "but to serve, and to give his life as a ransom for many" (Mk 10:45). That suffering would lead on to glory—the glory of his resurrection and his final return. Jesus painted his own autobiography in a parable about a man who planted a vineyard and rented it out. He sent servants to collect the fruit from the tenants, but the tenants beat them and killed some. Finally, he sent his son, whom he loved, saying, "They will respect my son." But the tenants said, "This is the heir. Come, let's kill him, and the inheritance will be ours." So they took him and killed him.

"What then will the owner of the vineyard do?" asked Jesus, rhetorically. "He will come and kill those tenants and give the vineyard to others. Haven't you read this scripture: 'The stone the builders rejected has become the capstone; the Lord has done this, and it is marvelous in our eyes'?" (Mk 12:1-11).

So Jesus unfolded his strategy step by step. First, he would be identified as the Messiah. Then he would show the kind of suffering Messiah he was—and the kind of people who would follow him. At last would come the final act. When he would return the revolution would be completed, and there would be great joy for some and eternal sadness for others.

The Leadership Style of Jesus

As we follow Jesus' ministry through the Gospels, we see his leadership in many ways: He preaches, he heals, he forgives, he challenges religious value systems. Does this mean that his leadership is only for religious leaders?

Not at all. For another theme weaves its way through the story. As Jesus touches the problems of people with the power of God, he is also creating a band of followers. He borrows the boat of a fisherman as a pulpit and calls the fishermen his friends. He sees a tax collector sitting in his place of business and recruits him. In his group, he includes women who help to support the cause out of their means. All of them are what we would call lay people; none was a priest or a scribe. Most of those who were among Jesus' first followers left their employment to follow him.

Jesus was teaching a vital truth. Not only did he come to be the Christ, he came to call others to make the kingdom of God their *primary* vocation. It was as if Jesus was saying to these fishermen and tax collectors and women, "You may leave your job, or you may stay in your job. But from now on your primary vocation is to use your second calling—your career or job, whatever that is—for kingdom purposes."

The leadership of Jesus is not a set of tools or ideas that is available for any cause we might choose. It is a kind of leading that is uniquely adapted for the cause God has chosen. Jesus' leadership was not a style he adopted, but a reality he expressed. So the question for us is not, Can I learn from Jesus certain techniques which will make me a more successful revolutionary or entrepreneur or counselor or evangelist? The question is, What ends did Jesus pursue?

Whatever our career may be, true leadership means to receive power from God and to use it under God's rule to serve people in God's way. Jacques Ellul has written often about the overwhelming power of technology in our modern world.[12] According to Ellul, technique becomes everything, and the clever leader is one who best masters the techniques in his or her field. People become means to use or they are ignored altogether. A leader is judged by how well he or she succeeds in using the techniques of leadership.

To such a style of leadership Jesus says, "Seek first the kingdom of God," not the kingdom of leadership. God rules, not leadership. People matter most, not techniques. The heart of leadership is not in mastering the "how-tos," but in being mastered by the amazing grace of God.

To the politician Jesus says, "Those aren't just *voters* you solicit; they are people God loves." To the doctor and the social worker he says, "Those aren't just *cases* you see; they are persons that Christ came to set free." To the preacher he says, "That is not just *an audience* to listen to your words; those are the blind I came to give sight." To the teacher he says, "Those students aren't names in a computer; they are persons made to know God and his truth for ever."

The Strategy of Jesus

Two millennia ago John the Baptist asked, "Are you the one, or should we look for another?"

I can imagine what a cynical reporter in our disillusioned age would feel compelled to ask Jesus, if he or she had the opportunity: "Aren't you rather disappointed after two thousand years? When you see the drug abuse and the homelessness, the wars in the world, even the divisions among your followers, don't you sometimes think you have failed? What were you aiming to do anyway?"

I can imagine Jesus quietly replying, "My aim is to extend the rule of my Father to all the nations and to set people free from all that binds them. I am accomplishing this by a radical transformation in the hearts of people, in those who know their need (the 'poor') and who are willing to be changed (the 'children').

"A strategy at once so global and so radical can only be carried out through a committed minority—men and women who leave all to follow me. I am sharing my life with them, and by being with me they are beginning to think and live like me. They, in turn, will change the world not by frontal assaults or by force or by slogans, but by infiltrating every nook and cranny of this world with God's salt and light and leaven.

"I am carrying out this strategy in two phases. The first was a phase of suffering, as I died for the sins of the world. The second will be a phase of victory, when I will return to overthrow the centers that still resist my Father's will.

"Meanwhile, I have gone back to him, and I have entrusted the work to my committed people. They are a preview of coming attractions by their love for one another. They are serving the poor and the children. They are suffering for me. Wherever they go they are preaching the good news, using words when necessary. They are inviting everyone—including you—to join our movement.

"And they *will prevail,* not in their own strength, but by the power of my Spirit in them and by the hope my promise gives to them.

"When they have finished the work, I will return. Those who have refused will be shut out, but those who have served and followed me will enter into my joy, and the everlasting celebration will begin!"

5

THE LEADER AS SEEKER

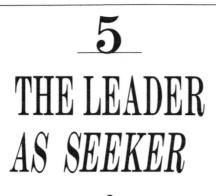

*Jesus had his own standard
of success—he stood for the
values of the kingdom.*

*"Seek first the kingdom
of God and his righteousness."*
JESUS CHRIST

*"My greatest fear for you is not that you will fail but that
you will succeed in doing the wrong thing."*
HOWARD HENDRICKS

*"Anyone can lead where people already want to go; true leaders
take them where only their better selves are willing to tread. That's where the
leaders' own values come in. They must want to do something
with their power, not just be powerful."*
JONATHAN ALTER

One hundred years ago, J. E. K. Studd, a well-known English athlete, was on a speaking tour of American universities. Studd was one of a group of devout student athletes known as the Cambridge Seven and brother of the more famous cricketer C. T. Studd. One evening he was booked to speak at the YMCA at Cornell University. A rather indifferent Midwestern student had been invited by a friend, and only at the last moment made up his mind to go. Entering late, the student was riveted when he heard Studd quote three short sentences from the Bible: "Young man, seekest thou great things for thyself? Seek them not. Seek ye first the kingdom of God." Those sentences proved to be the turning point of the young man's life, and they went straight to the springs of his motives.

That night he went back to his room, as he said, "not to study, but to fight." The next day he sought an interview with Studd, who suggested that he consult the source book of Christianity, the New Testament. Following this advice to take a hard, honest look at Christ's way, he undertook a thorough study of the resurrection. The day came when, his notes spread out on his desk and on the carpet, he was able to say with intellectual honesty, as the disciple Thomas had said centuries before, "My Lord and my God."

At once he wrote to his father, who had wanted him to join him as a partner in his law practice. He told him that he had seen a vision, the vision of Christ as Lord, and the only one who had the right to determine the investment of one's life. In his own words he began:

> I have glad news for you for your prayers have been answered. The past week has seen a great change in my plans for life. . . . I came to Cornell intending to devote my energies through life to the legal profession and the service of my country. . . . But since I have been here I have not been contented with my plans and there has been a constantly increasing impulse in me urging me to devote my whole life and talents to the service of Jesus.[1]

That student was John R. Mott, one of the greatest student evangelists and, arguably, *the* missionary statesman of the past century. Strongly influenced by evangelist Dwight L. Moody, Mott became perhaps the foremost student leader of his time. He was a prime mover in the Student Volunteer Movement, whose watchword was "The evangelization of the world in this generation." He was the architect of the Edinburgh Missionary Conference of 1910 and a founder of the International Missionary Council. As perhaps no one had since the time of the apostle Paul, Mott crisscrossed the world tirelessly in the cause of Christian unity, missions and student evangelism. He also became known as a diplomat. Late in his life he received the Nobel Peace Prize in recognition of his contribution to understanding among the nations.

Now, a century later, as the world prepares for another generational shift in leadership, it is of prime importance that the emerging generation of leaders become kingdom-seekers and not empire-builders, that they too are gripped by the challenging words John Mott heard as a student: "Young man, seekest thou great things for thyself? Seek them not. Seek ye first the kingdom of God."

"Empire-builders" is of course an epithet that can be misused to deride those who rise above the crowd. Sometimes leaders with great vision who attempt large things are called empire-builders out of jealousy. Some of my Australian friends bemoan a tendency in their country to "cut down the tall poppies," that is, to cut down to size anybody who rises head and shoulders above the others. And false leveling is found in many other cultures.

Christ's global cause should call forth great visions, for ambition in itself is not to be despised. Oswald Sanders wrote of God-sanctioned ambition: "Any ambition which centers around and terminates upon oneself is unworthy, while an ambition which has the glory of God as its center is not only legitimate but positively praiseworthy."[2] He cited as an example Jabez, who prayed to God with a holy ambition, saying, "Oh, that you would bless me and enlarge my territory! Let your hand be with me." And God granted his request (1 Chron 4:10). Jabez was singled out as being honorable because of such holy ambition, and his prayer remains as the shining epitaph of an otherwise obscure man.

The motive that lies behind ambition is the factor that makes it worthy or unworthy, and that was reflected in the words that gripped John Mott, "Seekest thou great things *for thyself?* Seek them not" (which was a word from the Lord to a man named Baruch, Jer 45:5). So Christ also counseled, "Do not store up for yourselves treasures on earth" (Mt 6:19). Sanders wrote, "The wrong lies not in the ambition itself but in its inspiring motive."[3] The kind of empire-building unworthy of Christ is that which exalts ego over Christ, rates visible success higher than God's invisible work, promotes rivalry rather than cooperation, and shows little concern for accountability.

The Shaping of Kingdom Values
If the primary task of a leader is to see and articulate the vision, it is nearly

as important to build the mindset and values needed to achieve that goal. Businessman David Rockefeller describes the role of a leader as seeing the vision, stating the mission and setting the tone. Leaders who bring meaning and commitment to our lives are those who help us to keep the faith. The leaders whom we most admire have always spent much time teaching their important values and vitalizing the shared beliefs of their followers. Moses did that constantly, and so did Lincoln, Gandhi and Martin Luther King. Effective leaders pass on these values not only through their performance, but also through their character.

The Center for Creative Leadership in Greensboro, North Carolina, is one of the most advanced in the world, committed to leadership development for both the public and the private sectors of contemporary society. Although the center is not specifically religious, those in charge believe strongly in the kind of creative leadership which is distinguished by vision, integrity and a servant spirit. When I visited the center I asked the president, Walt Ulmer, former commandant of the United States Military Academy at West Point, what he and his staff were doing to build values into future leaders.

General Ulmer told me of the fascinating studies they are conducting into how values are transmitted within an organizational culture, whether in business, education or government. Their research shows that the most effective transmitter of values is the use of value stories or parables. Written codes of ethics or standards are important, but the institutions that best set the tone do it by telling stories which embody their shared values. If, for example, a junior staff member hears about a veteran who "bucked the system" to bring about positive change or who refused to sign falsified expense accounts and who has been respected for that stand, that story will be a far more powerful influence than a code in a manual or a set of maxims hanging on the wall.

In the light of this discovery, it is intensely interesting that when Jesus sought to set the values of his kingdom-seekers, he did so in terms of value stories—parables!

This shows up vividly in Jesus' so-called parables of the kingdom, recorded by several of his biographers. (See Mark 4 for as good a summary as any of Jesus' value teaching.) Having set forth the kingdom as his goal, Jesus describes the mindset of the kingdom-seeker. The key value that runs through his teaching is *loyalty to another*. The kingdom-seeker is motivated to move beyond his or her own concerns.

Serving Another's Cause

The setting for these particular stories is significant. Jesus' family, his mother and brothers, had heard that crowds gathered to watch and hear him and that a controversy about his teaching had broken out. They thought he must be mentally unbalanced and went to take charge of him. Standing outside the house where he was teaching, they sent someone in to call him:

They told him, "Your mother and brothers are outside looking for you."

"Who are my mother and my brothers?" he asked.

Then he looked at those seated in a circle around him and said, "Here are my mother and my brothers! Whoever does God's will is my brother and sister and mother." (Mk 3:31-35)

This concern for God's rule and the spread of the good news is what Jesus singles out as most important. This, and not rank or blood relationship, brings us into Jesus' circle. The kingdom-seeker serves another's cause. This is borne out by the fact that Jesus taught his disciples to pray the great prayer, "Your kingdom come, your will be done on earth as it is in heaven" (Mt 6:10). To be in the kingdom is to do God's will.

Jesus not only told parables of the kingdom; he himself was the parable of the kingdom. In Jesus, God's powerful rule had come. As Stanley Jones used to say, Jesus is the kingdom personalized and the kingdom is Jesus universalized.

He had come as the Father's Son and the Father's servant. His vision was to see as his Father saw. His goal was to do not what pleased himself, but what pleased his Father. His food, he said, was to do the will of him who sent him, and to finish his work (Jn 4:34). He had come not to build up his own standing, but to serve another's cause. And so it follows that those who truly seek God's will are Jesus' people, the kingdom family.

One who later sought to do this with all his heart was Paul. He once wrote with sadness that "everyone looks out for his own interests, not those of Jesus Christ." But he also pointed gratefully to his young coworker, Timothy, as one who "takes a genuine interest in your welfare," and who "as a son with his father . . . has served with me in the work of the gospel" (Phil 2:20-22). Timothy was a kingdom-seeker who served another's cause.

So a key value-question that Jesus makes us ask ourselves is, What rules in my life? Is it my will? My family? My ambition or comfort? Or is it the Father's will? When visiting Mother Teresa in her shelter for the dying poor in Calcutta, I asked how she and the other sisters kept going in the midst of the squalor, poverty and the very smell of death. She replied, "We do our work for Christ, with Christ, to Christ, and that is what keeps it simple." She is a kingdom-seeker serving another's cause.

More than once I have been asked by young leaders how they can discern if their motives are pure. "I keep wondering, am I doing this work because I truly love God?" said a gifted young man. "Or am I doing it because of the fulfillment and the ego satisfaction I get out of it?" There is no simple answer, for we all have mixed motives. Desires to serve God, to help others, to find personal fulfillment are all so intertwined that it is difficult to separate them. Dealing with our mixed motives takes three elements— reflection, self-examination and bold faith.

From time to time, we need to pull aside from our busy activities and involvements and think about what we are doing and why we are doing it. We need times of deep exposure to Jesus Christ as we read the Scriptures or conversations with others who have a singleness of mind and heart. Times of reflection need to be joined with periods of self-examination, when in the presence of God we pray, "Search me, O God, and know my heart; test me and know my anxious thoughts. See if there is any offensive way in me, and lead me in the way everlasting" (Ps 139:23-24). After we have prayed this, we need to take time to be quiet, to listen inwardly, to note and perhaps write down what God says, and to face areas where our motives have been less than pure. "Purity of heart is to will one thing," said Søren Kierkegaard. And though we may aspire to it, if we are honest we know we have not attained it. In confession we need to bring before God areas of our thoughts, actions, motives and ambitions where there has not been integrity and purity. And then, having done that, we need to step out in bold faith.

There have been those moments in my own work when I have been preparing to speak to a group. At such times, I have found that as I get quiet I also become troubled. The inner voice of God's Spirit speaks to my conscience and reminds me of pride, or laziness, or impurity, or failure to pray or prepare. At moments like that, all I can say is, "My God, I come before you with mixed motives and an impure heart. I am a sinful man. Forgive me for Christ's sake. Fill me with your Spirit, and use me just as I am." Then I stand and speak and minister, confident that only God knows my heart well enough to sort out the pure from the impure. I give him all I know of myself and ask his forgiveness where necessary. If I were to wait until I was 100 per cent sure that my motives were pure, I would never speak or serve or minister! I would be completely paralyzed. Only one person was totally devoted to another's cause, and that was Jesus Christ, my leader. Since he has graciously called me, forgiven me and included me in his family, I seek, however imperfectly, to serve his cause.

So, too, humility is remembering that the gifts we have come through us but not from us. We have nothing that we have not received from above, and we give them back to God to use (John 3:28; 1 Cor 4:7). My friend Dick Halverson has for years written a letter to leaders, which he calls "Perspective." Hundreds of men and women in various walks of life read it and are helped by his seed thoughts. They are so well-done that a number have been published.

Once a friend suggested to Dick that he ought to have his letters copyrighted so that he could guard them for purposes of publication. That sounded like a good idea, so he set the process in motion to apply for a copyright on his materials.

That week he faced a deadline for the copy of the next letter. He had had a busy day and had not been able to formulate his thoughts. He sat late into the night, trying to get the ideas to come, and near midnight he became very frustrated because the typed material had to be ready for a deadline early the next morning. Finally, almost in desperation, he prayed, "God, I just can't get these ideas. They won't come. I'm frustrated. Please help me."

He says that it seemed as if the Lord replied to him, "Dick, if you are going to get this copyright so that you can say it is your material, that is fine. But then you do it by yourself. I am not going to help." Halverson decided on the spot that he was going to cancel the copyright proceedings. For other authors, copyrights might be fine. But for himself, on this particular project, he wanted to say that the ideas and the influence belonged to the Lord and not to him. He was serving another's cause. Then, the writer's block broke, the ideas came, and the next letter went on its way on time. Halverson had reaffirmed what John the Baptist said long before, "A man can receive only what is given him from heaven" (Jn 3:27).

Teaching Another's Truth

The kingdom-seeker also *teaches another's truth*. His message is received as a trust, not manufactured. Jesus told this in a parable while he was sitting in a boat teaching a large crowd of people gathered at the water's edge.

"Listen!" he said, "A farmer went out to sow his seed. . . ." In his parable (Mk 4:1-8), he told how the seed was scattered: some along a path, where birds ate it up; some on rocky places, where it sprang up quickly, but soon withered under the sun because the soil was shallow; some fell among thorns, which grew up and choked the plants; still other seed fell on good soil, where it grew and multiplied. And so he warned his hearers, "He who has ears to hear, let him hear" (Mk 4:9).

Jesus pictures himself—and by analogy his disciples—as a farmer scattering seed for the kingdom. That seed, he goes on to explain, is "the word" (Mk 4:15, 16, 18, 20). From the start of his work, the sowing of the Word has been at the heart of all that Jesus has done. He has proclaimed the good news of the kingdom (Mk 1:14). He has taught with authority in the synagogues (Mk 1:22). He has preached the Word in a house in Capernaum (Mk 2:2). He has told people at the synagogue in Nazareth that he is anointed to preach good news (Lk 4:18). Crowds have been down by the lake, listening to "the word of God" as he gave it to them (Lk 5:1-3). Those who obey his words are compared to a man who builds his house on a rock; on that foundation the house withstands battering storms (Lk 6:47-48).

But that same Word has also caused divisions. Some, like his townspeople at Nazareth, have rejected his message in anger, and certain religious leaders have even plotted to kill him (Mk 3:6). Others in the large crowds have listened with a minimum of interest and drifted off. There have even been those, like his own family, who have thought that he was out of his mind (Mk 3:21). But then there have been those—like the fishermen Peter, James and John, and the tax collector Matthew, and others—who have heard and left everything to follow him.

So now, as Jesus teaches the crowd, he explains that there are enemies of the kingdom. Satan, his invisible diabolic opponent, "snatches away what was sown," much like birds that pick seed off the path (Mt 13:19; Mk 4:15). Opponents persecute some who try to follow Jesus, like the sun which scorches seed growing in shallow and rocky ground (Mk 4:16-17). Some are interested in what Jesus has to say but are so preoccupied with worries and wealth and worldly desires that their initial interest is choked out, as weeds choke plants (Mk 4:18-19).

Jesus says, the only repellent against these enemies of the soul is the Word itself. In his brief explanation of the parable of the sower (Mk 4:13-20), the term *word* or *logos* occurs eight times. The farmer sows the Word. The Word is like seed sown along the path. Satan comes to take away the Word. Others hear the Word and receive it, but when it brings trouble they go away. Others hear but the Word is choked out. But then there are the Matthews and the Peters, who not only hear the Word, but also accept it into their hearts and let the powerful truth of the kingdom grow into their lives.

Be *attentive hearers* of the Word, says Jesus (Mk 4:9). "Let it in—hear it; let it root—accept it; let it grow, produce and multiply." But he also tells his followers to be *expectant sowers* of the Word.

Kingdom-seekers teach another's truth. They sow God's seed, not their own ideas. Different farmers may have different ways of sowing, but the seed is vital. So the kingdom-seeker is not preoccupied with style or method, but with communicating God's truth. And Jesus has already modeled this in his own life.

Leaders who seek to follow Jesus are reminded that cultures and styles change, but the one constant is God's Word. This is particularly important in our postmodern times, when the world has become so pluralistic in one sense with competing cultures and ideologies, and so monolithic in another, with instant communications that tend to produce fads, sensations and mere entertainment.

The early followers of Jesus learned their lessons well from their master-teacher. They "preached the word wherever they went" (Acts 8:4). Paul was living out Jesus' model when he wrote to the followers of Christ at Colossae that he had been commissioned to be a servant of the church, "to present to you the word of God in its fullness" (Col 1:25), and that the gospel they heard was the gospel "of which I, Paul, have become a servant" (Col 1:23). Kingdom-seekers are servants both of the church and of the gospel, and those who faithfully serve Christ and his people will sow the good seed so the "word of Christ" will "dwell richly" in the hearts of believers (Col 3:16).

Across the intervening centuries, kingdom-seekers have followed in the steps of the master-sower, showing the power of the Word. Two examples strike me, one from the eighteenth century, and one from our own time.

England in the 1700s had fallen into religious, moral and social decay. Voluntary societies had worked hard to improve conditions, establishing hospitals, publicizing the inhumane conditions of the prisons, legislating against alcohol, establishing free schools for poor children. Hard-line law-and-order advocates had sought to reduce crime by increasing the threat of punishment, making as many as 160 offenses subject to the death penalty. Scholarly books had been written to defend Christianity, yet little in the way of a profound moral change had taken place. In 1738 one high-placed religious leader, Bishop Secker, asserted that if the torrent of impiety did not stop, it could become "absolutely fatal."[4]

The historian and biographer Arnold Dallimore writes:

The successive failures of the several attempts to better conditions simply proved that the nation's trouble lay basically with the individual human heart and that the "torrent of impiety" would flow until some power was found that could stanch it at its source.

During the very months in which Bishop Secker wrote his foreboding words, England was startled by the sound of a voice. It was the voice of a preacher, George Whitefield, a clergyman but twenty-two years old, who was declaring the gospel in the pulpits of London with such fervor and power, that no church would hold the multitudes that flocked to hear.[5]

Before long the youthful Whitefield left the churches to go into the open air, and included in his preaching tours the miners, who were known for their poverty and brutality. In what has become a classic memoir, Whitefield wrote of preaching as he stood near piles of coal, surrounded by coal-grimed colliers' faces:

> Having no righteousness of their own to renounce, they were glad to hear of a Jesus who was a friend of publicans, who came not to call the righteous but sinners to repentance. The first discovery of their being affected was to see the white gutters made by their tears which plentifully fell down their black cheeks, as they came out of their coal pits. Hundreds and hundreds of them were soon brought under deep convictions, which, as the event proved, happily ended in a sound and thorough conversion. The change was visible to all, though numbers chose to impute it to anything, rather than the finger of God.[6]

The preaching of the word by Whitefield, the Wesley brothers and others proved indeed to be like God's finger, God's good seed, the sought-for power that could stanch evil at the source of the heart. The effect of this movement was described by the historian J. R. Green:

> A religious revival burst forth . . . which changed in a few years the whole temper of English society. The church was restored to life and activity. Religion carried to the hearts of the people a fresh spirit of moral zeal, while it purified our literature and our manners. A new philanthropy reformed our prisons, infused clemency and wisdom into our penal laws, abolished the slave trade, and gave first impulse to popular education.[7]

In a far different setting, but also in an age of moral and spiritual need, that same seed is at work. My wife Jeanie has for a number of years taught a women's Bible class in our home city. Some forty or fifty women meet every Thursday morning in a large room at the home of a doctor and his wife. They have no organization and no name, but affectionately refer to their group simply as "Bible," as in "I'll see you at Bible Thursday!" For two hours they read and discuss the Scriptures with a few minutes given to singing and prayer. Jeanie is a gifted teacher, good at making people feel involved and welcome, helping them to take part and drawing them out with questions. But the Word of God is the center. Week after week they read and study consecutively through a portion of Scripture. Jeanie uses reference books to prepare, but it is the Word of Scripture itself, not words about the Word, or books about the Word, which is the focus.

The effects are moving. No tears run down grimy cheeks as with Whitefield's miners, but the changes are just as deep. Most of the women who come have had little background in the Bible or in a personal walk with God. When a woman first comes, she is likely to attend out of curiosity, invited by a friend, to see what is so preoccupying the ladies on the tennis team and why they spend every Thursday studying the Bible. She may say that she has come out of intellectual interest. Often a first-timer will sit very rigidly for a number of weeks at the very back of the room, as if not to get overly involved. Within several weeks the welcome and warmth are such that she will begin to relax. She may move up two or three rows. After a few more weeks she may even ask or answer a question. One can almost see the change, as over the course of several weeks someone moves from the back to the front of the room as her heart is drawn to the message of the word. Lovingly, gently, but firmly and clearly, Jeanie presents Christ from the Word. More often than not, hearts are opened, minds understand, attitudes are changed. Loving friendships are established. Husbands and children begin to notice the difference. The Word has been received, and it multiplies and is fruitful.

Admittedly, George Whitefield was a great preacher, and my wife is an exceptional teacher. Yet the power has not been in their personalities, but in their message. They are kingdom-seekers, teaching another's truth.

Accepting Another's Results

The kingdom-seeker also *accepts another's results.* Jesus pictured this value in the parable of the sower and the soils. What happened in Jesus' work can be expected by all who lead as he did.

In Jesus' story, the farmer's seed fell on hard, rocky and weedy ground. Now a farmer would not deliberately sow in bad soil, but no farmer can fully control where seed falls. Nor can a leader fully control the environment. We can seek to understand our coworkers, our environment, and the trends in our world. But in a results-oriented world the kingdom-seeker realizes there is no way to be totally in control of the results.

Jesus' words apply particularly to those who are engaged in "the ministry of the Word." The preacher or teacher will come across the trampled soil, the hard hearts, the nonreceptive, who will not pay attention.

It is as if Jesus is saying, "Look, if you want to be a leader you have got to be a realist. I had mixed results. Some dismissed me, some ignored me, some laughed at me, some opposed me. Some followed me for a brief time. Some stuck with me, and their names will go down in history. If you are going to expect in your leadership to be in total control, you might as well stop now. A leader has to be a realist, not get discouraged when there is indifference or apathy or opposition, but keep on with determination. Above all, when you are serving God's cause you know you can't help but win in his time."

But Jesus' teaching applies not only to preachers. Anyone who works with people—whether a politician, an educator, a parent, a manager or a development worker—faces the whole range of human response from total resistance to enthusiastic acceptance.

General Charles Gordon once asked Li Hung Chang, an old Chinese leader, "What is leadership? And how is humanity divided?" He received this cryptic answer: "There are only three kinds of people in the world—those that are immovable, those that are movable, and those who move them!"[8]

Moving people to change is the essence of leadership. And those who are the movers need to understand people as Jesus did. The students of change tell us that about 10 per cent of any group will be early adapters who respond eagerly and enthusiastically to new ideas. At the other end will be 10 per cent who will never change. Their motto is "We never did it that way before," and they will drag, resist or drop out. The 80 per cent in between will move slowly in new directions.

Jesus, in his interpretation of the parable of the sower, adds to the natural human instincts of enthusiasm or inertia another factor, the reality of immense, subtle, spiritual pressure—led by the devil—that is opposed to God and his rule. Sometimes Satan works to compound inertia, leading people to resist the movements of God toward peace, justice, truth and faith. Or he may stimulate enthusiasm, making people rush to accept the latest fad or novelty, while ignoring the time-tested landmarks of history. The kingdom-seeking leader in any field must take into account the realities of environment and human nature and also continually be aware of underlying spiritual conflict.

In a technological age, we are constantly seeking better programs or improved techniques that are guaranteed to work. I suspect Jesus would be all for improved strains of seed and better methods of sowing! But I think he would also warn us that no technique is guaranteed to work where people are involved and spiritual forces are at work. When we have done our best, we should still be humble enough to accept the same kind of results that Jesus had.

Awaiting Another's Time

It follows that the kingdom-seeker also *awaits another's time.*

Jesus put this sense of timing in another parable:

This is what the kingdom of God is like. A man scatters seed on the ground. Night and day, whether he sleeps or gets up, the seed sprouts and grows, though he does not know how. All by itself the soil produces corn—first the stalk, then the ear, then the full grain in the ear. As soon as the grain is ripe, he puts the sickle to it, because the harvest has come. (Mk 4:26-29)

Sometimes we think that God's work depends so much on us that we become feverish, compulsive and overly involved—workaholics of the kingdom rather than disciples of the King. This kind of hyperactivism does not come from the obedience of faith but from the anxiety of unbelief. Fearful that if we do not "go, go, go," our plans—or even God's cause—will fail, we get into a kind of messiah complex, believing that it is up to us to save the world. And so we end up burned out.

To this Jesus counsels us to say, "Commitment, yes. Compulsion, no." In his story of the seed which grows whether a man sleeps or not, he is saying, "Sow the seed and go to bed. God doesn't need to sleep, but you do!" God's seed will reproduce itself powerfully and surely and, sometimes, slowly. So the Christlike leader learns to wait another's time.

Again, Jesus is giving insight into the nature of the kingdom: It is partly open and partly hidden; partly present, partly future; near because Jesus is here, but not fulfilled until he comes once more at the end of time. The Word produces results now; "the seed sprouts." At a later day the harvest will come.

If we want to be part of this work of God, patience is a must. The parable of the growing seed is meant to encourage the discouraged and to restrain the impatient. Sow the seed, wait, and sleep! The farmer cannot help the seed grow by digging it up and looking at it all through the night. Like that hidden seed, God's work goes on, often invisibly, and seemingly underground.

We are not to give up when nothing seems to happen, nor to force growth by trying to accelerate God's work. The secret of working in concert with God's timing is knowing when to wait for the growing seed and when to reap the ready harvest.

This sense of timing is essential to leadership. It was "when the time had fully come," wrote Paul, that God sent his Son into the world. At that precise moment in history, when Roman armies had pacified the Mediterranean world and created a communications network that stretched for hundreds of miles, when Greek had become the common language and made it possible to communicate widely, when belief in the ancient gods had died in people's minds and the world was ready for new hope . . . *then* God sent his Son.

Jesus showed an innate sense of timing. For thirty years he waited and prepared in the carpenter's shop, emerging at the right time onto the public scene. Intuitively, he knew when to speak to the crowds and when to withdraw in quiet. He would heal someone, then, when the crowds clamored for more miracles, say, "My time has not yet come." In him we see that superb sense of timing which marks all great leadership. He had a sixth sense that knew when it was time to wait, plan and marshal resources and a decisiveness that was able to move swiftly when the right moment came, to know what need to be done and then to take advantage of momentum when it had been created.

A good leader is neither overly cautious nor overly impetuous. So self-knowledge is something leaders should always be seeking.

Do I tend to be cautious? There are times when that is a strength. But I need to train myself to throw caution aside when the time comes and move.

Do I tend to be too impetuous? Then there is a need to exercise the discipline of thoughtful preparation, control and waiting.

Sometimes patience is the most difficult quality for a leader to possess. Charles Blair, the leader of a large religious organization and church in Denver, Colorado, found his ministry in serious trouble because he did not exercise patience. Blair had dreams and a plan for a magnificent retirement center for elderly people. But his impatience and his desire to push ahead made him unwilling to listen to the cautions of his close advisers and even of his wife. Soon his ministry was in financial jeopardy, his integrity was publicly questioned, and his enterprises near collapse. He held on, and after nearly a decade his work had not only survived and grown, but much of the debt had been paid off. But he learned hard lessons.

Blair tells of a time when, in near despair, he withdrew from his busy work for a time of solitude. As he prayed and read the Bible, it seemed God was saying to him, "It is difficult to talk to you on the run." In his heart Blair sensed that God was telling him that his love for the elderly was a God-given concern, but that God was also saying, "Son, there is more to my call than a shining vision." Each God-given dream, he sensed, had three ingredients: The *method* and the *timing* were equally important as the *goal*. God seemed to say, "And here is where you stopped listening, Charles. You caught my vision and galloped ahead without learning how I wished to bring it about."

Now chastened, but still a respected leader, Charles Blair says that his painful lessons taught him three questions the leader must ask about how a vision relates to God's will: Is the dream *his* vision? Is the method *his* way? Is the timing *his* moment?[9]

Dreaming of Another's Glory

Jesus taught still another quality of true leadership: The kingdom-seeker dreams of *another's glory.* Now, by definition, a leader must have some dreams. Too many young men and women have settled for too small a vision. A student leader once said, "In the 1960s students studied sociology to change the world. In the 1970s they studied psychology to change themselves. Now we study business to get a job." Business can be the place for carrying out God's call, but the kingdom-seeker looks beyond making a living, to fulfilling a sense of calling. Waiting on God's time is not smallness of vision, and patience is not apathy. Jesus illustrated this in another dramatic parable:

> What shall we say the kingdom of God is like, or what parable shall we use to describe it? It is like a mustard seed, which is the smallest seed you plant in the ground. Yet when planted, it grows and becomes the largest of all garden plants, with such big branches that the birds of the air can perch in its shade. (Mk 4:30)

Comparing the tiny seed to the great tree, it is as if Jesus is saying, "If you want to be a leader in God's kingdom, don't despise the day of small beginnings. But don't settle for less than the greatest dream God gives you."

Several years ago we launched a new organization, Leighton Ford Ministries. After thirty-one challenging and fulfilling years of working very closely with my brother-in-law, Billy Graham, I sensed that God was calling us to identify, develop, and network younger leaders for Christ's global cause. During the incubation of this new venture, I was reading a passage in the prophecy of Isaiah where God is speaking to his coming leader/servant, "It is too small a thing for you to be my servant to restore the tribes of Jacob and bring back those of Israel I have kept. I will also make you a light for the Gentiles, that you may bring my salvation to the ends of the earth" (Is 49:6). Those four little words, *"too small a thing,"* leaped off the page and into my mind and imagination. I read and reread Isaiah 49, which is, in effect, the autobiography of Jesus Christ, written hundreds of years before he came.

In those terse sentences the full career of Jesus Christ is set forth: his life pre-empted before his birth; prepared for thirty years in obscurity, like an arrow hidden in a quiver until the time came for it to be used; given a high purpose to glorify his Father; and yet allowed to go through the deep pain of rejection.

In the light of this, it is as if God says to his leader/servant, "What is worth what I have invested in you? What is worth the call and the preparation, the purpose and the pain?" The answer is plain: To restore only Israel is "too small a thing." He is being prepared as a light to the ends of the earth. God's servant would come with good news for Israel, but also for the nations.

So Jesus, fulfilling that prophecy, came from an obscure village in a small province of the Roman Empire to become a light for the world. Always having time for the smallest thing, he constantly dreamed of his Father's greater purpose. One can imagine him painstakingly crafting the tables and plowhandles in his earthly father's workshop, knowing the time would eventually come when he would shape human lives to be useful instruments in his heavenly Father's kingdom. He could tell the story of one lost sheep, yet have eyes and heart big enough to take in the huge, harassed and helpless crowds, like sheep without a shepherd. He could talk to one woman by a well and proclaim to the multitude on the seashore. He could pause to heal one blind beggar, yet not stop until he had died for the sins of the whole world.

Reflecting on that text from Isaiah and on Jesus, I have asked myself, What is "too small a thing"? What does it mean to say to the younger leaders whom we seek to develop, "Don't live for too small a thing"?

The smallest thing is not too small if it is done for the glory of God and the global purpose of Jesus Christ. Our friend Colleen Evans, whose husband leads a Presbyterian congregation in Washington, D.C., went to hear Mother Teresa when she spoke at a luncheon in that city. Afterwards, deeply moved, Colleen went up to her and said, "Mother, what can I do to help the world?" Mother Teresa said, "My dear, are you married? Do you have children?" When Colleen replied that she was and she did, Mother Teresa told her, "Go home and love your husband and love your children." That was not too small a thing! Now, Colleen Evans does many things. She writes, lectures, serves as a board member of World Vision, and chaired Billy

Graham's Washington Crusade committee. But the point is that the smallest thing—to love your spouse and your children—is not too small when done to the glory of God.

But the biggest thing is too small a thing when it is not done to the glory of God and for the global purpose of Jesus Christ. To build the biggest house, the biggest law practice, the biggest business, or the biggest church is too small a thing if it is not done to the glory of God and for the global purpose of Jesus Christ.

Was that what Jesus meant by his story of the mustard seed? Do not live for too small a thing? Let your dreams be big enough? "Give up your small ambitions," said Ignatius Loyola, calling the students of Paris to service in Asia. "Give up your small ambitions and come to the ends of the earth for Jesus Christ!"

To dream of another's glory is to let our God be big enough—the God of the whole earth. It means to let our prayers be big enough, asking not only for our personal desires, but also for the people of the earth to know the peace and justice of God. It means to let our jobs be big enough, working not simply to make a living or build a career, but as a vocation in which God may be glorified. It means to let our homes be big enough, not only as a shelter for us from the world, but as centers of renewal from which we go as Christ's ambassadors into the world. It means to let our retirements be big enough.

John Wright, the president of a bank, took early retirement at the age of sixty-two. He and his wife Ruth had enough to enable them to live in comfort for years to come in their hometown of Chattanooga, Tennessee. But John and Ruth were not willing to retire for too small a thing. In their active retirement, they spend part of each year in Australia, helping to plant churches in the burgeoning suburbs of Sydney and using their administrative gifts for various projects.

Kingdom-seekers are those, like William Carey, who "expect great things from God and attempt great things for God."

Kingdom-seekers will be like John R. Mott, who sought great things not for himself, but for the kingdom of God.

Kingdom-seekers are leaders marked by *loyalty,* for they seek another's cause; by *fidelity,* for they tell another's truth; by *humility,* for they accept another's results; by *constancy,* for they wait another's time; and by *expectancy,* for they dream of another's glory.

6

THE LEADER AS SEER

•

Jesus saw things clearly
—he had a steady vision.

•

"Your old men will dream
dreams, your young men will see visions."
J O E L

"Visions [are] the silent shapers of our thought."
T H O M A S S O W E L L

Vision is the very stuff of leadership—the ability to see in a way that compels others to pay attention. One day as I was walking the beach at Waikiki, in Honolulu, I saw several dozen people forming a tight circle as they watched something. I looked over their shoulders and saw a young man building a magnificent sandcastle, incredibly detailed and beautifully spray-painted. He was absorbed in creating what he saw, like a child playing in a sandpit, and that compelling vision made the rest of us pay attention.

As a student once put it, "Leaders point us in the right direction and tell us to get moving." Vision is like a magnifying glass which creates focus, a bridge which takes us from the present to the future, a target that beckons.

"Vision grabs," says leadership specialist Warren Benniss. He described vision as the commodity of leaders. Leaders, Benniss says, know how to get people's attention through vision, but "leaders also *pay* attention as well as catch it."[1]

Napoleon was described by a contemporary biographer as having a combination of idealism and realism "which enabled him to face the most exalted visions at the same time as the most insignificant realities."[2]

Henry Ford had the vision to gamble everything on the future of the automobile at a time when manufacturers turned out fewer cars in a year than they now do in a day or two.

Benniss says of William Paley, who built the CBS radio and television network:

> He could sit in New York in his tiny office with his almost bankrupt company and see not just his own desk . . . but millions of the American people out in the hinterlands . . . many of them in homes not yet connected to electricity. He would *envision an audience at a time when there was in fact no audience.* He not only had the vision, he knew how to harness it.[3]

By focusing attention on vision, says Benniss, leaders operate on the *emotional and spiritual resources* of their organizations, on their values, commitment and aspirations, rather than on their physical resources. But at the same time, visions often do not originate with the leader personally, but rather with others. "Successful leaders, we have found, are great askers, and they *do pay attention.*"[4]

Charles Swindoll writes in his *Quest for Character*[5] that vision is spawned by faith, sustained by hope, sparked by imagination and strengthened by enthusiasm. It is greater than sight, deeper than a dream, broader than an idea. Vision encompasses vast vistas outside the realm of the predictable, the safe, the expected.

By reading, talking, observing, asking, the leader gets the raw material which ignites into a vision that burns with an intensity that draws others to it.

Was Jesus a Visionary?

Some visionaries are entrepreneurs. Some years ago my friend Tom Cousins, one of the major developers in the city of Atlanta, Georgia, bought the rights to develop above the hundreds of sprawling acres of railroad yards in downtown Atlanta. He took me to see the place and described his plan for a huge complex of hotels, office buildings, parking decks and a great stadium which would rise in that empty space. In the transformation of that great city, his vision has now become a reality. I was impressed and overwhelmed. It was a tremendous vision.

Yet we never read of Jesus having grand plans, schemes and designs like that. Vision is not used in the Bible in our sense of an entrepreneurial "visionary." In the Scriptures, the word *vision* is commonly used of an ecstatic experience in which saintly people with an awareness of God receive a special word from him.

Those visions came to people waking and sleeping, at night and during the day, in dreams and through angels. Judges and prophets and kings had visions, but so did ordinary farmers and housewives.

Visions abounded during times of spiritual revival in the history of Israel. But in periods of decline there was a marked absence of vision. One of the Bible writers remarks, "In those days the word of the Lord was rare; there were not many visions" (1 Sam 3:1). A familiar proverb tells us that "where there is no vision, the people perish" (Prov 29:18 KJV). The thought behind "perish" here is of people casting off restraint (a point brought out more clearly in modern Bible versions such as RSV and the NIV). Righteousness and order in a society depend on a vision beyond our human horizons. The lack of moral vision in a society can be laid at the feet of those who ought to be speaking for God, his prophets. "Be stunned and amazed," wrote Isaiah. "The Lord . . . has sealed your eyes [the prophets], he has covered your heads [the seers]" [Is 29:9-10]. When the seers cannot see, that is stunning. The blindness of society reflects religion without reality, the loss of spiritual vision.

Now Jesus, so far as the records show, was not a visionary in the ecstatic sense. In his story we read of no burning-bush experience such as Moses had; no dream of the stars bowing such as Joseph had; no dream of a ladder going up to heaven such as Jacob had; no vision of wheels within wheels such as inspired Ezekiel. Yet Jesus has inspired more visions—in artists, composers, architects, leaders—than anyone who has ever lived. Without entrepreneurial plans or ecstatic experiences, Jesus stands all by himself as *the* transformational leader. He was able to create, articulate and communicate a compelling vision; to change what people talk about and dream of; to make his followers transcend self-interest; to enable us to see ourselves and our world in a new way; to provide prophetic insight into the very heart of things; and to bring about the highest order of change.

What Visions Did Jesus Have?
We might speak of four key events in Jesus' life which contained elements that could be called visionary.

1. At his baptism, Jesus "saw heaven being torn open and the Spirit descending on him like a dove," and a voice saying, "You are my Son" (Mk 1:10-11).

2. When his seventy-two disciples returned from a mission on which he had sent them and reported that even the demons had submitted to them in his name, he replied, "I saw Satan fall like lightning from heaven" (Lk 10:18).

3. At the pivotal point when his follower Peter confessed that Jesus was the Messiah, Jesus told him and his other disciples that he must suffer and die; then he took Peter and two others with him to a high mountain, where he was transfigured before them and his clothes literally glowed (Mt 16:13—17:13; Mk 8:27—9:13; Lk 9:18-36).

4. Finally, we may include Jesus' vision of the future, as recorded, for example, in Mark 13. On a trip to Jerusalem, his disciples looked around at the temple buildings with awe. He asked them, "Do you see all these great buildings?" Then, in a grand forecasting of events, he gave them his vision of when the temple would be thrown down, of the conflict of good and evil through history, of the spreading of the gospel, and of the final time when

"men will see the Son of Man coming in clouds with great power and glory" (Mk 13:26).

So at the beginning of his ministry (his baptism), at the inaugural mission of his disciples, at the pivotal point in the middle (the great confession and transfiguration), and as he comes to the climax, Jesus is a seer. He shows visions of who he is, God's Son, the one who sends and empowers his representatives; of his mission as the suffering servant; and of the end of history with the triumph of his kingdom.

Where Did Jesus' Visions Come From?

Earlier I referred to the book *Servant and Son,* J. Ramsey Michaels' fascinating discussion of Jesus' sense of identity and mission and where it came from. Michaels believes that Jesus is "undeniably presented in the Gospels as a visionary or seer," although the Gospel stories give little detail about the mechanics of his visions. He describes vision as

a way of seeing, a way of perceiving reality, whether that reality is a supernatural revelation direct from God, or simply the everyday world in which we live. A visionary may see extraordinary things that no human eye has ever seen or may bring new perspectives to commonplace things that the rest of us have seen all along, but taken for granted.[6]

Jesus, says Michaels, did both. He *told* stories about everyday activities like planting and harvesting, fishing and baking, buying and selling. And he *acted out* stories—eating with sinners, forgiving them, healing them. In so doing, he lifted up "his profound and peculiar vision of what is real."[7]

Where did Jesus' visions come from? First, says Michaels, they came from the images of the Scriptures, for Jesus was steeped in the Old Testament Scriptures. So when at his baptism Jesus heard the voice of the Father saying, "This is my beloved Son," he was likely seeing in his mind the picture of Abraham ready to sacrifice his beloved son Isaac, or the picture of the beloved servant from Isaiah 42.

Michaels makes another intriguing suggestion that Jesus' parables "are a retelling of what he himself has heard, or seen, from God. They may be described as stories his Father told him, or images his Father showed him."[8] Is it possible, wonders Michaels, that the stories Jesus told and acted out in time were stories his Father had told him in eternity? This is, of course, just speculation.

What it does underline, however, is Jesus' insistence that everything he taught he had first learned from the Father. This is especially brought out in the Gospel of John. For example, "My teaching is not my own. It comes from him who sent me" (Jn 7:16).

So Jesus was far more than an entrepreneur. He was not just another ecstatic prophet. His visions were not created or invented; they were truths that he saw from his Father and truths he lived. He himself explained this: "I tell you the truth, the Son can do nothing by himself; he can do only what he sees his Father doing, because whatever the Father does the Son also does. For the Father loves the Son and shows him all he does" (Jn 5:19-20).

Jesus was a leader who paid attention. *Vision for Jesus was seeing how the truth, as his Father showed it, touched life as Jesus lived it.*

I can imagine him looking at fishermen pulling in their nets or at the man with a dreaded skin disease asking for healing or at the magnificent temple which had been commercialized or at religious institutions like the sabbath day, and saying, "Father, how do you see this?" Out of the intimacy of his Father's presence and the compelling word of Scripture, Jesus the Son and servant saw how God wanted people and the world to be. If we are going to be leaders in Christ, our vision must come from the same place as Jesus'. It must come from the Word of our God, and from Spirit-filled minds and imaginations, and from asking, "How does Jesus see my world and my life and the people around me?" Our task is not to dream up visions or to develop strategies, but to see Jesus' visions and understand what the Father's strategy is for our lives.

As Terry Fullam asks, "Who originates vision? God, humans, or both?" His answer:

> Vision is a product of God working in us. He creates the vision and we receive it; it becomes a rallying point, a goal toward which we move as his people. . . . Vision arises out of our burden to know the will of God. . . . Vision is something that elicits a response from us, that calls us forth. Goals, on the other hand, are things we project. . . . If I am part

of the body of Christ, it is not really a matter of "Where do I want to go?"—but rather, "Where does he want to take me?"[9]

What Were the Marks of Jesus' Vision?

If Jesus' vision was not primarily an entrepreneurial scheme or an ecstatic experience, what characterized him as a seer?

1. *Jesus was a seer who lived by the unseen.* Our contemporary world is preoccupied with what can be seen, counted and appraised. At least in the West, we are a results-oriented world. Leadership effectiveness is judged by the ability to set objectives and to reach measurable goals. How many? How much? and How often? tend to be our questions about any enterprise, even about Christ's cause. As a result, we too often become the "victims of the visible."

In contrast, Jesus' vision was mystical—even, in a sense, secretive. To his disciples he spoke in parables describing "the secrets of the kingdom of God." He described a heavenly Father who saw "in secret" and was not impressed with showy prayers or public displays of charity. He said that he saw "heaven opened." Did anyone else? He announced that he saw Satan fall. Did anyone else?

Once, when asked by religious leaders when the kingdom of God would come, he replied, "The kingdom of God does not come with your careful observation, nor will people say, 'Here it is,' or 'There it is,' because the kingdom of God is within you" (Lk 17:20-21). Vision, in this sense, is simply the seeing power of faith. Faith enables us to see with our mind and imagination what we do not yet see with our eyes and experience. Moses had this kind of vision when he endured the wrath of the king of Egypt, because by faith "he saw him who is invisible" (Heb 11:27). Vision is the heart of the great conviction that "what is seen is temporary, but what is unseen is eternal" (2 Cor 4:18).

Walter Cronkite always closed his evening news summary by saying, "That's the way it is." Jesus would never say that. He would close by saying, "That's the way it *appears!*"

If we see as Jesus does, we will not be the victims of the visible, swept away by apparent success or swept under by present suffering.

Billy Graham and his wife, Ruth, returned to the part of China where she grew up as the daughter of a missionary surgeon. When her father first arrived to begin his medical work there, he had been greeted by James Graham (no relation), a veteran missionary who had been there a quarter of a century. James Graham would often come home in the evening covered with the spittle of those who had jeered at the "foreign devil" as he preached in the marketplace. His wife would frequently find him black and blue from being pelted with stones. In twenty-five years that man had seen twenty-five converts to Jesus Christ. Today, in that same region of China, there are an estimated 140,000 followers of Jesus Christ.

Commenting on the patience that is called for in God's work, Ruth Graham quotes the Prayer Book version of Psalm 27:16, "O tarry thou the Lord's leisure." She laughs as she says, "The Lord is too leisurely for me sometimes."

Compared with some success stories, the measurable results of James Graham's twenty-five years in China seem pitiably small, hardly a success at all. Some church buildings are being created in Korea and America that will seat upwards of ten thousand people. Other little village churches in India have room for only a handful of believers to gather. How does Jesus look at them? Bigness or smallness is not the issue. In God's sight, it is not the presence or absence of numbers that counts, but whether the kingdom is present in reborn hearts and remade relationships. When we see as Jesus does, then the mystery of "Christ in you, the hope of glory" (Col 1:27) will be the unseen central secret of our lives.

2. *But Jesus' vision was also practical and very much "down-to-earth."* It was of the eternal in the everyday. See how his parables touched everything—fishing, sewing, reaping, trading, investing, cooking, partying. He looked at everything through his Father's eyes. Jesus' visions were not "religious." They were ways of seeing life itself lived out in the reality of God.

Just as Jesus said that he had come to bring abundant life, not religion, so the visions of leaders who follow Christ are not just related to religious and churchy matters. The vision of a surgeon, a scientist, a teacher, or a businesswoman in Christ is just as spiritual as that of a pastor or an evangelist. If we take seriously the truth that Jesus Christ lives in all of his people and in every part of their lives, then nothing a person in Christ does can be called secular.

Dr. Ida Scudder saw life in that way. Her father and her grandfather had both been missionary doctors in India, but she had decided that India was the last place she wanted to have a career. A visit back to India to help with her sick mother changed her vision. Two Hindus and a Muslim had come requesting help for their wives who were giving birth, but they had refused the assistance of her father because customs forbade contact with the opposite sex.

For Ida Scudder that night was long and traumatic:

I could not sleep that night—it was too terrible. Within the touch of my hand there were three young girls dying because there was no woman [doctor] to help them. I spent much of the night in anguish and prayer. I did not want to spend my life in India. My friends were begging me to return to the joyous opportunities of a young girl in America. I went to bed in the early morning after praying much for guidance. I think that was the first time I ever met God face to face, and all the time it seemed that He was calling me into this work.[10]

When she awoke, she learned that the women had died. Later that day she told her parents she would study medicine and return to India to help such women. After graduating from Cornell Medical College, she left for India and began a women's medical complex in Vellore. Today the complex has become known as one of the best medical centers in all of India. The sight of three anguished husbands became a vision from God that thrust Ida Scudder into a lifetime career of medical practice and development.

3. *Jesus' vision was total and compelling, a vision of the largest and widest scope.* Some years ago a British communist worker, Douglas Hyde, came to faith in Christ. In his book *Dedication and Leadership,* he analyzed why the communists were so successful and what others could learn about leadership development from them:

Marx concluded his Communist Manifesto with the words "You have a world to win." Here is a tremendous aim. In material terms one could hardly aim higher. The belief that the world is there to be won and that

Communists can win it is firmly implanted in the mind of every Communist cadre. It is with him all the time.[11]

Communists, says Hyde, believe that if you make big demands on people you will get a big response.

Theirs is a goal which has captured the imagination of millions, but Jesus' vision was even wider. See, for example, how Jesus' vision of the kingdom he proclaims actually goes into action in the first two chapters of Mark's Gospel.

Jesus shows his followers that his kingdom is *God's total answer* for their total need. He calls fishermen to follow him, drives out an evil spirit and heals many of diseases. He teaches with authority in the synagogue and cleanses a man who has leprosy. He forgives and heals a paralyzed man and calls a tax collector to follow him.

Here was a total kingdom. It offered teaching for the ignorant of mind, deliverance for those oppressed spiritually, healing for the diseased, forgiveness for the sinner, and reconciliation for all to God. Here was good news for all the world!

There is a well-known presentation of the gospel which begins "God loves you and has a wonderful plan for your life," and indeed he does. But Jesus set that personal promise in the context of a wider vision, "God loves the world and has a wonderful plan for it."

A gifted young Japanese pastor went to an international conference for emerging Christian leaders. Afterward he was asked what difference the conference had made to him. Thoughtfully he replied, "I used to see my church which is in the world. Now I see the world in which God has placed my church." It was a paradigm shift caused by catching Jesus' vision.

4. *At the same time, Jesus' vision was personal.* People were the focus of his purpose. His vision was wide and compelling; yet it led him to see not fire in the sky but people at the next corner. Look again at the way in which Jesus followed up his preaching that the kingdom had drawn near.

He *saw* "Simon and his brother Andrew casting a net into the lake." A little further along, "he *saw* James son of Zebedee and his brother John in a boat, preparing their nets." He called them all to follow him (Mk 1:16, 19). A few days later, several men brought to him a paralyzed man, and "when

Jesus *saw* their faith," he told the paralytic that he was forgiven (Mk 2:5). Again, "as he walked along, he *saw* Levi" sitting at the tax collector's booth and called him, too, to follow (Mk 2:14).

The great kingdom was in the smallest happening. He looked through his Father's eyes, and he saw a vision of the power of God at work in individual persons. World Vision, the humanitarian child care organization, has the saying "How do you feed a hungry world? One at a time!" That is how Jesus saw.

When he was transfigured on the mountain with Moses and Elijah, Jesus immediately went into the valley, saw a distraught father and his ill son, and said, "Bring the boy to me" (Mk 9:19).

Months later, he issued his great mission statement: "The Son of Man did not come to be served, but to serve, and to give his life as a ransom for many" (Mk 10:45). But he was not preoccupied with working out the scenario of his death; he immediately stopped for one blind beggar by the road who called for help (Mk 10:46-52).

When asked about greatness, he did not give a speech. He simply said, "If anyone wants to be first, he must be the very last, and the servant of all" (Mk 9:35). And he stood a child among the disciples to illustrate that true greatness welcomes the little ones who have no power (Mk 9:36-37).

At a student conference, I heard two talks on the needs of the great megacities of the world. One was informative, mind-stretching, full of statistics. The other centered on the story of one boy who wanted to go out and preach to the drug addicts on the street. The statistics were challenging, but it was the story of that one boy that stayed with me. For the vision was personalized, as with Jesus.

5. *Jesus' vision was realistic.* Thomas Sowell, a Harvard political scientist, has written of "a conflict of visions," which makes for a constant and creative tension in society.[12] "Visions," says Sowell, "are the silent shapers of our thoughts," which grip the actors in history and determine how they act. One way of seeing things is what he calls the "constrained" vision, which takes very seriously human evil and self-centeredness. Adam Smith, for example, regarded the moral limitations of humanity as such an inher-

ent fact of life, such a basic constraint, that any attempt to change human nature is pointless. The other perspective Sowell identifies is the "unconstrained" vision of human potential. Underlying the French Revolution was this unconstrained idealistic vision of humanity. When Rousseau said that humanity "is born free" but "is everywhere in chains," he was expressing the unconstrained vision, which sees the fundamental problem not in human beings, but in human institutions.

Using Sowell's terminology, we can say that Jesus' vision was both constrained and unconstrained. It was realistic, giving insight into the potential for good *and* the power of evil.

When Jesus was asked whether what one eats makes one "clean" or "unclean," he answered, "What comes *out* of a man is what makes him 'unclean.' From within men's hearts come evil thoughts, sexual immorality, theft, murder, adultery, greed, malice, deceit, lewdness, envy, slander, arrogance and folly. All these evils come from inside and make a man 'unclean' " (Mk 7:20-22). When a paralytic was brought to him for healing, Jesus saw beyond the man's withered limbs to his withered soul and offered him forgiveness. Knowing the potential for evil in people, "Jesus would not entrust himself to them" (Jn 2:24). That was constrained vision.

Yet Jesus could see a moral outcast or a disreputable, despised tax gatherer like Levi and call him because he knew what he could become. He held back from a naive trust in others. But he could also look at the rough-and-ready fisherman Simon and say, " 'You are Simon. . . . You will be called Cephas' " (which, when translated, is Peter) (Jn 1:42). In his vision he saw an unstable "reed man"—implied in the name Simon—who would become a sturdy "rock man," which is the meaning of Peter.

It was said of Luther Burbank, the famous horticulturist, that he looked at every weed as potentially a flower. Jesus looked at people in the same way. That was the unconstrained part of his realistic vision which took into account both the tragedy of the human condition and the enormous possibility of human change by God's power.

William Clark had that kind of vision when he went as an educator to Japan in 1876. Clark was president of the Massachusetts Institute of Agriculture when he was called to undertake a special one-year teaching assignment for some young Japanese. En route to the Far East, he stopped off in Hawaii, where his parents were missionaries. After telling them about his assignment, he walked alone on the beaches, praying that God would use him to bring moral as well as agricultural and educational changes.

When he arrived at his post in a remote western province of Japan, he found the governor in despair. A dozen promising young men had been selected for the special course and had been transported in a river boat to meet their American tutor. But on the trip they had proved to be so immoral, unpredictable and drunken that the governor had already given up on them and was ready to send them back home.

Clark persuaded the governor to give him a chance with them and asked if he might also provide them with some religious and moral education. The governor replied that Clark could do so only outside the classroom, during free time, and that he could teach them morals but not Christianity.

So Clark met with these rowdies every day for one hour before official classes began. Through an interpreter, he taught them ethics and morals by using material from the Bible. Little by little the vision of a higher and different life seeped into the hearts, minds and consciences of those young men. By the time the year was over, Clark had become far more than a teacher of agriculture; indeed he was their mentor and champion. When the time came for him to leave, he rode on horseback as they accompanied him on foot to the place where he was to catch his boat. They begged to leave with him, but Clark told them to go back and in words that became famous said, "Young men, be ambitious for Christ."

The impact of Clark's teaching and life never left those young men. One became the treasurer of Japan; another eventually became Japan's representative to the League of Nations; a third became the greatest evangelist in Japan in his day.

The story of William Clark and those young men is still legendary in that country. Japanese children still learn the story of the young men who were told, "Be ambitious." (Though the qualifying words, that they were to be ambitious *"for Christ,"* are usually forgotten.)

A more naive or more cynical teacher would have given up in despair. But the realistic vision given by Christ to William Clark took into account both the conditions and the potential of the Japanese youths, and transformed them.

6. *Jesus' vision was as radical as it was realistic.* It was radical in that it enabled him to see through tradition and institutions to what lay at the heart of their original intent.

I once had the privilege of visiting one of Japan's most famous sculptors and was paid the great honor of being served tea in the Japanese style by his wife. As we looked at the beautiful cups, which dated back hundreds of years, I quoted to the sculptor the words of Jesus, "Cleanse the inside of the cup, and the outside will also be clean." The sculptor meditated thoughtfully on that, then answered, "That is very profound. I know that I must be clean on the inside before I create."

Jesus saw through traditions and institutions in this radical way. That is, he saw right to the center and the core of their meaning and purpose.

Can we therefore describe Jesus as in some sense a revolutionary radical? Yes, if we understand that Jesus began no campaigns of defiance and approved no violence in his kingdom. He was what Stephen Neill, in his remarkable book *A Genuinely Human Existence,* has described as "the courteous rebel."[13]

Neill believes that the problem with many young people today is that they need to be taught *how* to rebel. Violent or sullen rebelliousness is useless. "What is required is to learn how to be the courteous and constructive rebel after the pattern of Jesus Christ."[14]

Jesus never held the view that tradition was bad *in itself.* Tradition can be likened to the habits that we have adopted in our personal lives. If we had on each occasion to think through every move we need to make when tying our shoes or opening the door or walking to the bus, we would be exhausted before half the day was over! Like our daily habits, tradition preserves what we know and frees us to concentrate on learning what is new.

During his ministry Jesus positively affirmed many traditions from the past. But he came into conflict—sometimes violent conflict—when he saw that a tradition or a system had twisted a law and made it into a rigid legalism which could even end in cruelty to people.

For example, one sabbath day he went into the synagogue and saw there a man who had a shriveled hand. The Pharisees, we are told, "watched him closely to see if he would heal him," so that they might accuse him of breaking the sabbath (Mk 3:2). Knowing their critical spirit, Jesus asked, "Which is lawful on the Sabbath: to do good or to do evil, to save life or to kill?" (Mk 3:4). When they remained silent, "he looked round at them in anger and, deeply distressed at their stubborn hearts, said to the man, 'Stretch out your hand.' He stretched it out, and his hand was completely restored" (Mk 3:5).

Jesus' radicalism was to call people back to see basic reality. He kept the sabbath, along with most of the many rules associated with it. But he also asked the radical question, What is the sabbath for? Was it just meant to preserve the past, or to be a day that afforded people genuine freedom and fulfillment, and the opportunity to serve God and others?

So he kept the sabbath, yet filled it with new meaning. He became furious at a system which *kept people from seeing* things as they really were. As Stephen Neill says:

> Jesus, the realist, is troubled by the way in which they have allowed their system to come between them and reality. . . . The whole of the ministry of Jesus is filled with an urgency . . . trying to get men to see things in their stark reality. . . . He could see with dreadful clearness the doom his people were preparing for themselves.[15]

Jesus reverenced the past, yet at the same time, wrote Neill, he had "an uncompromising maintenance of his right to his own vision of reality and his right to criticize the existing order in the light of that vision."[16]

Further, adds Neill:

> What all this adds up to is the probability that even the most courteous radical will get crucified. When the system is all important, in church or state, it is likely that the man who criticizes any part of it will be branded heretic or traitor . . . and yet perhaps the most important people in history are the courteous rebels. They are the mature and creative people.[17]

Once Jesus "sat down opposite the place where the offerings were put and watched the crowd putting their money into the temple treasury. Many rich people threw in large amounts. But a poor widow came and put in two very small copper coins," prompting Jesus to say, "I tell you the truth, this poor widow has put more into the treasury than all the others. They all gave out of their wealth; but she, out of her poverty, put in everything—all she had to live on" (Mk 12:41-44). It was his radical vision that enabled Jesus to see through the system and to judge how it had departed from God's initial purpose for the temple as a place of worship and dedication.

7. *Jesus' vision was hopeful, but not optimistic.* He saw history as the arena in which a crisis is taking place, a divine judgment (or *krisis,* the Greek word for judgment, from which we derive the English *crisis)* in which both salvation and condemnation come upon the people and institutions of the world.

The prostitution of the temple's original purpose (from a place of prayer into a place of profit) also played its part in this aspect of Jesus' vision: "As he was leaving the temple, one of his disciples said to him, 'Look, Teacher! What massive stones! What magnificent buildings!' " (Mk 13:1).

"Do you see all these great buildings?" Jesus replied (Mk 13:2), as if to say, "Is this the limit of your vision—great monuments which have outlived their purpose?" He then told how the buildings would be thrown down, leaving not one stone on another. Sitting opposite the temple, on the Mount of Olives, he gave his followers his prophetic vision of current events and future history (Mk 13:5-27). There would be a succession of false prophets and wars, earthquakes and famines, persecution and betrayal, until the end, when "men will see the Son of Man coming in clouds with great power and glory," to gather his elect "from the four winds" (Mk 13:26-27).

In Jesus' vision, history is a battleground, a stage where historical events reflect the dynamic conflict of the kingdoms of this world and the kingdom of God. As Jesus' coming to Jerusalem precipitated a crisis, whereby the city would stand or fall, depending whether it received or rejected him, so Jesus' historical crisis was a rehearsal for the last judgment.

His vision was more than the setting in motion of goals and action plans for the days or years to come. Jesus, the visionary realist, knew the kingdom would bring both good news for those who believed and a struggle with those who rejected him. He always set his priorities in accordance with this sense of conflict. So, after he had shown them this vision of the future, he gave a characteristic final order to his followers:

Be on guard! Be alert! You do not know when that time will come. It's like a man going away: He leaves his house and puts his servants in charge, each with his assigned task, and tells the one at the door to keep watch.

Therefore keep watch because you do not know when the owner of the house will come back—whether in the evening, or at midnight, or when the rooster crows, or at dawn. If he comes suddenly, do not let him find you sleeping. What I say to you, I say to everyone: "Watch!" (Mk 13:33-37)

Simone Weil, who died in 1943 at the age of thirty-two, was part of the French Resistance movement during the Second World War. After the war she became known as an apostle of the spiritual life. Weil defined prayer as *attention*. So, too, Pascal, her spiritual forebear, felt that the greatest enemy of the spiritual life was inattention, complacency. Their thoughts echo Jesus, for whom vision meant being awake and alert to see what God is doing.

Visionaries in Christ are not overly impressed with institutions, although they know they are often needed. They are neither optimists when everything is going well nor pessimists when everything is a struggle. Visionaries in Christ are realists who lift up their eyes to watch for the signal flares—the acts of faith, hope and love—that signal the Father's kingdom is coming, and who carry out their assigned tasks as servants in their Father's house. They share the mindset of Martin Luther, who once said, "I live as though Jesus died yesterday, and rose again today and is coming again tomorrow."

What, Then, Is It to Be a Visionary in Christ?

For Jesus, as we have seen, vision meant that he saw his mission, the people he met, and everyday life in the light of his Father's kingdom. This "seeing" was expressed in dynamic acts full of faith, hope and love.

If we want to be visionaries in Christ, we will long and pray to see as Christ sees.

We will seek that vision through the disciplines of reading, of praying, and of thinking originally and radically in ways which may be painful.

We will obey that vision, recognizing that vision has its outflow in acts of service, both great and small.

We will understand that vision is costly, for we cannot have Jesus' vision without the vision of the cross in our hearts. Bob Pierce, the evangelist who started World Vision, saw the orphans in war-torn China and Korea and prayed, "Let my heart be broken with the things that break the heart of God." That was Christlike vision.

And yet we will know that, along with the cost, following Christ's vision will bring joy, as it did in the life of the missionary Amy Carmichael.

Amy Carmichael went from England to India, dedicated herself to a single life and gave herself to rescuing the young girls of India from temple prostitution. Sometimes sick, and often misunderstood, she quietly lived a life of sacrifice for others. Sherwood Eddy, who knew Amy Carmichael well, wrote of her, "She was the most Christlike character I ever met, and her life was the most fragrant, the most joyfully sacrificial, that I ever knew."[18]

Developing a Vision

At Leighton Ford Ministries we ask the young men and women who join with us to go through a process of observing, reflecting and acting.

This threefold process was practiced by a Roman Catholic bishop in Belgium, who, following the two great world wars, took little orphan waifs off the streets to shepherd them. He would never tell them what to do; instead, he taught them to read the Bible, to pray and to ask God to show them what he wanted to do. He would tell them to look around them and see what the needs were, to wait until God spoke to them, and then to do something about it.

This process can be a key to learning to see as Jesus does.

We must *observe* carefully and prayerfully where people are hurting and suffering and longing, and what God is doing in the world, until in our hearts we are drawn to an area which may be God's vision for us.

We need to *reflect* on what we have observed, praying and reading, thinking and talking, and perhaps writing in a journal, until our sense of call begins to emerge and we "see" what it is that God would have us do.

Then we must begin to *act* on that vision, even if it is just in small ways to begin with.

A Visionary in Christ

E. Stanley Jones was one of the great visionary communicators of this century, to India, to America, and to the world. His thoughtful and passionate presentations of Jesus and the kingdom challenged American Christians to break out of their cultural blinders and see a bigger Christ. He challenged Hindus and Muslims in India to find in Jesus a fulfillment and a reality which their own aspirations and cultures had not given to them. Whether he began his message with a social problem or with a personal story, he always aimed at presenting Christ. Stanley Jones' vision began when, as a boy, he went to a series of evangelistic meetings at a little Methodist church in Maryland. On the third night of the series, he ran a mile to the church and could hardly wait to kneel at the altar to pray:

I had scarcely bent my knees when Heaven broke into my spirit. I was enveloped by assurance, by acceptance, by reconciliation. I grabbed the man next to me by the shoulder and said: "I've got it." "Got it?" What did I mean? I see now that it was not an "it": It was a him. I had him—Jesus—and he had me. We had each other. I belonged. My estrangement, my sense of orphanage were gone. I was reconciled. As I rose from my knees, I felt I wanted to put my arms around the world and share this with everybody. Little did I dream at that moment that I would spend the rest of my life literally trying to put my arms around the world to share this with everybody. The center of being was changed from self to Savior. I didn't try by an act of will to give up my sins—they were gone. I looked into his face and I was forever spoiled for anything that was unlike him. The whole of me was converted. There was nothing the same except my name. It was the birthday of my soul. Life began there.[19]

So too, when we see Christ, we may begin to see with the eyes of Christ, to be visionaries in him.

117

7

THE LEADER AS STRONG ONE

*Jesus showed strength—
of character—he had the moral
authority to move others.*

*"Charisma without
character leads to catastrophe."*
PETER KUZMIČ

*"The lost image of God in man can be restored. But before
it can be restored, that true human reality into which man is to be
transformed must be visibly set forth before his eyes. This is what was
accomplished in the life and death of Jesus of Nazareth."*
STEPHEN NEILL

*"When a strong man, fully armed, guards his own house, his possessions are
safe. But when someone stronger attacks and overpowers him, he takes away
the armor in which the man trusted and divides up the spoils."*
JESUS CHRIST

*I*magine that a modern television journalist could go back to the first
century to produce a program on "the real Jesus." Suppose she did a series
of interviews with those who knew Jesus, and she asked, "What one or two
words sum up your impression of Jesus?" I can imagine the answers going
something like this:

James, his disciple: "Authority. That's what made me get up and follow
when he called me. And what I saw when he stood up in the teeth of the

storm on the lake and told the winds and the waves to stop raging—and they did."

Unnamed citizen: "Authority. I was one of the crowd on the mountain that heard him preach one day. I never heard anybody speak with such authority."

Unnamed woman: "Power. I'd been sick with a hemorrhage for years, and when I came out of the crowd and touched him I was healed, and I actually sensed power flowing out of him to me."

Policeman: "Authority. I was sent out to arrest him, but I had never heard anybody speak words like his. We turned around and came back without him."

Unnamed citizen: "Authority—and power. I'd been paralyzed for years, and my friends brought me to Jesus. He looked at me and said my sins were forgiven, and then healed me. None of us had ever seen such authority."

Samaritan woman: "The power of his mind. When we were talking one day, he knew and told me everything I ever did."

Roman centurion: "Authority, of course. I am a man under authority. I tell one of my soldiers 'go' and he goes, and another 'come' and he comes. I know authority when I see it. One of my valued servants was sick, and I asked Jesus to heal him. I told him I wasn't worthy for him to come to my house, just to say the word and he would be healed. I knew he could do it, and he did."

The Quality of the Person

Growing up as a boy in Canada, I wavered between two pictures of Jesus. One was of a Jesus who was rather pale, anemic and insipid. He was at home in the tame atmosphere and the drab rooms of our Presbyterian Sunday school at three o'clock on a Sunday afternoon. But was he hearty enough to be out on the playing fields where a boy longed to be? Later, I was captivated when I heard some eloquent speakers of my teenage days depict a much more appealing Jesus, sun-bronzed, with rippling muscles, calves and thighs hardened by years of walking over rough terrain.

Now, after years of reflection, I realize that both of those pictures are inadequate. Was there a gentleness about Jesus? Of course. A physical strength? Quite likely. But if I were asked what prime quality strikes me in the Jesus I meet in the pages of the Gospels, I would reply without hesitation, "compassionate power."

Students of leadership like to distinguish between power and authority. Power, they often say, is the ability of a leader to control others; authority is the leader's right to use that power. Tony Campolo suggests that *"power is the ability to make others do your will even if they would choose not to. Authority* is the ability to get others to do what you want because they recognize (through your life and words) that what you ask is legitimate and right."[1]

With Jesus, it is not as easy to separate power and authority. For in him, both are intertwined in the most impressive strength of character.

As Bishop Stephen Neill has written in his fine study, *A Genuinely Human Existence:*

> The Jesus who strides through the Gospels is a man of immense and terrifying power. He is the master of every situation. He speaks with authority and not as the scribes. He is never at a loss for an answer. His glance can quell and put to flight the crowd of buyers and sellers in the Temple. He knows how to draw men and women to himself in a devotion which will prove stronger than persecution and death.[2]

Fortune magazine recently carried an article that profiled "America's Toughest Bosses." The article depicted a series of chief executive officers whose leadership strength was seen in terms of toughness. One banned green plants from his corporate headquarters because they were too costly to feed and water. Another is reputed to have pulled the pin on a fake hand grenade during a business meeting, to see which of his subordinates would pale! Few of these bosses had any personal life to speak of because of the long hours they worked.

Admittedly the article was selective, and not all bosses are tough in that way. But successful leadership in our competitive world is said to demand toughness of that sort. Maybe it is now time for second thoughts.

Half a century ago, Virginia Woolf wrote about people who are highly successful in their professions but who "lose their senses":

> They make us of the opinion that if people are highly successful in their

professions they lose their senses. Sight goes. They have no time to look at pictures. Sound goes. They have no time to listen to music. Speech goes. They have no time for conversation. They lose their sense of proportion—the relations between one thing and another. Humanity goes. Money making becomes so important that they must work by night as well as by day. Health goes. And so competitive do they become that they will not share their work with others though they have more than they can do themselves. What then remains of a human being who has lost sight, sound, and sense of proportion? Only a cripple in a cave.[3]

Does strong leadership need to be inhuman? Or can it be superhuman?

There was in Jesus Christ a strength which was awe-full and at the same time appealing. Those who met him encountered a power which was often overwhelming.

Jesus asked to borrow Simon Peter's fishing boat as a pulpit. When he had finished speaking to the crowds on the shore, Jesus got Simon to put the boat out into the deep water and let down his nets to catch fish. Simon protested that they had fished all night and caught nothing. But in response to Jesus' command he let down the nets. They became so full of fish they were about to break; at which point, Simon threw himself at Jesus' feet, saying, "Go away from me, Lord; I am a sinful man!" (Lk 5:1-8). Yet, that strength of Jesus was appealing rather than foreboding. He made goodness attractive, so that when he replied to Simon Peter, "Don't be afraid; from now on you will catch men" (Lk 5:10), the fisherman obeyed in an instant.

Many mistake toughness for strength, precisely because they lack inner security and have to project a brazen image. Jesus, on the other hand, possessed a remarkable force of personality and character and was secure enough that he could be remarkably open. He showed his emotions and concealed neither his tears nor his anger. He enjoyed people and allowed them quickly to establish intimacy. Children loved him, and ordinary people could approach him in the marketplace.

In Jesus, strength and compassion were joined so that his strength became a transforming, liberating force, not one which frightened and crippled others.

122

Christ the Strong One

Gentle, compassionate, at times withdrawing, yet filled with power and authority. That was Jesus. And that is how he saw himself, as the powerful agent of God's kingdom.

Once, after driving out a demon that made a man mute, Jesus was accused of operating by the power of Satan. In that case, he replied, Satan would be working against himself! Rather his questioners should have known that if he drove out demons by the finger of God then the kingdom of God had come in power to them (Mt 12:22-28). For Jesus, God's rule was seen not in beautiful phrases, but in strong deeds and power-filled words that overthrew evil and set people free.

In fact, he boldly cast himself as strong: "When a strong man, fully armed, guards his own house, his possessions are safe. But when someone stronger attacks and overpowers him, he takes away the armor in which the man trusted and divides up the spoils" (Lk 11:21-22). In this vivid picture Jesus is the actual leader of an assault force, the "stronger one" who attacks the very fortress of evil ruled by "a strong man" (that is, Satan) and sets the prisoners free. Armed with the power of God's Spirit, Jesus' hands were God's fingers at war, disarming the arsenal of evil.

To see Jesus as a passive figure is to misjudge him totally. The picture of God's leader as a "strong man" runs throughout Scripture. In ancient days, Isaiah had asked, "Can plunder be taken from warriors, or captives rescued from the fierce?" And the Lord had answered, "Yes, captives will be taken . . . and plunder retrieved. . . . Then all mankind will know that I, the Lord, am your Savior, your Redeemer, the Mighty One" (Is 49:24-26).

The early followers of Jesus picked up this portrait. They saw him as *Christ the captain,* leading his followers through the world in triumphal procession, like a Roman general who had won a victory and was given a triumphal march through the streets of Rome (2 Cor 2:14). Or as *Christ the victor,* allowing himself to be crucified, then disarming the very powers and authorities who opposed him, making a public spectacle of them, and triumphing over them by the cross (Col 2:15). Or as *Christ the warrior,* supplying his foot soldiers with the full spiritual armor of God, in order to stand against the spiritual forces of evil (Eph 6:10-18). Yet he did all this without taking up the sword or even using threats to retaliate. Even when he suffered as *Christ the martyr,* by that very death he overcame sin and evil and became their leader—the overseer of their souls (1 Pet 2:24-25).

The Unexpected Power of Jesus

Jesus came from humble parents. There was little in his lineage or early life to suggest the kind of power his peers found in him. In fact, as one of the ancient prophecies had said, God's leader would be a "root out of dry ground" (Is 53:2). In years to come the people of his hometown who had known him as a boy would be offended at this background. When they saw his miracles or heard his gracious speech, they sniffed, "But isn't this the carpenter's son? Isn't this Joseph's son? Aren't these his brothers?" (All said with a wink, a sly elbow in the ribs, and perhaps the unspoken innuendo that his parents were not yet married when his mother became pregnant.) "We know his family." That was all that needed to be said by those who dismissed his power.

Jesus' authority was not something *imposed* on others, but rather a force he *exposed.* He was not one to strut around saying great things, pulling off tremendous miracles, demanding attention, even passing judgments (until he felt it necessary, toward the end). Rather, his authority was the exposing of an inner spiritual power that was released little by little—through words, actions, attitudes and his very presence—until finally his character itself seemed to be as wonderful as his greatest miracle.

Jesus' strength of character is demonstrated in many dimensions of his personality and experience: in purpose, speech and balance; in spirit, in suffering and in dedication.

Firmness of Purpose

From the boyhood incident when Jesus told his parents that he must be about his Father's affairs, right through to his execution, there emerged an unswerving sense of purpose. His intensity burned like a laser beam. Once, on a hot and dusty day, he had a lengthy conversation with a seeking woman. Afterward, his disciples urged him to eat, but he told them that he had food to eat which they knew nothing about (Jn 4:32). Had somebody else brought him food, they wondered? He said, "My food is to do the will of him who sent me and to finish his work" (Jn 4:34).

On another occasion he said, "Night is coming, when no one can work" (Jn 9:4). He set his face to go to Jerusalem, in spite of the efforts of the disciples to deter him from danger; for he knew his destination. "I must keep going today and tomorrow and the next day," he responded when the Pharisees warned that Herod wanted to kill him (Lk 13:33). The cross that was his death was also his goal. Even though he prayed on his last evening that "this cup" might pass from him if there were any other way, he still did not flinch from the cross until in his final breath he could say, "It is finished" (Jn 19:30), and hang his head and die.

"Why are we so different from Jesus? Why is weakness as characteristic of us as power was of him?" asks Stephen Neill. And he answers that Jesus was strong "because he lived every moment with the full intensity of all that he was."[4] Occasionally we read in the newspapers of someone who under pressure achieves a superhuman feat, like a woman who single-handedly lifts a car under which her child has fallen. I am sometimes conscious of moments when I seem to be speaking or writing or playing a game at my very best. Far more often I know my brain and body are operating at far less than full capacity. So often, we ordinary humans are held back by the checks of our own fears or scars, our failures or pride, our laziness, uncertainties and conflicts. But Jesus seemed to have none of that. At every moment he was free to be the best he could be, and that freedom was the primary reason his power was so uniquely focused and evident.

Force of Speech

When one of the policemen sent to arrest Jesus returned, shaking his head and saying he had never heard anybody speak like that man, it was because he had known firsthand that power of speech which Jesus commanded. Simplicity, integrity, clarity, force—all these and more describe the impact of Jesus' speech, a strength we shall examine more fully in another chapter. With Jesus there was neither the contrived style of the professional orator nor the cliches that pass for much of our everyday conversation. His speech had the directness and vividness of a country man. "Go tell that fox. . . ."

125

was his reply to a threat from King Herod (Lk 13:32). As a Jew, he spoke in Aramaic, a language that was not flowery, but very flexible. As a result, his words have been translated into hundreds of the world's languages without losing either force or effect.

Those who have had the experience of speaking through interpreters know what a struggle it can be to tell a story or make a point across the language barrier. Yet a simple quotation or metaphor from Jesus retains its vividness, losing nothing in translation. His language was simple and spare. He could sketch a parable in fewer than a hundred words, and yet leave the likenesses of the parable's characters etched in his hearers' minds for ever. Some of his sayings are, of course, difficult to understand. And likely, he deliberately made them that way. While he usually wanted to reveal truth, there were times when he wished to hide his meaning from those who were not ready to receive and act on what he said. His words are so simple that my young grandchildren can grasp them, like picking up pebbles on a beach. Yet they have such depth that scholars can spend their lives exploring them, as miners dig for an underground lode of ore.

Balance of Character

If, as Jesus said, our words reveal our heart, then his words show an immense inner power, a force marked by utter simplicity and integrity. Yet the strength of Jesus was also marked by complexity, by a balance and blend of characteristics held in dynamic tension. Just as music is not produced without tension, so there is no greatness of personality without an ordered tension, a balancing of different characteristics.

Jesus' authority, for example, is without pushiness. Those who most impress us as having authority are not those who always have to prove themselves. Instead they have a kind of inner balance wheel, giving them a confidence that speaks for itself. A thoughtful reading of the first three chapters of Mark's story shows that Jesus possessed this balance. He presents himself as the heart of the gospel—the kingdom personalized. He asks his disciples to follow him and they do. He commands evil spirits to leave oppressed people and they obey. He shows his authority over illness by healing, over sin by forgiving, over religious custom by letting his disciples pick grain to quell their hunger even on the sabbath day.

Underlying all of these actions is that inner authority, the sense that Jesus is not driven by his needs, but called by his mission. He does not always have to be with the crowd in order to be vital; he finds renewal in solitude. He is able to set priorities and timetables rather than reacting to pressure. He permits neither evil spirits nor those he heals to reveal his identity prematurely. Nor does he permit others to set his agenda. When his disciples tell him, "Everyone is looking for you," Jesus replies, "Let's go somewhere else." He himself discerns the greatest need of those he meets. When a paralyzed man is lowered through the roof to be healed, Jesus sees the less obvious—a festering in the man's soul that needs forgiving. Many leaders are driven by their own inner needs and anxieties: they *must* sense applause; they *must* continually meet needs; they *must* be recognized. Jesus shows no such compulsions; he is the compassionate king. From the unending pressures of time, needs, people and criticisms, he selects only those things he is called to do. Here is the selectiveness of true authority.

That inner balance is constantly present in the Jesus who walks through the Gospels. In him we find both courage and sensitivity. He is ready to go to Jerusalem and to his death; yet his is not the courage of ignorance. He knows what will befall him. In the Garden of Gethsemane he prays that the cup may pass from him, sweating great drops like blood, showing the pain he can feel in his spirit. And yet, with that most sensitive imagination, he goes to Jerusalem calmly and without haste.

In Jesus we see both authority and the willingness to serve. He gives commands with every indication that he expects them to be obeyed. And yet he lived out his master principle that leadership is to be marked by service. John records a remarkable scene in which Jesus—knowing who he was, that he had come from God and was going to God, and that the Father had put all authority into his hands—rose from the table at supper, took the apron and bowl of a servant, and washed the dirty feet of his followers. "I have set you an example," he told them, "that you should do as I have done for you" (Jn 13:15). Here is a startling paradox, a leader who puts his own authority at the very center, and yet acts with such unself-centeredness.

G. Studdard-Kennedy, the British writer, once described Jesus as

a mad fanatic who played with children . . . a ridiculous visionary with his eyes fixed on heaven who was always telling people that their first duty was to love one another and do good in this world . . . a megalomaniac madman who was always talking about himself as king of heaven, and always thinking about other people and living the simplest and humblest life of kindly service. He made himself equal with God, and forgave the men that spat in his face. He was impossible and immensely appealing.

Forcefulness and humility, both admirable qualities, are rarely found in the same person. But in Jesus we see both at their finest and fullest.

In Jesus, severity is also linked to gentleness. On a final visit to the temple at Jerusalem he plays the part of chief inspector. He looks carefully at everything, reads the actions and motives of the worshipers and the leaders, and drives the mercenary businessmen out—all with the confidence of one coming to inspect his own place. He speaks as the stern prophet and denounces the Pharisees for their hypocrisy, likening them to vipers that cannot escape the damnation of hell. Yet he fills this role not with diatribes of personal hatred but with the tragic sense that a nation has lost touch with the reality of God. Like a tree cut from its roots, it will wither and die. Then, instantly, he shifts to the role of the loving mother who longs to gather her children together "as a hen gathers her chicks under her wing." But he weeps over the city that was not willing to respond (see Mt 21—23).

Jesus' balance can also be seen in the way he combined patience with decisiveness. Great leadership is almost always evident in an unusual sense of timing. Jesus knew when to wait and when to move. In the early days of his ministry, he told those he had healed not to spread the news around. He did not want to be followed as a wonder-worker or a miracle-man before people understood that he had come to die for sin and to bring about radical spiritual change. Yet at the moment when he sensed his disciples had realized he was the Christ, the pace of the story quickened and he moved swiftly toward Jerusalem and the betrayal that awaited. At one point his brothers urged him to go to the Feast of Tabernacles in Jerusalem and "go public" with his ministry. If he really is the prophet he says he is, why hide it in the backwoods? Why not go to Jerusalem to make it known? He replied, "You go to Jerusalem. Your time is any time. My time is not yet come." Yet halfway through the festival he suddenly appeared at the temple and riveted the crowd with his claim to offer the water of life that would satisfy all who came to him (Jn 7).

One final paradox needs to be noted: Jesus was both accessible and withdrawn. It is often said that he was always available to those who sought him. But he was not always so. Again and again he would either send the crowds away or withdraw from them. True, he knew how to socialize. Luke's account shows him spending a great deal of time going from one dinner party to another (although he could be a very disconcerting guest who brought up uncomfortable topics). Some criticized him for being a glutton and a winebibber, in contrast to his ascetic cousin John, who lived off locusts and honey in the desert. But that same openness was balanced with the choice to be alone.

It has been said that Jesus knew the importance of safe times and safe places and safe people. At the very moments when the crowds were pressing in upon him, he understood the need to withdraw to a solitary place for renewal. He had places to go where few demands were placed on him. One of those was the home of his friend Lazarus and his sisters Mary and Martha. Apparently, he would often go there for a little while, to be away from the pressing crowds and rest with friends who would just let him be.

Stephen Neill makes a comment about this contrast between availability and withdrawal, one that we easily overlook:

> Jesus doesn't make a compromise between the contrasting needs for fellowship and for solitude. Each is felt in full intensity, and for each provision must be made. . . . It is precisely the loss of this dimension of intensity that is at the root of many of the ills of modern society. Modern man is a little afraid of being alone and of being still. . . . Because we are afraid to know ourselves, we find difficulty in knowing one another. Because we do not know how to withdraw into ourselves, we find it hard fully to go out to other people. . . . The recovery of the rhythm of life as it is in Jesus, both in its withdrawnness and its openheartedness, might

be the first step towards the deliverance of Western society from a number of the ills that so heavily oppress it.[5]

Jesus' withdrawal also had a positive purpose. He went apart not only to be away from people but also to be with his Father. Luke particularly notes the place of prayer in the life of Jesus: "One of those days Jesus went out to a mountainside to pray, and spent the night praying to God. When morning came, he called his disciples to him and chose twelve of them" (Lk 6:12-13). This is one instance from a regular pattern—a pattern which tells us that Jesus was strong because he was *strong in spirit.*

Son of God that he was, Jesus did not operate on his own. The Spirit had moved upon his mother Mary when she was still a virgin, and had formed the infant Jesus in her womb. That Spirit overshadowed him from the beginning, came upon him in his baptism and anointed him to preach. When he saw the good results of his disciples' work he was "full of joy through the Holy Spirit" (Lk 10:21). Power could go out of him in acts of healing, and yet, though he was spiritually pressed and physically tired, his inner reservoir was constantly renewed and overflowing.

The strength of Jesus came from this dimension of depth, the deep-rootedness of his life in unbroken fellowship with his Father. Our modern world is hungry for leadership. Yet it has grown weary and cynical over so much hype, so much image-making, so much emphasis on the appearance and positioning of leadership. What about depth of heart? Where are the deep leaders?

In the light of Jesus' example, those called to leadership might well ask each day:

Am I becoming more informed? Am I also getting deeper? Am I getting broader? Am I also getting deeper? Am I getting better known? Am I also getting deeper? Am I gathering more resources for my work? Am I also getting deeper? Am I getting older? Am I also getting deeper?

A young American leader took a cue from Jesus at this point. He headed a rapidly developing organization which was having a very effective ministry in Eastern Europe. To many of his friends' surprise, he curtailed his activities and became the minister of a small church for several years. When his friends asked why, he answered, "My ministry outgrew my character." He had learned, like Jesus, that busier and bigger does not always mean better and that continued strength of spirit only comes from going deeper.

Courage in Suffering

A leader may appear strong in action and accomplishment. But the most acute test of moral authority comes when facing testing and hardship. Is there enough strength to stand then?

How does one endure suffering, especially when it is undeserved? No question has been more widely or poignantly asked. Many of the great religions have developed in answer to this heart cry. Hinduism has its doctrine of *Karma* of fate deserved, of endless cycles of reincarnation in which suffering is supposed to expiate failure and guilt. The Buddha's quest for illumination centered on that same question: Why do all suffer? His answer was that suffering is caused by passion; therefore, the response is to eliminate desire from our lives. Some, like Socrates, have faced suffering with stoic resignation. Others have shaken their fists in rebellion at the fates, or pretended that suffering is an illusion, or simply shrugged their shoulders at the cruelty of an indifferent universe.

And Jesus, how did he confront suffering? Never as an illusion to be exposed or as a misfortune to be accepted passively. When his friend Lazarus died, he wept (Jn 11:35). The term used to describe his emotion suggests that he "snorted" in his spirit like a warhorse snorting before battle. Evil, sin, suffering and death were enemies that had spoiled the beautiful world he and his Father had made, and he was angry. Neither did he look upon suffering as a friend to be welcomed, nor did he play the martyr who invited trouble. Rather, he saw suffering as a necessary part of putting right a broken and a fallen humanity, an experience neither to be denied nor to be sought. If he were to fulfill his mission, it could not be avoided. Some things, he knew, could only be accomplished through suffering.

In Isaiah's prophecy there is a remarkable picture that shows suffering and triumph linked in the career of God's servant. Isaiah 49 gives one the impression of reading an autobiography of Jesus written hundreds of years before his birth:

Before I was born the Lord called me;
>from my birth he has made mention of my name.
He made my mouth like a sharpened sword,
>in the shadow of his hand he hid me;
he made me into a polished arrow
>and concealed me in his quiver.
He said to me, "You are my servant,
>Israel, in whom I will display my splendor."
But I said, "I have labored to no purpose;
>I have spent my strength in vain and for nothing.
Yet what is due to me is in the Lord's hand,
>and my reward is with my God." (Is 49:1-4)

Here is the servant whose life is pre-empted before his birth, and who is prepared from his birth for a very special task. He is given a high purpose, "to display God's splendor," yet allowed to go through deep pain: "I have spent my strength in vain and for nothing." Yet his faith, though tested, does not waver; for he is sure that "my reward is with my God."

Finally, there comes the triumphant affirmation of a purpose fulfilled through suffering:

I am honored in the eyes of the Lord
>and my God has been my strength—
[the Lord] says:
"It is too small a thing for you
>to be my servant to restore the tribes of Jacob
>and bring back those of Israel I have kept.
I will also make you a light for the Gentiles,
>that you may bring my salvation to the ends of the earth."
>(Is 49:5-6)

Jesus and his followers saw his career as the perfect fulfillment of Isaiah's words and of other prophecies about the suffering servant. Jesus knew that he had been called before his birth and sent into the world to carry out his Father's purpose. Like the sharpened sword or polished arrow, he had been carefully crafted and made ready through thirty long years of obscurity in a carpenter's shop, until the time came for him to be pulled from the scabbard, drawn from the quiver, and launched into his mission. In himself, he embodied Israel, a nation compressed into one person, who perfectly showed forth the splendor of his Father in every word and action.

He was the one who on the cross cried out, "My God, why . . . ?" (Mt 27:46). Had he labored to no purpose? Had he spent his strength in vain? As he was assaulted by his enemies and deserted by his closest friends, his faith, too, was tested. Yet he commended himself into his Father's hands so that the darkest moment in his life became the brightest moment in all history. Jesus did not detour around suffering. He went straight through it in order to be God's light for the nations.

From the beginning to the end of his life, Jesus was tempted to take the path of least resistance. In the wilderness, the devil promised him the kingdoms of the world if only he would bow down to Satan's power (Mt 4:8-9). When Jesus told his disciples that he had to suffer and die, Peter rebuked him for such a thought. Jesus turned on him almost fiercely: "Get behind me, Satan! You are a stumbling-block to me; you do not have in mind the things of God, but the things of men" (Mt 16:23).

The cross was his destiny, yet Jesus had no illusions about the cruelty of death by crucifixion. On his travels he had seen the agonies of criminals and rebels in their final hours on a Roman stake. So in his prediction that he must suffer and die, there is no trace of a morbid interest in suffering. His final prayer in the garden before his arrest was with great sweating drops of blood as he asked his Father to take the cup of suffering from him. But there was no other way. So he did not evade his destiny. He did not shake his fist in impotent rage. As long as he could avoid suffering, he did; but when the hour came, he waited quietly for those who came to arrest him.

During his trial, Jesus protested in the clearest terms against the injustice of false accusations. He reminded those who were judging him that they themselves had a judge that they would meet. Yet there was no complaint or self-pity. Peter recalled that "when they hurled their insults at him, he did not retaliate; when he suffered, he made no threats. Instead, he entrusted himself to him who judges justly" (1 Pet 2:23). The way in which Jesus met suffering shows the strength of God's power in human character as perfectly and fully as it can be expressed.

Even more, Jesus "is convinced that suffering itself is something that can be turned to creative purpose in this strangely confused and troubled universe."[6] He put the law of spiritual multiplication in this way:

Unless a grain of wheat falls to the ground and dies, it remains only a single seed. But if it dies, it produces many seeds. The man who loves his life will lose it, while the man who hates his life in this world will keep it for eternal life. Whoever serves me must follow me. . . . (Jn 12:24-26)

Jesus was deeply convinced of the place of suffering and death in God's plan. This sets his understanding of leadership apart from the slick success-oriented versions of leadership that abound in our modern world. When we plan our strategies for our life and work, we do not program an element of suffering. Nor should we, for it would be morbid. Yet Jesus saw suffering as fertile ground for leadership. The seed must fall into the ground and die. Reflecting on this, someone, I think perhaps the great Augustine, said: "God had one Son without sin; he has no sons without suffering."

In his last battle with sin and evil, Jesus showed his strength most authentically. Dying for the truth and for the world's sin, he showed where true greatness lies. Those who have followed his leadership since have known that the leader who is willing to suffer is the greatest servant of all. Almost every advance in human history has been costly, achieved through difficulty and testing that was willingly accepted.

Power for What Purpose?

Jesus made staggering claims for his own authority. He quoted the provisions of ancient law, then set them aside, saying, "You have heard that it was said . . . but I tell you . . ." (Mt 5:21-22). He claimed immortality for his teachings: "Heaven and earth will pass away, but my words will never pass away" (Mk 13:31). He saw himself as the central figure in history, the Son of Man who had come to bring a new conclusion to the human story (Mk 13:26; 14:62). His death, he said, would make possible the ransom of many (Mk 10:45). At the end, he said, all nations would be gathered before him, and he, the King, would judge all humanity, welcoming some into his kingdom and sending others into the punishment of eternal fire (Mt 25:31-46).

Yet he saw this power as directed not to his own glory, but beyond himself. Power in Jesus' day (as in every age) was largely used to lord it over others. Religious leaders bound their followers to live by standards which they themselves did not obey; Roman soldiers used their power to press the peasants into service; tax collectors used their powers to extort; little bands of revolutionaries sought power to overthrow their oppressors, and in turn became oppressors. But Jesus firmly rejected power as "lording it over others" (Mk 10:42-45).

Stephen Neill has compared and contrasted the leadership of Jesus with the genius of Napoleon:

It is not difficult to recognize in Jesus certain Napoleonic traits. Here once again we find fearlessness in decision and execution, resolute firmness in the face of opposition, quickness to see the significance of occasion and to make the best use of it. Here too are a profound knowledge of human nature and the power to make use of other men for his own purposes. In Jesus also all the powers of thought, of imagination, and of action are at the service of a concentrated and inflexible will. This will also is directed to one single, over-mastering purpose. But it is here that the parallel breaks down; the purpose of Jesus was related to something outside himself. The fulfillment of his purpose is intimately connected with what he is and what he does. But he is always the servant, the messenger, the one who can command only because he first obeys.[7]

In Jesus, power, truth and grace were uniquely joined. He had come to bear witness to God's truth. He had come to use his power for God's glory. And he had come for the service of others. He was not a dominator but a developer, and he showed that the true leader uses power to make his followers twice the people they were before.

Contemporary writers and speakers sometimes present Jesus merely as the supreme inspirational leader. If we model ourselves on him, we are told, we can accomplish anything. If we harness our energies to follow a vision as he did, we will most certainly succeed.

But the strength of Jesus as we see it in the Gospels is not a magical

135

inspirational power to be harnessed in self-serving ways. His power is 180° removed from the powers of this world. It is a power which can truly be realized only in those who can say as one of Jesus' followers said, "When I am weak, then I am strong" (2 Cor 12:10). And that is why the power of Jesus ultimately appeals most strongly not to the powerful, but to the weak. For his power "is made perfect in weakness" (2 Cor 12:9).

Robert Coles, a Harvard University child psychiatrist, has spent much of his professional life studying children from very rich homes and from very poor homes. In 1979 Coles and his son were working their way up the slopes of one of Rio de Janeiro's shanty towns that had been built on a hill. The higher they went, the poorer the people were. There was no electricity, no heating, no plumbing, no water, no medical care.

They noticed that from every point in the *favella* they could look out on the dramatic monument to Christ the Redeemer which stands on the top of another of Rio's hills. Coles' teenage son wondered whether the Savior depicted there had any special care for the rich or the poor. They decided to ask one of the mothers, and this was her reply:

Can you imagine Jesus Christ living in one of those buildings in Copacabana, or Iponema [where the rich of Rio live]? Can you imagine him boasting that he owns many cars and boats, has lots of money in the bank, and owns a big house on the ocean? . . . I clean for them, the big shots. I know how much they own. There is only one piece of property they don't own: Heaven! They can't buy it.

The woman did not deny that she would like to be rich. She did not deny that she and her family needed bread and education. But this is how she looked at the world:

I look at Christ every day—over there, across the city, on the hill. I think of how hard His life was. He was crucified, even if He was God. No, He was crucified *because* He was God. Oh, I can't figure out why He was crucified! I can't figure out why I was born so poor. But I do know this: Jesus is someone for all of us. He lives in my heart. But those who killed him did so a long time ago, and no one knows them. It is best to remember that, and I do. He loved us, the poor, and He lives. The big shots who ran the country where He lived cared nothing about Him, or us, and they disappeared. I tell my children: That is lesson number one for them to learn, and never, never forget, however long they live.[8]

More eloquently than any theologian, that mother from Brazil's *favella* described how the authority of Jesus, because it was shown in humility, suffering and death, offers power to live to all who trust and obey him.

8

THE LEADER AS SERVANT

●

Jesus knew the price
of leadership—he was willing
to give himself.

●

"I am among you as one
who serves."
JESUS CHRIST

"Ministry is what we leave in our
wake as we follow Jesus."
GERALD HARTIS

*E*li Black, an entrepreneurial businessman, was well-known for two things. The high point of his life was when he engineered the takeover of the United Fruit Company. The end came when he jumped from the forty-second floor of the Pan American Building in New York.

One of his executives, Thomas McCann, wrote about Black in his book *An American Company.* He describes a luncheon meeting with Black and two other managers.

As they sat down, Black smiled and asked if they were hungry. McCann replied that he was starving. Moments later a waiter came with a plate of cheese and crackers. Black reached out and took it, but instead of passing it around he placed it before him and clasped his hands in front of it.

"Now," he asked, "what's on the agenda?"

For several minutes they talked about a building they were going to put up in Costa Rica. McCann, who had not had breakfast, kept his eyes on the cheese and crackers. The only way he could get to them would be to reach across his boss's arm, and Black's body language made it clear that that would be a violation of his territory.

At a brief pause in the discussions, McCann said, "How about some cheese and crackers?" Black never even glanced at McCann, so he rephrased it. "You're not planning on eating those crackers and cheese all by yourself are you, Eli?" Again, no answer. The conversation continued, and McCann leaned back in his chair, giving up all hope of a snack.

Moments later Black made it clear that there was nothing wrong with his hearing. He continued to question and make comments.

Then, says McCann:

He unclasped his hands and picked up the knife. . . . I watched the knife dig down into the bowl of cheese; the other hand reached out and selected a Ritz cracker from the plate and Black poised the cracker on his fingertips as he carefully stroked a rounded, tantalizing mound of cheese across its face.

The cracker remained balanced on the fingertips of Black's left hand for at least the next five minutes. He asked questions about the height of the building from the street and its height above sea level . . . the color and materials . . . the size of the lobby. . . . My eyes never left the cracker. . . .

I leaned back again, this time accepting my defeat.

It was then that Black reached across the table and placed the cracker on my butter plate. He put the knife down where he had found it, and he refolded his hands before him, keeping the food within their embrace for himself alone to dispense or to keep. Black didn't say a word, but his expression made it clear that he felt he had made his point.[1]

Eli Black symbolized perfectly one use of power. Next to truth, the power question is the most important issue for the leader. And it is precisely in relation to power that the leadership of Jesus stands in the greatest contrast to popular understandings of leadership.

Leadership and Power

In his essay "Leadership and Power," John Gardner defines power as "the capacity to ensure the outcomes one wishes and to prevent those one does not wish."[2]

The ability to bring about through others the consequences that we intend is power. In our complex modern world the sources of that power are widely varied.

Today we generally equate position with power. A delightful story illustrates positional power. A new factory owner went to lunch at a nearby restaurant which featured a "blue plate special" that allowed for no substitutions. When he asked for a second pat of butter, the waitress refused. Irritated, he called for the manager, but she also refused him. "Do you know who I am?" he asked indignantly. "I am the new owner of the factory across the street." The woman smiled and said, "Do you know who I am, sweetie? I am the person who decides whether you get a second pat of butter!"

In addition to position, there are many other sources of power. Money can buy access to an influential politician. Muscles can give us the strength to knock others down. "Power goes out of the barrel of a gun," said Chairman Mao. Knowing how to work the system and understanding how to tap into people's beliefs are also sources of power. Hedrick Smith, a Washington newsman, has written a penetrating study of the "power game" in the capital. He describes "the soft sides of power," those intangibles that are vital ingredients:

> Information and knowledge are power. Visibility is power. A sense of timing is power. Trust and integrity are power. Personal energy is power; so is self-confidence. Showmanship is power. Likability is power. Access to the inner sanctum is power. Obstruction and delay are power. Winning is power. Sometimes, the illusion of power is power.[3]

Power and the Powers

Like anyone else, followers of Christ, whether they are in "religious" or "secular" life, may or may not have access to the levers of power. But those who seek to think in Christ's way recognize some other insights into power.

Because of creation, power can be creative. "Rule over the earth," said the Creator in conveying to his human creatures the authority to develop the earth's resources (Gen 1:28).

But because of human failure, power can also be destructive. As the story of Genesis relates it, in the wake of our ancient ancestors' spiritual rebellion the earth was cursed, the battle of the sexes was under way, and in a jealous rage Cain used his power to kill his brother Abel.

From the perspective of the biblical writers, power is not *value-neutral,* that is, an innocent force that can be used for good or misused for evil. Rather, power is actually *value-driven.* For example, Jesus said that, far from being a mere commodity, money—which he personified as Mammon— is in fact a rival god.

In a speech at the Harvard Business School, Ivan Boesky, the Wall Street trader who went to prison for insider trading, blatantly confessed, "My God is my pocketbook." President Bok of Harvard later said that the Business School had shamed the university by inviting Boesky. But why is it that so many young investment bankers have found that making a million is not enough, that they need two, three or four million? It seems they are driven not only by greed, but also by a power beyond their control.

Author Richard Foster lists greed, racism, sex, technology, skepticism and narcissism as some of the powers which have a life of their own today. "Power can be an extremely destructive thing in any context, but in the service of religion it is downright diabolical. . . . when we are convinced that what we are doing is identical with the kingdom of God, anyone who opposes us must be wrong."[4]

Several years ago I had lunch with Richard Dortch, who had just been chosen to become the executive vice president of the PTL Club, a multi-million dollar religious televangelism network. Dortch had headed his denomination's work in Illinois and had an outstanding track record. I was frankly very impressed with what he had to say and with his seeming sincerity and competence. He planned to recruit a strong finance director and several MBAs to establish some fiscal sanity. "It's going to be like turning the _Queen Mary_ around with a teaspoon," he said. "It won't be easy, but I plan to do it." I wished him well and watched from a distance.

Eventually, Jim Bakker, the head of PTL, resigned in disgrace over a sexual liaison and its cover-up. Both he and Dortch were convicted for the misuse of funds. How, I wondered, could a man with such seemingly good intentions go so wrong? So I read with interest a later interview in which he described how the managers of PTL came to define success:

> It is all tied to how many stations we have on our network or how big our building is. It is so easy to lose control, to compromise without recognizing it. At PTL, there was not time taken for prayer or family because the show had to go on. We were so caught up in God's work that we forgot about God.

He also talked about the impact of television on preachers:

> A television camera can change a preacher quicker than anything else. Those who sit on the sidelines can notice the changes in people once they get in front of a camera. It turns a good man into a potentate. It is so easy to get swept away by popularity: Everybody loves you, cars are waiting for you, and you go to the head of the line. That is the devastation of the camera. It has made us less than what God has wanted us to become.[5]

In PTL's case, the TV camera, the show, even the ministry itself, had become ends in themselves; they were powers which could have been creative but which in the end actually became destructive.

For those of us not in the public eye, it is easy to point the finger at the Jim Joneses and the Jim Bakkers. But power can be just as seductive to the teacher in a classroom, the physician in an examining room, the boss in a union meeting or the leader of an average church.

Jesus and Power

Those who are called to be in Christ are also called to look at all things, including power, in Christ. To see power as it was "in Christ," and to be able to use power righteously when we are "in Christ," acknowledges its creative or destructive potential and also admits the possibility that power itself can be redeemed from evil to good.

No one ever had at their disposal greater powers than Jesus. Think of his ability to sway the multitudes through his Sermon on the Mount, or to calm the raging storm with a word, or to cast out demons, or to open blind eyes, or, for that matter, to curse a fig tree and have it wither. One of his biographers describes his calm confidence: "Jesus knew that the Father had put all things under his power, and that he had come from God and was returning to God" (Jn 13:3). Yet he held these powers not with a closed and clenched fist, but with an open hand, as something received and to be given.

One of his earlier followers, the apostle Paul, understood the significance of Jesus' death as an unmasking of the "powers" of the world. In a vivid passage Paul wrote, "And having disarmed the powers and authorities, he made a public spectacle of them, triumphing over them by the cross" (Col 2:15). The picture Paul has in mind is of a Roman general who, having won a battle and disarmed his enemies, returns to Rome to be greeted by the crowds. He leads a triumphal procession in which his vanquished prisoners walk in chains and disgrace behind the commander's chariot. Paul seizes on this image to make the point that what seemed to be a defeat for Jesus on the cross was actually a triumph in which he exposed the "powers" that oppress the human race—whether sin or death, rulers or priests, sex or greed. He showed them to be posturing weaklings, authorities that pretend to be powerful but have only the appearance, and that, by the powerful weakness of the cross, are exposed as the pretenders they really are.

The cross was the climax of a lifetime in which Jesus disarmed the powers. And how did he do it? He showed the greatness of the servant. He showed the power of the last place. He showed the triumph of the cross.

Jesus Turned the Power Scale Upside-Down

One day Jesus was walking with his disciples and teaching them about his coming betrayal, death and resurrection. They did not grasp at all what he was saying.

On the road as they walked, Jesus had overheard them bickering as the line stretched out behind him in single file. He waited patiently to talk with them, not to humiliate them, but perhaps to surprise them that he had overheard. At the end of the day when they had reached Capernaum and had found shelter, he asked them, "What were you arguing about on the road?" (Mk 9:33). They kept quiet, "because on the way they had argued about who was the greatest" (Mk 9:34).

Can we imagine them glancing uneasily at each other as he asked, "What were you arguing about?" Can we sense the shame that lay behind their silence? It is hard for me to think of Jesus' disciples arguing not over theology or the best methods of healing but over who was number one! Jesus had been telling them that he was going to die; were they, therefore, trying to decide who might take his place? Or perhaps they were remembering that only hours before he had taken Peter, James and John to a high mountain to see him transfigured, and they were wondering which of them was closest to him. In any case, there is pathos in the thought that while Jesus was saying he was going to the cross his disciples were arguing about who was the greatest.

"Who is the greatest?" the disciples asked. The answer was obvious. Jesus was the greatest. Now he was going to show the disciples that the "greatest" acts differently from what usually passes for greatness in human society.

Sitting down and assuming the posture of a rabbi about to teach, Jesus called them and said, "If anyone wants to be first, he must be the very last, and the servant of all" (Mk 9:35). Then followed incidents illustrating this essential truth: Those who truly desire spiritual greatness should choose the last place.

We generally measure our greatness by how many supporters and helpers we have. Instead, Jesus took a child in his arms and said, "Whoever welcomes one of these little children in my name welcomes me; and whoever welcomes me does not welcome me but the one who sent me" (Mk 9:37). A child has no influence at all, no power to do anything for us. It is the other way round. So Jesus says, "If you welcome those who have no influence, you welcome me and God."

We also measure greatness by the ability to include and exclude, to control access to power. No one has much more power than the appointments secretary who allows people in to see a great leader—or keeps them out. But notice what follows next in Mark 9, for Jesus gives us some important insights into what a truly transforming leader should want his or her followers to do.

After Jesus put the child down, his disciple John immediately recognized they had done something wrong.

"Teacher," said John, "we saw a man driving out demons in your name and we told him to stop, because he was not one of us" (Mk 9:38). If to receive a little child is to receive Christ, John wonders what they had done when they stopped this man.

"Do not stop him," Jesus said. "No one who does a miracle in my name can in the next moment say anything bad about me, for whoever is not against us is for us. I tell you the truth, anyone who gives you a cup of water in my name because you belong to Christ will certainly not lose his reward" (Mk 9:19-41).

The principle is "Whoever is not against us is for us." There are two corollaries. First, do not cut out potential friends or allies. No one can invoke Jesus' name and the next moment badmouth him. And second, do not rob them of their potential reward and blessing. Anyone who gives you a cup of water because you belong to Christ will not lose his reward.

But Jesus is still building his description of true greatness. Greatness in the worldly sense is usually judged by how well we can build ourselves up, develop ourselves, or, in that grating modern term, "self-actualize" ourselves.

So Jesus next adds a warning against causing the "little ones" to sin: "If anyone causes one of these little ones who believe in me to sin, it would be better for him to be thrown into the sea with a large millstone tied around his neck" (Mk 9:42). Then he repeats his radical teaching (first stated in the Sermon on the Mount): "If your hand causes you to sin, cut it off. . . . If your foot causes you to sin, cut it off. . . . If your eye causes you to sin, pluck it out" (Mk 9:43-47). It is better to enter life maimed, crippled and with one eye than to have two hands, two feet, two eyes and be thrown into hell!

Such is the leader's radical discipline. Eternal life is more important than physical life. Christ calls his followers who desire greatness to practice a radical discipline in their lives so they will not stumble or cause others to stumble. Christ's followers are to know that their hands, their feet and their eyes are their Lord's.

Now let us put this all together and see how Jesus turns the world's power scale upside-down.

Nothing will destroy a movement faster than disunity among those who are at the center. And being around greatness (including the greatness of Jesus) may corrupt us if we grasp for the glory and fail to understand the spirit of the leader. Our attitudes to the unimportant person, the outsider and the other followers show our grasp of our leader's mission.

"Who is the greatest?" argued the disciples. The one who acts like Jesus, comes the answer.

He takes a child in his arms and says that welcoming a child is welcoming him. Here there is no superiority or isolation complex.

He not only tolerates but commends someone who is "not one of us" yet who does a miracle in his name. Here there is no intolerance, no perfectionism or need to control.

He warns against causing a "little one" to sin. Here there is no defensiveness. His "little ones" are to be protected and guarded, but he himself is to practice ruthless discipline.

Through all these stories there is a common thread. The relationship to Jesus' person is decisive (whoever welcomes _me,_ gives water in _my_ name, believes in _me_), but his primacy is neither touchy nor demanding.

It is impossible to ascribe to Jesus too high a place or too great a name. But what does such a leader want his followers to do? We followers may think we serve the leader best by publicizing him, by making sure important people surround him, by insisting that only those who fit organizational policy are recognized, even by sacrificing ourselves for his approval. But what does he actually want? He wants his followers to treat the child as they would the king, to reward any who act in his name, to sacrifice themselves for the "little ones," and to be at peace with one another.

Here is how Jesus turned the power scale upside-down. Greatness is measured by taking the last place, by a total commitment to welcome the "little ones," by a breadth of sympathy and an openness to all who name his name, by a passion for personal purity, by toughness with ourselves but gentleness with others. Here are the questions he gives to measure our greatness:

Not "How many people help me?" but "How *deep* is my commitment to others?"

Not "Whom do I let into the circle of influence?" but "How *long* and *broad* is my circle of fellowship? Whom can I include and still be loyal to Jesus?"

Not "How can I best develop myself?" but "How *intense* is my passion to be pure and useful?"

Jesus Took the Role of a Servant

My friend Truett Cathy is an unassuming Georgia businessman and a devoted Christian who has built his chicken sandwich business into a national enterprise. Truett has a great love for young people, especially young boys who have been disadvantaged. His mission in Chick-Fil-A is not only to serve his customers, but also to develop his staff. His business provides college scholarship funds for young people who have worked for his company for several years, and he places a strong emphasis on developing leaders throughout his corporation. I asked Truett what he felt constituted leadership. He gave a very simple answer, "To be a good leader, you must be a good follower. That is the very first thing."

In discussing the marks of spiritual power Richard Foster also highlights submission as a key mark:

> There is a power that comes through spiritual gifts and there is a power that comes through spiritual positioning. The two work in unison. Submission gives us spiritual positioning under the leadership of Christ. Submission is power because it places us in a position in which we can receive from others.[6]

Jesus knew what it meant to submit. "The Son can do nothing by himself," he said. "He can do only what he sees his Father doing" (Jn 5:19). And he extended the theme of turning the power scale upside-down not only by showing the greatness of the last place but by taking the role of a servant. In Mark 10 we see Jesus and his disciples "on their way up to Jerusalem." As the path winds up from the Jordan Valley and the countryside rises, so does his followers' tension. The disciples are astonished, while those who follow are afraid (Mk 10:32). They sense that the final act in Jesus' story is about to close in. Again, he takes the twelve aside privately and tells them what will happen; he will be betrayed and condemned, mocked and spat at, flogged and killed, but three days later he will rise again (Mk 10:32-34).

A Leader's Mission Statement

This was Jesus' fourth prediction of his death (see Mk 8:31; 9:9-10; 9:31 for the others). But from the beginning he had surely known where he was heading, and from the time that Peter and the other disciples openly avowed him as the Messiah he had been telling them about his destiny. It is particularly noteworthy that even though Jesus must have known or felt that his death was only a short time away, he was still very much future-oriented.

As John Stott has said, "Jesus was not looking back at a mission he had completed. . . . he was still looking *forward* to a mission he was about to fulfill." He did not regard his death as bringing an untimely end to his mission but as actually necessary to accomplish it.[7]

"We Want You to Do for Us . . ."

At this point, two of Jesus' followers, James and John, came with a request: "Teacher, we want you to do for us whatever we ask" (Mk 10:35).

"What do you want me to do for you?" he asked. And they replied, "Let one of us sit at your right and the other at your left in your glory" (Mk 10:36-37). They were asking for positions of power, to be his number two and number three. Perhaps they thought they deserved these positions since they had already been selected along with Peter to be in his inner circle of three. What about Peter? Were they trying to preempt him? Were they afraid that Peter might be closer to power if they did not get there ahead of him? The way Jesus handled this request is intriguing. First, he drew out of them—as he has a way of drawing out of all of us—their hidden motives. "What do you want me to do for you?" It would have been very easy for them at that point to have put on a pious act and said something like, "Well, Jesus, we would like to volunteer to do the laundry or cook the supper or be sent out to some needy people." But something about Jesus made them reveal their true desires. And then he told them, and us, some very important things about leadership and the kingdom of God.

For one thing, *leadership involves suffering.*

"You don't know what you are asking," Jesus says to them. "Can you drink the cup I drink or be baptized with the baptism I am baptized with?" (Mk 10:38). To informed Jewish minds, the cup was a symbol of wrath, as baptism was a picture of the anger of God at human sin.

So closeness to Jesus means to share in his cup and his baptism, his suffering and his death. "Can you do this?" he asks James and John. They glibly reply, "We can," not realizing that one would be martyred and the other exiled.

Jesus adds, "You will drink the cup I drink and be baptized with the baptism I am baptized with, but to sit at my right or left is not for me to grant. These places belong to those for whom they have been prepared" (Mk 10:39-40).

So Jesus says that leadership in the kingdom involves a *sovereign* assignment. Leadership is a call from God, not a position we choose for ourselves. Certainly we may prepare and offer ourselves for service. Long before Abraham Lincoln was in public life, he saw a slave being traded at a public market in New Orleans. The sight, he said, went like "steel into my soul," and he told himself that if he ever had a chance to do something about it he would. "I will prepare myself," he resolved, "and some day my chance will come." And his time did come.

But there is a difference between preparation for service and seeking for promotion. When the ten other disciples heard about James and John's presumption, they were indignant (Mk 10:41). They must have felt that theirs was a righteous indignation. After all, who did James and John think they were? But their reaction was no better; it was just the flip side of James and John's. They were indignant only because James and John thought of the idea and got to Jesus first!

All twelve disciples were still ignorant of what really matters in kingdom leadership. It is easy to get upset at "pushiness" when we see it in others. But how much of our indignation is because someone else got in line ahead of us?

Jesus' response got to the essence: Leadership involves not only suffering and sovereignty, but also *servanthood*.

He brought the indignant ten together with the pushy two and said:

You know that those who are regarded as rulers of the Gentiles lord it over them, and their high officials exercise authority over them. Not so with you. Instead, whoever wants to become great among you must be your servant, and whoever wants to be first must be slave of all. (Mk 10:42-44)

Jesus says that if you want my way, you must know the relation between "wants" and "musts." We like to think much more about our wants than our musts. The "must" that Jesus brings to us is not arbitrary. It is an essential of kingdom leadership.

Then he wrapped it all together in what J. Oswald Sanders once called the Master's Master Principle: "For even the Son of Man did not come to be served, but to serve, and to give his life as a ransom for many" (Mk 10:45).

Luke's Gospel gives a slightly expanded account of Jesus' discussion of greatness, this time at Jesus' final supper with his disciples. Again, he tells them not to be like the Gentile kings who would lord it, exercise authority and call themselves benefactors: "Instead, the greatest among you should be like the youngest, and the one who rules like the one who serves. For who is greater, the one who is at the table or the one who serves? Is it not the one who is at the table? But I am among you as one who serves" (Lk 22:26-27).

Earlier Jesus had elevated the child to greatness. Now he elevated the table waiter to power. He pictured his kingdom as a community of fellow servants in which the older would serve the younger; the greater, the lesser; the powerful, the weaker.

When our daughter Debbie married, our son-in-law, Craig, sang to her as part of his vows a beautiful folk hymn:

Sister let me be your servant

let me be as Christ to you

Grant that I may have the grace to

let you be my servant too.

That could be the theme song of Jesus' community, one in which we freely give and receive from one another and in which we never get to the point of being too important to do menial things.

Mahatma Gandhi periodically retreated from his public campaigns for India's independence and went back to the little village where he grew up. There he sat at a wheel, spinning thread, as if to remind himself and his followers that he was representing the peasants and villagers of India and that great causes should never elevate us above simple duties. Though he made no claim to follow Jesus, in that symbolic act he was showing a Christlike spirit.

When I read Jesus' words about the older servant and the younger I think of my long-time friend Bishop A. Jack Dain, a former British naval officer who later served as a missionary to India and then as an Anglican bishop in Sydney, Australia. Jack Dain is not afraid to command. I served under him when he was the executive chairman of an international conference called by Billy Graham. It was my first experience working with him. While I admired him deeply and looked up to him with great affection, I confess, there were times I was afraid of him! He could ask for a report, correct a lax attitude or note an omission with an authority that made those working with him sit up straight. And he rarely missed a detail. At the same time, he had a deep abiding concern for all those who worked with and under him.

My work sometimes took me to Sydney while he was a bishop there. Despite his hectic schedule, he always insisted on meeting me at the airport, and to my embarrassment he would carry my heaviest suitcase to the car. Yet he never put on a show of humility. He was just Jack. And in him I saw Christ expressed in the most unself-conscious way.

Jesus' master principle, "Whoever wants to be first must be slave of all" (Mk 10:44), was a dash of cold water to the disciples, who expected to attain "superstar status." There is sovereignty, suffering and servanthood in spiritual leadership; through these comes greatness. Only by becoming a servant can we achieve first place.

Only One Example

Have you ever realized that only once did Jesus say he was leaving his disciples an example? That was when he washed their feet and had an evening meal with them just before he died. "Do you understand what I have done for you?" he asked them.

You call me "Teacher" and "Lord," and rightly so, for that is what I am. Now that I, your Lord and Teacher, have washed your feet, you also should wash one another's feet. I have set you an example that you should do as I have done for you. I tell you the truth, no servant is greater than his master, nor is a messenger greater than the one who sent him. (Jn 13:12-16)

But perhaps we need to point out what servant leadership is not. It is not giving up our own personhood. In the story of the foot-washing Jesus knew "he had come from God and was returning to God" (Jn 13:3). He operated out of a sense of being deeply secure in his identity. It was not weakness that forced him into being a servant. Rather, his offering of himself came out of that strong self-image.

Nor does being a servant mean that we abdicate responsibility for leadership. Jesus also knew "that the Father had put all things under his power" (Jn 13:3). He had a strong sense of destiny. Read on in the rest of the story and you will find him reassuring his disciples, boldly confronting those who came to arrest him, behaving calmly before his judge, and being in command at the very end when he "bowed his head and gave up his spirit" on the cross (Jn 19:30).

Note, too, that when Jesus told his disciples not to be like the Gentile leaders, he said that "the one who rules" should be like the one who serves (Lk 22:26). He did not say *the one who gives up ruling* should be that way, but *the one who rules*. When it is a God-given call, the exercising of leadership cannot be evaded. But it is a call that needs to be exercised in the spirit of serving; indeed, the leading itself is a way of serving.

Some years ago the leader of an evangelistic team talked with me about this whole principle of leadership. The team consisted of a number of young men and women of similar age. He and they had been influenced by egalitarian ideas of shared leadership and community decision-making. But it had become a frustrating exercise, and they were muddling about with no sense of direction. I pointed out to him that just as nature abhors a vacuum, so a team cannot operate with a vacuum of leadership. Leadership is a God-given gift to human communities. While all may be consulted, and a leader should not be a dictator who thinks he or she has all the answers, someone must take the lead, set the direction and the tone, and move the group ahead in making fundamental decisions. I predicted that if he did not exercise that kind of leadership they would fall apart. He grasped the nettle and began to lead. Even though one or two of his team later drifted away, the ministry went on to have a growing, long-term effectiveness in their chosen field. My friend learned to lead, but as one who served.

The Essence of Leadership

If the kingdom is Jesus' master thought, then servant leadership is his master principle. For him, the essence of leadership is:

1. that kingdom leadership is in contrast to worldly patterns, in so far as they involve "lording it over" others;

2. that kingdom leadership is internally consistent with the very nature of a community which seeks to live in Christ—where greatness is ranked by service, and primacy through voluntarily being last;

3. that kingdom leadership takes its ultimate model from "the Son of Man [who] did not come to be served, but to serve, and to give his life as a ransom for many" (Mk 10:45).

To understand leadership as set forth in Christ, we must discern when power is misused and when leadership patterns are inappropriate; we must be committed to the building up of the community of the followers of Jesus; and we must grasp the significance of Jesus himself.

His Trump Card Was the Cross

There is a story about a painting which depicted the story of Faust, a man who gambled with the devil for his soul and lost. The artist had pictured the story as a chess game. On one side of the table was Faust with only three or four chess pieces left in front of him and despair on his face. On the other side was the devil with a look of triumph. The artist titled his work *Checkmate*. A chess master came to the art gallery and studied the painting for a long time. Then he exclaimed, "It's not over! It's not checkmate. The king and the knight have another move!"

In a world dominated by the lust for power, God had another move—Jesus. His mission statement of Mark 10:45, "The Son of Man did not come to be served, but to serve, and to give his life as a ransom for many," is really the climax of Mark's entire story of the one who began his leadership as Son and servant.

The heart of the story, the essence of leadership, is found in Mark 8—10. Until that point, Jesus had consistently hidden his identity as Son and Messiah. When those he healed had said he was the Messiah, he told them to be quiet.

It is fascinating to notice how this section begins with the story of a blind man (Mk 8:22-26) and ends with the story of another blind man (Mk 10:46-52).

In Mark 8:22-26, Jesus heals the blind man in two stages (the only two stage healing recorded in the Gospels). After Jesus first touches him, the man can see people who "look like trees walking around." But when Jesus touches him a second time, he sees everything clearly.

There was a special symbolism in this healing. Up to this point, the people, and even Jesus' disciples, had only a dim idea of who he was—teacher, healer, wonder-worker—but from now on he would reveal very clearly the meaning of his cross. So immediately he asked his disciples, "Who do people say I am?" (Mk 8:27). They replied that some saw him as John the Baptist or Elijah, or one of the prophets. Peter then spoke for them all, saying, "You are the Christ" (Mk 8:29). Then Jesus warned them that they still must not tell anybody about him, and he "began to teach them that the Son of Man must suffer many things and be rejected . . . and that he must be killed and after three days rise again" (Mk 8:31).

Everything that follows in Mark's Gospel shows how the principle of servanthood and the cross touches Jesus' life and the life of the disciples.

There is the story of the distraught father whose son the disciples cannot heal because they do not know how to pray (Mk 9:14-29). Jesus is asking: Has the cross touched your prayer life?

There is a controversy among the disciples over who is the greatest (Mk 9:33-37). He asks: Has the cross touched your judgment of others?

There is his teaching about cutting off our rebellious hand and plucking out our wayward eye (Mk 9:42-48). He asks: Has the cross touched your self-discipline?

There is the welcoming of children (Mk 10:13-16) and the question, Has the cross touched your attitude to the little ones?

There is the story of a rich young ruler who will not give up his many possessions to follow Jesus (Mk 10:17-23), and the question, Has the cross touched your attitude to money?

There is the request of James and John to sit at his left and right (Mk 10:35-45), and the question, Has the cross touched your ambition?

All comes to a climax in the master statement "For even the Son of Man did not come to be served, but to serve, and to give his life as a ransom for many" (Mk 10:45).

In this one terse, seemingly simple statement, a host of pictures of Jesus the leader are combined. The *Son of Man* is that wonderful heavenly figure who appears in the Psalms and in the prophecies of Daniel and Ezekiel. Daniel, for example, recorded the vision of

> one like a son of man, coming with the clouds of heaven. He approached the Ancient of Days and was led into his presence. He was given authority, glory and sovereign power; all peoples, nations and men of every language worshiped him. His dominion is an everlasting dominion that will not pass away, and his kingdom is one that will never be destroyed. (Dan 7:13-14)

The *servant* title showed the other side of God's leader, the one of whom the Lord said to Isaiah, "Here is my servant, . . . my chosen one in whom I delight. . . . He will not shout or cry out, or raise his voice in the streets" (Is 42:1-2). The idea of a *ransom* offered to set people free, one that only God can pay, comes from Psalm 49:7, "No man can redeem the life of another or give to God a ransom for him. . . ." And the thought of *the many* who will be ransomed comes directly from the suffering servant of Isaiah 53, who "poured out his life unto death, and was numbered with the transgressors. For he bore the sin of many, and made intercession for the transgressors" (Is 53:12).

Suddenly it all came together—in one life, in a few brief months, and in one picture-packed sentence. The glorious heavenly mission of the Son, the humble earthly task of the servant, the compelling life-giving ransom by the cross, and the worldwide salvation of many all combined to define the essence of leadership.

And yet, leadership is much more than a concept to be defined: It is a call to be acted out. And so it happens that, just as this key section of Mark opens with the story of one blind man, so also it ends with that of another (Mk 10:46-52).

Still on their way to Jerusalem, they come to Jericho. A blind man, Bartimaeus, is begging by the roadside. When he hears that Jesus is nearby, he begins to shout, "Jesus, Son of David, have mercy on me!"

Many rebuke him and tell him to be quiet, but he keeps on shouting until Jesus says, "Call him." Throwing his cloak aside, he jumps to his feet and comes to Jesus. "What do you want me to do for you?" Jesus asks (the same question, incidentally, that he had asked James and John when they wanted to sit at his left and his right).

The blind man says, "Rabbi, I want to see."

"Go," says Jesus, "your faith has healed you." And, Mark tells us, "Immediately he received his sight and followed Jesus along the road."

Not only did the blind man receive his sight. The disciples of Jesus received their sight. They saw the vision of what made a true leader. On Jesus' way to accomplish a great thing, going to Jerusalem to die on a cross for the sins of the world, he still had time to stop for one blind man.

If he went this way, who are we to go differently?

Here is the heart of leadership in Christ. We do not start at the cross and go on to bigger and better things. We start there and go deeper and deeper, but there we also find the power, the living power, of that same Jesus. Every day brings "a chance to die,"[8] but also a chance to rise with Christ. "We always carry around in our body the death of Jesus," wrote Paul about his discovery of this master principle, "so that the life of Jesus may also be revealed in our body" (2 Cor 4:10). Helen Roseveare, an Irish medical missionary to Zaire, told a large conference of students how she learned this lesson. She was the only doctor in charge of a large hospital where there were constant interruptions, constant shortages, and constant

157

red tape and interference from the government.

There came a time when she had been working so hard, but so impatiently, that her irritation was showing all around. One Friday afternoon the African pastor of her church took things into his own hands. He went to the hospital and gently, but firmly, insisted that she come with him.

In his ramshackle car he drove her to his humble house and ushered her into a small room. Then he told her that she was to make a weekend retreat to be quiet and away from all the bustle and noise. She was to pray until her spirits were restored for the work ahead.

All that night and the next day, she struggled alone. She prayed, but it seemed as if her prayers got no further than the thatched hut of the little building.

Late on Sunday, she ventured outside to a spot where the pastor and his family were sitting around a fire, cooking their evening meal. Humbly, almost desperately, she told him that she was getting nowhere and asked him to help her.

"Helen, may I tell you what's the matter?" he asked. She nodded.

The pastor stood up and with his bare toe drew a long straight line in the dust.

"That is the problem. There is too much _I,_ too much _Helen,_ in what you are doing."

Then he went on, "I have noticed you in the hospital. A number of times during the day you will take a brief break and ask for a cup of hot coffee. You hold that cup of coffee in both of your hands while it cools off, and then you drink it."

Again he took his big toe, and this time he drew another line across the first one.

"I want to ask you to do this," he said kindly. "Every time you stand cooling that cup of coffee, why don't you say in your heart, 'Lord, cross out the _I,_ cross out the _I_'?"

In the dust of that African ground, Helen Roseveare learned the master principle of Jesus. She had let her service become more important to her than those whom she was serving and than the Lord himself.

The story of Eli Black, with which this chapter began, shows us the secular definition of power: "The capacity to ensure the outcomes one wishes and to prevent those one does not wish." This is a leader who keeps the cheese and crackers.

The story of Jesus shows us the kingdom definition of power: the freedom to surrender what one wishes in order to serve the purpose of God and the good of others; the faith to believe that God's power will be at work through our weakness, as it happened in Jesus, who offered himself as broken bread and poured-out wine for the world.

9

THE LEADER AS SHEPHERD-MAKER (1)

●

*Jesus had a strategy
to develop leaders—he aimed to
reproduce himself in them.*

●

*"A student is not above his teacher,
but everyone who is fully
trained will be like his teacher."*
JESUS CHRIST

*"The final test of a leader is that he leaves behind him in other
men the conviction and the will to carry on."*
WALTER LIPPMAN

*"Of a good leader, when his work is done, his aim
is fulfilled, the people will say: 'We did this ourselves.'"*
ANCIENT CHINESE PROVERB

*T*he name Peter Drucker is legendary among executives throughout the world. When he is announced as the speaker at a seminar, it guarantees top attendance and interest. Born in Central Europe, he has lived and traveled throughout the world and has been a journalist, a businessman, a government official, a consultant, a lecturer and an author. His books, such as *Managing in Turbulent Times*,[1] are benchmarks in their field.

I once had the privilege of attending a seminar for leaders where Drucker was the key resource person. As we discussed the challenge of leadership development, he listened carefully. When it came time to respond he remembered who had said exactly what, and then gave fascinating responses, drawing on his wide reading of history, from the rise of the symphony orchestras in the early 1800s to the experience of the British civil service in India. I can still remember some of Drucker's memorable maxims:

On learning by doing: "Don't put people just in learning experiences, put them in doing—achieving enables people to grow."

On staying with someone: "If someone is willing to try hard you have an obligation to help, but if they are not willing to try you are under no obligation."

On the teacher/disciple mix: "No one is able to develop everybody; the mark of a good teacher is knowing whom he can develop and whom he cannot."

On choosing models: "Don't put your people to work with people if you are not willing for them to model themselves after them. Augustine said that in picking a teacher for your gifted son you should ask whether you want your son to take him for a model."

On problems: "All you know when you choose someone is that they will bring problems! The rest you hope for."

One night I sat opposite Drucker at dinner. For two hours I talked—or rather listened—to this master mentor (two hours for which many executives would gladly have paid handsomely, but which I received for the price of a dinner someone else paid for!). I heard from him a running account of his varied interests. Toward the end of our time together I asked, "Peter, you have had an amazingly diverse career. Has there been a common thread that has run through everything you have done?"

"Of course," he came back immediately. "At the heart of everything I have done has been the thought of enabling others, getting the roadblocks out of the way, out of their thinking and their systems, to enable them to become all that they can be."

The Leader as an Empowerer
That theme of enabling lies at the core of all genuine leadership. "Leadership is not so much the exercise of power itself as the empowerment of

others," is Warren Benniss' way of saying the same thing.[2] And at its very heart the leadership of Jesus was an empowering, transforming leadership.

Of course our modern term *empowering* was not in common use then, though the idea was present. Paul wrote, "I can do everything through him who gives me strength," that is, who "empowers" me (Phil 4:13). He spoke of Jesus having given gifts to his leaders for them to "prepare [that is, equip and empower] God's people for works of service, so that the body of Christ may be built up" (Eph 4:12).

Shepherd is a key biblical term for the leader who empowers others. In the Gospels, Jesus refers to himself as "the Good Shepherd," the one who leads, saves and protects the sheep (Jn 10:11); who is sent at first "only to the lost sheep of Israel" (Mt 15:24); who looks upon the harassed crowds as "sheep without a shepherd" (Mt 9:36); who goes into the wilderness for his one lost sheep (Lk 15:4-7).

When Jesus pictures himself as the gate through which the sheep may "come in and go out, and find pasture," the one who has come "that they may have life, and have it to the full" (Jn 10:9-10), we see Jesus liberating people to empower them to experience life to the full. This picture echoes his inaugural speech in the synagogue at Nazareth. Then he said that the Lord had anointed him "to preach good news to the poor . . . to proclaim freedom for the prisoners and recovery of sight for the blind, to release the oppressed" (Lk 4:18). The empowerer came to take away all of those forces which keep people from living out God's dream for their lives. But the model of Christ as shepherd-leader has another side to it. He saw his task not only as saving and leading the sheep, but also as developing undershepherds. One might say that he wanted to transform sheep into shepherds!

"Shepherding people," writes Klaus Bockmuehl, "means to help them grow; it demands thoughtfulness about 'how to make the other one great' and it implies nothing less than the act of true friendship for others."[3]

That mentality marks the shepherd mindset.

In recent years, however, the corporate mindset has become more and more dominant. My friend Richard Halverson has said that Christianity began in Palestine as a relationship, moved to Greece and became an idea, went to Rome and became an institution, then came to America and became an enterprise! I believe the enterprising spirit of taking risks as Christ calls us is all for the good. But to the extent that we have become so results-oriented that we are driven by the bottom line of "getting the job done," we have sacrificed the shepherd mentality.

As I understand Jesus, his bottom line was not just getting the job done, but *growing people and getting the job done.* It has been said that transformational leaders work themselves out of a job as subordinates are converted into leaders. One can almost read Jesus' thoughts running through the three years of his ministry: "How am I going to reach all the people with the good news of God's rule? I can only do it as I develop under-shepherds. I want to find the people who see others as I do, who think as I do. I want to leave behind not just a set of principles, but a band of people who will continue to feed my sheep."

In this sense Jesus' leadership can be called a transforming, empowering, enabling leadership. His goal was to plant and grow his own "mind" in his people.

In his training the twelve disciples, that thought comes out most clearly at the point when Peter rebukes him for talking about dying. In his turn, Jesus rebukes Peter, "You do not have in *mind* the things of God, but the things of men" (Mk 8:33). Later, Paul grasped this when he called believers to "be transformed by the renewing of your mind" (Rom 12:2). More specifically, he wrote, "Your attitude [mind] should be the same as that of Christ Jesus" (Phil 2:5).

Jesus' use of his time and influence was both extensive and intensive. He divided his energy among the many and the few, in line with his strategy of saving the sheep (the crowds) and building up the under-shepherds (the disciples). In Matthew's Gospel we see the pattern. He mentions Jesus' contacts with his disciples roughly twice as often as contacts with any other group. At a quick count there are fifty-four to fifty-five references to contacts and relations with his disciples, compared to twenty-seven mentions of encounters with his opponents, while instances describing his mingling with crowds or dealing with individuals occur an equal number of times—twenty-one or so each. And these contacts are in addition to his

164

intensive teaching of his twelve disciples, which takes up four long sections of Matthew's Gospel.

A Key Transition

The third chapter of Mark's account of Jesus notes a key transition in his strategy. Three features are obvious at this point. First, he has been traveling, speaking and teaching widely, and has become so popular that he can no longer enter a town openly. Second, he has selected certain individuals who are recognized as his disciples, though he has not yet chosen the twelve. Third, a clash has begun to develop between Jesus and the religious leaders over the issues of Jesus' right to forgive, the failure of his disciples to fast (as John's disciples and the Pharisees' disciples did), and the question of healing on the sabbath.

Jesus now makes a strategic withdrawal with his disciples, first to the lake and then up into the hills (Mk 3:7, 13). (Luke adds that he withdrew to pray and spent the entire night praying to God [Lk 6:12].) Clearly, Jesus senses he is at a critical point in his work, and he wants some time to think and pray about it. I can imagine him walking, sitting, looking up at the night sky, perhaps talking out loud to his Father.

Since the day he had been baptized in the Jordan by John and heard the Father's voice saying, "You are my Son," and since those forty lonely days in the desert, he had rarely had a moment to stop. The days had been absolutely breathless, filled with healings, preaching, travels and personal encounters. Three questions must have been uppermost in his thoughts as he talked with God:

Father, how can I *multiply* what I am doing? There are so many needs, so many people. If I had ten lifetimes I couldn't speak to them all or heal them all. Just this morning, as I healed several people, the others rushed on me so I didn't have space to breathe, and I had to get into a boat and speak from there and then get away just for a little rest. Father, there are so many people out there. And beyond them, how many? My heart breaks for them. What can I do to reach them?

Then I can imagine his thoughts moving on:

Father, how can I *deepen* the work? I know you haven't sent me only

165

to heal bodies or feed stomachs. I know how important that is. I feel your power go out of me when I touch people and heal them. Our dream is that they should be forgiven of all that stands between you and them. Father, I don't want to be just a miracle-worker. I want these people to be freed from everything that keeps them from being like you. I want them to be people who know you so well that your glory is seen in them—and that all the world will see it!

Then I can see him pacing, looking up, and speaking again:

Father, there is something else. There is danger. I wish you could have seen the faces of some of those Pharisees when I forgave that fellow in Capernaum, or could have heard their voices when I healed the man in the synagogue on the sabbath. It wasn't just hostility I saw in them. It was hatred. The rumors have come back that they are already talking about how they can kill me. Father, that doesn't surprise me. I know I am going to end up dying. That is why you sent me, so I'm not afraid.

But how do we _continue_ what I am doing after I am gone?

Through the night he thought and prayed. How would he multiply his work, deepen it, and continue it? By the first light on the hill he knew the answer. The time had come to focus on a few. He could not handle all the needs; others must be trained. If the opposition could not be won over, it must be countered by having a loyal core who would carry on, regardless of what happened to him. He had to share the responsibility and ensure there was a succession of leadership. But he also had to be sure that those he chose were clear about the mission. Otherwise, the movement could dissipate through mistaken notions of what they were about.

The conversation with his Father had clarified his mind. (And perhaps we can allow our imaginations to picture what might have happened.)

Firmly and resolutely, he walked to the spot where his disciples were making breakfast. After eating, he said, "Please listen, in a tone that told them this was important. Did he tell them what he had prayed and thought about on the mountain? We do not know. What we _do_ know is that when he saw the harassed and helpless crowds, like sheep without a shepherd, he said, "The harvest is plentiful but the workers are few. Ask the Lord of the harvest, therefore, to send out workers into his harvest field" (Mt 9:36-38).

So now he told them, "I am appointing twelve of you to be my special workers. I am going to call you 'apostles,' ones I have chosen to send out on special assignment.

"You will have three responsibilities. First, I just want you to be with me. I want you to travel with me. I want you to stay close and hear what I say. I want to tell you what is in my heart. I want you to watch what I do.

"Second, I am going to send you out to preach. I can't preach to everybody, so I am going to send you, at the time that I choose, when I think you are ready.

"Then, I am going to give you authority to drive out demons. You have seen how harassed those people are. They have all kinds of physical problems, and they also have some deep spiritual conflicts. You are going to be my team to help set them free.

"Now, here are the men I have chosen," his eyes went around the circle. Then pointing with his finger, he began to single them out. "Peter . . . James and John . . ." Those choices everyone expected; they were the first three that he called at the start of his ministry. Quickly he added, "Andrew, Philip, Bartholomew, Matthew. . . ." The former tax gatherer sighed. He had been amazed that someone like Jesus had wanted someone like him, a despised collaborator. He had been even more amazed when Jesus accepted an invitation to his house to meet his friends. And now Jesus had included him among his inner core!

Very quickly the roll-call came to completion: "Thomas, James, Thaddaeus, Simon. . . . No, I don't mean you again, Simon Peter. I am talking about this other Simon over here. . . . Let's see, we'll call you Simon the Zealot, to distinguish you from Simon Peter!" Everyone chuckled. It was a good nickname. They all knew what a zealot Simon had been in his political agitation against the Romans. They had even heard it rumored that he might have slipped a knife into one or two Romans in the days when he used to hang around with some of the young gangs who talked revolutionary ideas at night.

Matthew caught Simon's eye, and he smiled. Frankly, he had been a little nervous when Simon had joined the band. After all, Matthew had collaborated with the Romans and had received his position from them. If they had met each other before they met Jesus, there could well have been some blood shed—and it might have been his! Now they were partners. He reached over, and with a grin he clapped Simon on the shoulder.

Eleven had been chosen. One more was needed. Israel had originally been made up of twelve tribes. Jesus wanted to reconstitute Israel, to pull together a new community, people who would let the world know that there was a God, that he was just and good and loving, and that life lived in his way and under his rule was good.

So he would pick a twelfth. These twelve would symbolize the new kind of people.

His voice rang out, "Judas." There was a little murmur of surprise, but the twelfth man looked up, his eyes alight. Since his youth, there had been a restlessness in the soul of Judas. He was a man who wanted to rise above the common crowd, to make a difference in his world. Now his chance had come.

"Now, you know who you are," Jesus said. "You know what I am asking you to do. There is a big task ahead, but I won't ask you to do anything I haven't done, that I won't help you to do. The rest of you will not be among the twelve, but I need you. There is a place for you! So, come on, let's get going. There's work to do today."

Quickly they broke camp. As they were putting out the fire and picking up their bags, Judas sidled over to Peter, "Peter, I don't know where all this is leading, but it's exciting, isn't it? I think Jesus knows where he is going, and I want to go with him. All the way."

Peter looked at his counterpart. He and Judas had not always been of the same mind: Peter, with his impetuous outgoing nature and his salty fisherman's manner; Judas, quieter, with his accountant's bent for figures. But what did it matter? Now they had a common cause.

"Yes, Judas," he said, "I agree with you. I am going all the way."

So they started down the mountain: Jesus first, followed closely by Peter. The rest of the twelve stretched out behind him, with Judas bringing up the rear. And others followed on the way.

10

THE LEADER AS SHEPHERD-MAKER (2): A CASE STUDY

•

*W*hat makes a good leader, especially a transforming and empowering leader? The study of this issue has become complex, sometimes even confusing. As noted in chapter one, some students of leadership have focused on the *traits* of outstanding leaders, some on the *situations* which produce leadership, and others on the *process* by which leaders go about their task.

In my reading I have been helped most by those who have talked with leaders, or those who follow them, to seek out the reasons for their effectiveness. So it occurred to me that it would be valuable if at this point we could include a case study of a leader developed by Jesus. The man whom I most wanted to consider was Simon Peter. Several reasons make him the prime candidate. Most obviously, he was Jesus' own Number One choice for a disciple. Also, he is mentioned and quoted by name far more than any of the other disciples—more times, in fact, than all the rest put together. Also, my primary reference for this book has been Mark's account of Jesus, and we know that Mark was very close to Peter and used Peter's preaching and recounting of Jesus' story as the primary source for his Gospel.

Even more important, Peter was clearly Jesus' own test case for his leadership development. After Jesus' death, resurrection and ascension, Peter emerged as one of the three most prominent leaders of the early church. Further, in his own writings Peter showed that he had absorbed and was passing on certain keys to leadership that he had learned from Jesus.

What follows is an imagined interview with Peter which seeks to bring out the key elements in Jesus' style of transforming leadership development.

Interviewer: Thanks very much for agreeing to take the time to talk with me. I know you are a busy man, and I will try not to take too much of your time.

Peter: You are welcome, and not to worry—I've got all the time there is. I really don't think of myself as busy any more.

I: I understand! Thanks anyway. Now, Peter . . . by the way, what do I call you? Simon? Peter? Simon Peter? I've never been quite sure.

P: Anything you want. I go by either name or both of them. Peter is just fine.

I: Right. Now, Peter, let me give you just a bit of background. I am doing a study on leadership. The movement on Planet Earth is going fine in some areas, not so well in others. We are going through a transition right now. Many of our older leaders are getting ready to come and join you, and we have quite a crop of young ones coming along. We know the Lord left behind a first generation of leadership that has never been equaled. We want to find out how he did it. So I have come to get your thoughts on how he did it. Will you talk with me about it, Peter?

P: Of course. But I have to make two things clear at the outset. First, he never called us leaders. He never used that word. "Disciples," yes. "Apostles," yes. Most often "servants." Never "leaders." Second, I am not sure I would go along with you in thinking that we were such a great crop. The raw material Jesus chose wasn't that promising to start with. We missed the mark a lot. I know I made more than my share of mistakes. I'll let the others speak for themselves, but you know we didn't always get along that well. Even Paul and I had our problems, and Paul once had an unholy row with Barnabas over something. . . . Oh yes, it was when young John Mark let him down. But I am willing to talk as long as you don't paint too exalted a picture of us.

I: With all due respect, Peter, we think a lot more highly of you than that, and I think there are good reasons for doing so, but I accept what you say.

Let me start by reading something that you wrote in one of your letters. I quote:

> I appeal as a fellow-elder, a witness of Christ's sufferings and one who also will share in the glory to be revealed: Be shepherds of God's flock that is under your care, serving as overseers—not because you must, but because you are willing, as God wants you to be; not greedy for money, but eager to serve; not lording it over those entrusted to you, but being examples to the flock. And when the Chief Shepherd appears, you will receive the crown of glory that will never fade away.
>
> Young men, in the same way be submissive to those who are older. All of you, clothe yourselves with humility toward one another, because, "God opposes the proud but gives grace to the humble." Humble yourselves, therefore, under God's mighty hand, that he may lift you up in due time. (1 Pet 5:1-6)

Peter, your words have been quoted again and again as a classic statement of the values of leadership. Give me a bit of background as to what was in your mind when you wrote that.

P: Well, it wasn't just I that wrote it. Jesus had promised that his Spirit would guide us, and I believe that in a real sense those were not only my words, but the words he gave me. But as I recall, I wrote that at a pretty rough time. We had been all over the ancient world. Lots of people had

171

turned to the Lord, and there were fellowships scattered all throughout the Mediterranean. Some were growing and had all the problems of growth. Others were stagnant. Many were being persecuted. We had even had some stoned to death.

I guess we were in a situation like yours. Many of us older ones had been around a long time, and we knew we weren't going to be there for ever. Our senior leaders, our elders, had been working a long time. Some of them were just plain tired and ground down and had lost their motivation. A few, I felt, had lost the heart of their work and were just doing it because they were paid to do it. Some who had been in office a long time really were lording it over the others. They wanted everybody to bow to them and serve them and do what they said, and jump at their every order. At the same time, we had a crop of young turks coming along who felt that the older leaders had lost their vision and served their time and ought to step aside and let them take over. They had some great new ideas, but they were impatient, aggressive even, and if they could they would have pushed the older men into retirement.

Now, that's not the kind of leadership I saw in Jesus . . . not what he taught us to be. We all had the same tendencies, but he taught us to think a different way.

I: Peter, that's what I'm interested in. How did you learn to think in Jesus' way? Walk me through the story from the beginning.

He Chose Me

P: Well, very simply, the first thing is that he called me—he called us, that is. First me, then James and John. This came out of the blue. One day I was down by the lake, fishing. Jesus came by and looked at me and said, "Follow me." I remember he had a twinkle in his eye, and he said, "From now on, Peter you're going to be fishing for men instead of fish!" So I left what I was doing and followed him.

I: Just like that? Just up and left everything, without knowing anything about him?

P: Oh, I knew something about him. I had heard about him, and I think I had heard him talking to a couple of groups. But I didn't know that much about him. And I surely didn't know where it was all going to lead. If he had told me, I don't think I would have gone.

I: But what made you do it?

P: It's hard to explain. There was something about him . . . his manner, his voice, the way he looked at you. The way he looked at me, that is. I never had anybody look at me like that. Who was I? The skipper of a fishing boat. None of the big people around there wanted anyone like me around, except to pay my taxes on time. All I know is, all of a sudden, I just got up and followed him. I suppose at that time I thought it might be for just an hour or two. I certainly didn't think about leaving my livelihood. But he just picked me. That is all there was to it, and he didn't let us forget that. I remember one time—it wasn't long before he left us —he looked right at us and said, "You know, you didn't choose me. I chose you." And he was right.

I: Would you have chosen you? Or the others?

P: Not a chance. All I knew was fishing. I was pretty brawny and could hold my own in a fight, but I had a temper. Everybody knew that. I was up and down a lot. No, I wouldn't have picked me. For that matter, I wouldn't have picked Andrew, my brother. I had never seen any leadership in him. James and John, I knew them pretty well, and I would have said that they would have put their own interests above anything or anyone else.

I: Thomas?

P: He had a good mind. But he was always questioning everything. I wouldn't have wanted him in my crew.

I: And Matthew?

P: Definitely not. No. He kowtowed to the Romans. Milked widows dry. Lined his own pockets by gouging and chiseling people for more taxes than they owed. Matthew had been blacklisted by every self-respecting business-man in Capernaum. I'd just as soon have seen Matthew go to hell back then.

I: And the others?

P: No, I wouldn't have picked them. Some were too politically radical for me. John was a dreamer and I am a practical man. Judas—he had a good mind for figures. I can see why Jesus wanted a good money man, but even then there was something about Judas that never felt right to me.

As a matter of fact, I know you use a lot of consultants these days, and you have all these high-powered tests. That makes me laugh. If Jesus had had consultants and tests and profiles and motivation stuff back then, he would never have picked a single one of us.

I: So why did he do it?

P: Because he believed in what he was about. You see? He really believed people could be changed. Not our differences of personality, but *us*—what we were inside. He had this uncanny way of seeing through us, but then seeing what we *could* be, not what we *had* been.

I: What made him so good at picking people?

P: Let me think about it. (Pause.)

Well, first, he had the ability to accept people as they were. He could approach them in terms of the present and the future, rather than the past. Also, once we started being with him he paid attention to us. This is an important thing. I think most of us pay more attention to strangers and casual acquaintances than we do to those close to us. Jesus really focused on us. One more thing: Even if it seemed risky, we always knew that he trusted us.

I: Keep going. He called you; what else?

He Named Me

P: He named me. Renamed me. Nicknamed me, I should say. I remember the day he looked straight in my eyes and said, "I know you. You are Simon. You are going to be Peter."

Now that may not mean much to you, but where we lived your name or your nickname said what you were. My first name, Simon, had the idea of a weed or a reed, shaking in the wind. Everybody knew I was like that, blowing hot, blowing cold. When Jesus called me Peter, I felt a shiver down my spine. I knew that "Peter" meant a rock. At that moment I stood taller than I ever had before. And I really believed that was what I was going to be.

I wasn't the only one. One day James and John got into a big argument, and Jesus threw his hand up and said, "I know what I am going to call you: Boanerges, Sons of Thunder!" That was a laugh. *Donner und Blitzen,* that was James and John. Did they have hot tempers! Thaddaeus. That meant big-hearted. He was that. "The Zealot." You know, the other Simon? That was a fellow who went all out for whatever he did.

One nickname I could never quite figure out. He called Judas "Iscariot." I used to think that was the town he came from. But I got to thinking about it. It also sounds like the word for "knife man" or "dagger man." I always wondered if he suspected. . . .

Well, anyway, you get the picture.

I: Interesting. So he picked you. Understood you. Paid attention to you. He even gave you a nickname. That is some kind of motivation. What else?

He Teamed Us Up

P: He made us a team. James, John, Andrew, the rest of us. That was important. I know how important it is to have a good crew in a boat. Some with a sail, some with a line, some with an eye on the weather. Without good teamwork you can go broke. And when we started fishing for men, the same thing. I know I wouldn't have made it without the others, and I don't think they would have made it without me.

Jesus really believed in this team thing. He never sent us out alone. Always by twos. After he left and we started going out to other parts of the world, we did the same thing. Always at least two. Oh, I think there were a couple of times when people went off on their own. I remember Philip was sent to talk to some Ethiopian all by himself down in the desert, but that was an exception. We learned that lesson from Jesus. Old Paul would sometimes almost have his own rabbinical school with him. He even had his own personal doctor and writer traveling with him. But Jesus taught us that.

I: Why do you think Jesus emphasized a team so much?

P: Oh, a lot of reasons. We had to balance each other off. You know I was a pretty emotional chap, impulsive. If I hadn't had the others to stand up on the other side we could have made some pretty bad decisions. It kept us honest. We had some women traveling with us, you know. If there had been one man, we could have gotten into some trouble. Jesus knew we were pretty strong personalities, too. As most leaders are. We all would have wanted our own way, our own ambitions. We had to learn there were others who could do things better than we did.

Sometimes you can get lazy too. If you don't want to get up and get going in the morning, start praying, start working, it can help to have someone around to give you a good swift kick in the rear end. You know, Andrew used to do that for me. I liked the big crowds. Andrew liked individuals. He would always see some foreigner or some little boy and bring him to Jesus. I wasn't good at that. Andrew would keep after me. Matthew and John were a lot better at writing than I was. I could preach pretty well, but I just had a block about getting those words down on parchment. That is why I was so glad when Mark came along and wrote down what I said.

I: Anything else about a team?

P: Sure, it helps to have someone else there to share the good and the bad. Sometimes we'd come back from a project and we were so high. Having someone else to share it with just doubled the joy. And we could get down too. Sometimes the work was just backbreaking. It would break your soul more than your back too. I would get down when things were tough, but someone would always take me for a walk and talk to me, and things would be better. And, of course—

I: Yes?

P: There was the time I . . . when I . . . I guess you know. You've heard? How I let him down? If one of the brothers hadn't come and got hold of me . . . I don't know where I would have ended up. . . . Back where I started or worse. My point is, he had joined us together, for better or for worse.

I: So you needed each other?

P: And we needed him. I'm telling you. It wouldn't have worked without him. He was the center. We were so different. Different personalities. Different loyalties. The only way to keep us together was by someone bigger than ourselves. And he was that. Bigger than us? Bigger than anybody! Big enough to be the center of everything.

I: A leader has to be able to bring about a workable unity. Can you describe for me how Jesus did that?

P: It's like I said. He knew us, trusted us, motivated us individually. He gave us a higher cause than any other causes. Someone bigger than ourselves to be related to. Somehow he took our partial loyalties and our lesser talents and put them all together. A unifying passion. I guess that is what he would say he gave us. A unifying passion that brought out the best of each of us.

He Motivated Me

I: Peter, it seems to me so far we have been talking about motivation. You said that Jesus picked you, named you, joined you with others. Gave you a cause bigger than yourselves. Before we leave this, is there anything else you can think of that motivated you?

P: Oh sure, he met a genuine thirst in me. Anybody else I have ever met wanted to use me, have me feed their stomachs, pay their taxes. Roman soldiers wanted me to carry their baggage and keep out of the way. Jesus had a cause. He wanted to enlist me in that, and he didn't make any bones about it. But he also brought out a genuine thirst in me. That's something I learned from him. The key for a leader is to look for thirsty people. People want different things. Meaning. Approval. Belonging. Something worth doing. Love. Forgiveness. A cause. I needed those things. I needed a cause. Approval. A bigger life. Jesus talked a lot about water for thirsty people. Well, most of us have one thirst down deep, and we usually go through our lives looking for someone to meet that thirst. Jesus understood my thirst. He had the water to satisfy it. He taught me when I went out to recruit anyone to ask: Am I just wanting to use these people for what I want, for what's important to me? Or am I also giving them an opportunity to do what is important to them? Jesus was like that. He always kept his eyes both on the job and on the people who were doing the job.

He Taught Me

I: Peter, I would like to move on to another area now. Every great leader, I believe, has been a great teacher. I heard someone say that outstanding leaders create a "learning environment." I am sure that was true of Jesus. Talk to me about that.

P: You're absolutely right. We never used those words, but a place for learning is what he brought to us. And you have got to remember that all of us were grown men when he called us. We weren't little kids. You move adults by letting them in on what is going on. Letting them be a part of it. If you just give me routines, one, two, three, I may do them, but I won't have my heart in them. But if you let me feel that I'm part of the action, understand that I'm on the inside, then I'm with you all the way.

I: And Jesus did that? How?

P: By everything he did. What he was, what he said, what he did, where he took us, what he asked us, what we overheard as well as what he said to us. It was all learning. That's what made it exciting, interesting. We always sensed there was a purpose. He was using everything to lead us on to what it was all about. It wasn't like school. It wasn't like learning. It was life.

I: Spell that out a little bit more for me. There were times when he sat you down and just taught?

P: Oh, sure. Let's see, I can remember, oh, maybe a half dozen times at least that stuck with me. One was on the mountain, when he gave all the "blesseds." Another was down by the lake when he told all the stories about the seed and the fishing and the lamp. Those were two. Then in the temple in Jerusalem he talked about the Pharisees and the future. Those of us who were there gave names to them—one was "mountain talk," another was "lake talk," another "temple talk." That was our code, you see? They were milestones that stuck in our minds, times when he tied it all together. Those are the building blocks that we were to refer back to.

I: So he did sit you down and teach. What else?

P: We discussed what he had talked about. He would explain it to us. We would ask him questions and he would ask us questions. Like down by the lake, when he told those stories, we weren't all clear on the point. So we just walked up and said, "Explain it to us." And he took us away from the crowds, sat down and told us what he meant—the seed was the Word, the birds were Satan, the sower was like the heart. Then he said, "Have you understood?" And we did. He was a great explainer. All the time explaining, and he never made us feel stupid for asking. We only felt stupid when we didn't ask or didn't think.

I: Such as?

P: Well, when he took us across the lake and there was a big storm. We thought the boat was going to be swamped, so we woke him up. He looked at us and said, "Why are you so afraid?" We should have known by then to trust him, but we didn't. Another time, he was having a big discussion with the Pharisees about why we didn't wash our hands before we ate. He said it isn't what goes into our mouth that makes us unclean but what comes out of our mouth. He also said the Pharisees were like a blind man leading a blind man and both of them falling into a pit. Well, big mouth old me, I didn't try to think about what he was saying. I just said, "Explain the parable to us."

And he looked at me. And could he look at you! There was a long pause. Then he said, "Are you still so dull?" I felt about as big as the widow's mite, and he was right. I wanted him to do all the work. I didn't want to think. Then he went on to explain that it's not out of the mouth but out of the heart that all the evil comes. It was all there. But he wasn't going to spell it out for me. He was saying, "Look, Peter, you're a grown man. I've given you all you need to know. Think it through for yourself."

I: So he didn't tell you everything to think and do and say?

P: Well, yes and no. It depended on what we needed. I can remember the first time he sent us out to preach and heal while he stayed behind. He sat us down and briefed us.

Some of the things he told us were very specific. Don't go to the Gentiles. Don't go to the Samaritans. Go to Israel. What to preach, how to heal. Not to take along any money or extra clothes. When he wanted to be, he was very clear and specific. He didn't leave you wondering.

But he didn't try to anticipate everything and give us a manual for every situation. I remember once he said we were going to be sheep among wolves, so we had better be as wise as the snakes and as innocent as the doves. Now that was a mixed metaphor. But we got the point.

And he said that if we were arrested by the authorities we weren't to worry about what we would say. He said we'd know what to say. He said he'd given us the Holy Spirit and the Spirit would speak through us. He didn't try to give us the answer for every situation. Then after he'd told us what to expect, he spent a long time dealing with our attitudes and feelings.

He told us we'd feel fear but we didn't have to. He gave us some thoughts. "I didn't come to bring peace but a sword" was one thing he said. So we weren't expecting everybody to love us. And the thing that really got to me was when he said, "He who receives you, receives me." I thought that when it came to my business, I didn't want just anybody representing me or speaking for me. I wanted to be there myself. And here Jesus was trusting old Peter, the big-mouth fisherman, to speak for him.

I: So he treated you like . . .

P: Apprentices. That's what we were. Apprentices to Jesus. You see, that was the way he'd learned in his dad's carpentry shop. His dad would do something, and Jesus would watch. Then Jesus would do something, and his dad would watch. His dad would let him do something on his own, and then he'd come back and check up on it. Then when he was a little older, his little brothers would come in and Jesus would do it and they'd watch. That's the way I trained my fishermen. That's how he trained us. Not like they do at the synagogues.

I: How so?

P: Well, you know the way the rabbis are trained. They get with an older rabbi and they learn out of books. They memorize all those hundreds and hundreds of passages and rules. I guess that's OK, if you need it. There are some things we need to learn that way. But that's not how you learn life, and life was what Jesus knew.

I: All right, let's move on. What else did he use to create this learning atmosphere?

P: Stories. Was he a storyteller! He had a story about everything and for everything. I used to think I was a pretty good storyteller when we were around the fire cooking our fish. Learned it from my father. But Jesus— I never heard anybody tell stories like he did. He'd use anything to make his point. He'd see something or think of something and out would tumble a story. Weddings. Funerals. Houses that fell in the flood. Towers that collapsed. Shepherds. Doctors. Children dancing. Making wine. And not a one of them was about religion. They were all about life.

I: Give me an example.

P: Well, there was the time I asked him how many times I had to forgive my brother. Some of us disciples grated on each other! So I asked him if I had to forgive seven times, and he said, no, seventy *times* seven. Well, that's not what I wanted to hear, and I guess I could have forgotten it. But then he told a story about a fellow who owes several million pounds and is about to go into bankruptcy. He goes to his knees and begs and promises to pay, so he gets his debts canceled. Then he walks right out and sees someone who owes him a few pounds. He tries to choke him to make him pay. Well, he got what was coming to him. Then Jesus looked right at me and the rest and told us that was how the heavenly Father would treat us unless we forgave our brother from our heart. I couldn't look him in the eye, and I couldn't look one of the men in the eye. And you know, every time I am tempted to come down hard on someone because of what he or she has done to me that story pops back in my mind.

I: So, you got the point?

P: I got the point. In his movement there is no seniority. And every one of his stories had a point. Forgive from your heart. Watch and pray. The first will be last. Those points stuck in my mind, and when I need them they come back.

I: I am interested in what you say about how he used everyday things to teach. Can you tell us more about that?

P: It wasn't just what he taught us or even the examples he used. It was where he taught us and how he did it. You see, the whole world was his classroom. Let me go back to the rabbis again. If you want to be a rabbi, you attach yourself to an older rabbi, you live in a seminary several years and you learn a lot, but it's not like real life. It takes some of those rabbis a long time after they finish to understand common people. Some of them never do. They sit in ivory towers. They dream up the rules for doing this and not doing that. They don't know what it is like to fish three nights in a row, never catch a thing, with three crying kids and a wife at home who are running out of food, and a crew that expects to be paid and you are down to your last penny.

But that's not how Jesus taught. If he wanted us to learn about faith, he didn't sit down and read it out of a book. He took us on a lake and let us learn what it was like to trust him in the middle of a real-life storm.

I remember this one day we were really hungry and we were walking through some grain fields, and it was a sabbath. Now the religious leaders in their ivory towers say that no matter how hungry you are, you don't pick one grain on the sabbath day. So, because we'd eaten some grain, they got all over him. What did Jesus do? He quoted the Bible right at them. Some story about David who was hungry and went into the temple and ate the bread that only the priests were to eat. And then Jesus told them that God wanted mercy, not sacrifice. Well, that got them mad. But I want to tell you, we learned something. I learned that the Scripture is about life. And when I saw how he knew his Scripture, I decided I'd better know it. That is when I started reading. It wasn't easy. I was not a reading man. But I learned that God's Word was important—and I learned that in a grain field, not a synagogue.

I: So he could relate to you as a working man.

P: Or as a parent. You know, he loved children. He could never pass a child without picking it up. And he knew people loved children and weren't threatened by them, so when he had to make a hard point, he turned to a child. One day we were having a big argument about who was the greatest, and Jesus heard us. He turned around, and here was this little boy, about three or four years old. He picked him up and held him and said, "You want to be great in God's kingdom? Well, you won't even enter the kingdom unless you become like this little child. How important is he? How much influence does he have? How much money does he have? I will tell you who is the greatest. It is anyone who humbles himself like this child."

I: So he taught in little everyday things.

P: But he could be demanding when he had to! When we were making our last trip to Jerusalem, he was so disgusted with the buying and selling in the temple. And on the way back to the place where we were staying, he saw this fig tree. He went up, as if he were going to pick some fruit off it, but it only had leaves, you know? He said, "May you never bear fruit again!" And the next morning, when we came back, that fig tree was withered and dead from the roots. The only time I ever saw him do anything like that. He was really upset that day. Then he explained to us how the temple system was dead at the root, like the fig tree was dead at the root.

There wasn't any faith there; it was all show. And it was cursed too.

I: I suppose you remember that day!

P: You bet! Actually, I got a little awed inside. I thought if he could see my roots as he did that fig tree—I mean, I know he knew my heart—and if he'd seen that I was dead, then he could curse me just like that tree and I would be gone overnight. It made me a little bit sober, but it made me grateful.

I: Let me ask you to do this. Go back over the whole time you spent with Jesus. In a nutshell, what was he doing to help you learn?

P: Teaching me to think as he thought. I don't mean brainwashing me. I mean teaching us to look at life and ourselves and God and other people as he did. He brought us along a little bit at a time. He would say something and let it soak in. He would give a parable, let us think about it. He would ask a question. He didn't force-feed us when we weren't ready. I think he was watching to see our minds and our hearts grow. Sometimes he would be pretty rough on us. He would keep asking questions to lead us on. A high point for me—a low point too—was when he asked us who we thought he was. He had just fed this big crowd of four thousand people with bread. Then the Pharisees came to him and asked him for a sign, and he wouldn't give them one. Right after that we were crossing a lake in a boat, and he said, "Be on your guard against the yeast of the Pharisees." We thought he was talking about bread. He knew what we were saying, and he said, "You of little faith, do you still not understand?" Then he reminded us how he fed the crowds with bread—five thousand once, four thousand the next time. He said, "I'm not talking about bread. I'm talking about the yeast of the Pharisees." We got it then. He was talking about their teaching, their hypocrisy.

Right after that, he asked us who people were saying that he was. We told him we had heard some say he was John the Baptist come back to life, or Elijah come back from the old times, or maybe he was Jeremiah. Then he asked us straight out, "What about you? Who do you say that I am?"

Everyone looked at me, so I said, "You're the Christ; you're the Son of the living God."

Now, he'd been that all the time. We didn't make that up, we discovered it. But he let us find it out for ourselves. He could have told me that on the first day, when he called me by the lake: "I am the Son of God come to earth." I probably would have said, "Oh sure, and I am Noah, and this boat is my ark!" But he was patient. He let me watch and listen to him and talk with him When he healed people he would tell them to be quiet about it. I wondered why. I thought that was a great thing; you would think he'd want everybody to know. Little by little, I and the other brothers began to realize he was real and that he was bigger than life.

He could bleed like I could. He could get hungry like I could. And he could get bone-tired like I could. But he was so unlike me. He would forgive someone's sins, then he would make the fellow walk to prove he could do it. And yet, you know, I never once saw him do anything that I'd call a sin. He'd break all the little petty rules about the sabbath day and then say he was the Lord of the sabbath. I heard him tell someone that before Abraham was, he was! What he said, what he did, and what he was . . . it was all one piece.

And it began to fit together. He wasn't just talking about God's kingdom. He was the King. He was God come in the flesh, to show poor sinners like me what God was like.

I know now that what I said that day was true. He was the Son of God. He is the Son of God, and he told me then that my flesh and blood didn't make that up. I know that. God showed me. But Jesus understood my flesh and blood, so he took his time and he went slowly. He didn't push. He pulled me. Always questioning. Always showing. Always telling me things. Always explaining until. . . . Well, I saw him touch a blind man's eyes, twice he touched them actually, and the man could see. That is what happened with me. I could see.

I: And I see. So, let's try to sum up his teaching. He let you learn by listening, by watching . . .

P: And by doing! You know, when I was a young boy I grew up with my daddy fishing. Sometimes I'd be hungry and I'd ask him for something to eat, but he'd always make me finish what I was doing first. I can remember he used to say, "Son, if I give you fish, you'll eat for one meal. If I teach you how to fish, you'll eat for a lifetime."

I: So Jesus was like your father in that . . .

He Trusted Me

P: He put me to doing. He trusted me. At the very beginning he told me to follow him and he'd make me a fisher of men. And when he called us twelve, he said that we were to be with him, then he was going to send us. He picked us for a purpose. He taught us by living with us. Let us listen. Let us watch. Then he taught us by going and doing. I tell you, I was scared when he sent us out on our first preaching mission. I was a little less scared when he sent us as part of a group of seventy. By the time he left and sent us into the world, I was still scared, but I had some confidence because he started us off in a small way. He let us go first to the people we knew around us in Israel before he sent us to others. You know, one of the people I helped to bring to Christ was a Roman army officer. His name was Cornelius. He and his whole family became part of the movement. But I want to tell you, if I hadn't started off by going to some of my fishermen friends and some of the neighbors, I never would have been ready to go to Cornelius.

I: So first he picked you to be alongside him, to watch him teach, listen to him. How long did that go on?

P: Weeks, months, years I suppose. But then he trusted us to do what he did. That's where I learned how to develop other young leaders. I tell them what we are about and why. I let them go along with me, and I show them how I do it. Then I give them a task and trust them to do it.

I: As he trusted you? And tested you?

He Tested Me

P: Tested me, sure. Terrified might be a better word! Before he sent us out on our first project, he took us across a series of hurdles that almost took the socks off every one of us. First was the night he took us in the boat and the big storm came up while he was asleep, and he said, "Where is your faith?" That was a big thing with him. He was always asking that over and over again, "Where is your faith? Where is your faith?" I remember the time we came down from the mountain with Jesus and there was this father of a little boy. Some thought the boy was epileptic, but he had a demon. The other disciples had been trying to cast the demon out, but they couldn't. Jesus got so exasperated, and he said, "O you of little faith." And then the time he cursed the fig tree, he talked to us about how if we had faith we could move mountains. More than anything else he wanted our faith to grow, and he had to test it.

He knew that if we had faith we'd see God's kingdom and we'd do great things for God's kingdom if our faith had grown enough—I don't mean big enough. He always reminded us that it wasn't how big it was, that mustard-seed faith was enough—but if we had faith in God, that was better than all the money in the world or all Caesar's armies or all the Pharisees' rule books.

I: So he tested your faith.

P: Deliberately. And again and again. I don't know how we could have been so thick-headed, maybe the word is thick-hearted. He'd have to put us in the same situation twice. We went through two storms when the boat almost foundered at night. Twice he asked us to feed big crowds. Each time we told him we didn't have enough bread, and he took a little boy's lunch and multiplied it. And he kept saying, "Do you still not understand? Where is your faith?"

I: But you learned?

P: I thought I did. I thought I was learning. But I had several low points with Jesus. Once he came walking to us in the middle of the night on the water. I kid you not! I know it's hard to believe; we made jokes about it, but it's true. After all, he made the water. He made the storm. Why shouldn't he walk on it?

Well, anyway, meek old Peter. I couldn't be satisfied to sit there with the others, so I told him if it really was him to let me walk on the water too. And he told me to come, and I stepped out.

I: And . . .

P: And I had gone about five steps, and I felt the wind and saw the waves. I started to sink. But he reached out and got me and pulled me up.

I: What did he say?

P: Same thing, "You of little faith. Why did you doubt?"

I: So you learned to walk on water?

P: No, I didn't. That was the only time he ever walked on water. I sure wasn't going to try it again. But I think he did it just that one time to say, "I'm not calling you to walk on water. You don't have to do that. I am calling you to go out there and love the sinners and heal the sick and bring good news to the poor and cast out the devils and announce the kingdom and not be afraid of your enemies."

I: So he tested you and challenged you?

P: Challenged us beyond our limits. He took us out of our comfort zone. Sent us to preach when we had never done it. Told us to feed the crowds when we didn't have enough food. Called me to walk on water.

I: And when you made a mistake?

P: Told us, leveled with us. If he had to, he rebuked us. He was always straight. He never let us get away with anything. But he never shamed us publicly. He always picked a moment when we were alone to correct us. I know some people blast you in public. Others will just hold it all inside, and while you know there is something wrong, they won't ever tell you. He would tell us, believe me. I have never known anybody that could tell it so straight. But he never held it against us. And he was always more interested in the next chapter, not the last chapter. I didn't like what he said, but I knew he did it because he cared for me.

He Selected Me

I: Peter, let me move on to something else. This may be a little sensitive, but as I read the story Jesus seems to have a number of circles. One was his family. Another was the large crowds that he spoke to. There was a real hard-core group of enemies. But then there were those who followed him most of the time. There were at least seventy?

P: That's about right. Some of those left at one point or another. Others came along. Later there were more.

I: And some women?

P: Yes, the women. They were important. They were helpers. They did the cooking and the laundry. Some of them, like Susanna, had some family money, and they helped buy food for us. But Jesus never treated them like helpers. He treated them like anybody else. Speaking personally, I had never seen a man treat a woman like that at that time, not in our time and place. Women were supposed to cook, clean, have babies. He treated them like equals. And when he was preaching to a big crowd, afterward we'd talk with the men; the women would gather around and our women would explain to them and answer their questions and help them to believe. I don't think any of us realized then how important it was to Jesus that the women were along.

I: Then there were the twelve. And there was an inner three—you and James and John?

P: Right.

I: And then of those three, if I read the record right, Jesus talked to you more and paid more attention to you than perhaps the others?

P: Maybe. You have to remember, though, that when I gave Mark the story to write it down it was from my viewpoint. So it's natural that I told more about what I knew. Also, I just talked more than anybody else. But maybe it is true that he focused on me. I think we all felt we were special to him.

I: It seems to me that this was pretty selective on Jesus' part. Out of the crowds he had seventy, and twelve, and three, and then you. It doesn't sound very democratic.

P: Don't kid yourself. We didn't know anything about democracy then, but he certainly didn't believe in lording it over other people as our kings and the Romans did. He had this knack of making everybody feel equal. He was one with us. He would never ask us to do anything he wouldn't do. He would take his turn cooking and fishing. If it were a dangerous situation he'd be out front. But he did believe that the Father was Number One, and, though he was perfectly equal with the Father, he would do what the Father said. So, we should do what he said, and others should do what we said, but only if we were really following him. He was the leader, but he was also the equalizer. No question. And I'm glad he picked me to be close to him.

I: What did that do for you?

He Included Me

P: It was the sense that he wanted me, associated with me, included me.

I guess that is it. He didn't just tell me what to do; he opened himself up to me. James and John, I know, felt the same way. I remember the first time he took the three of us with him. This synagogue ruler asked him to come and pray and heal his daughter. When we got there Jesus made the others stay outside and he took James and John and me inside. Maybe it was just because he didn't want to be crowded. But there was this little girl about twelve years old. They thought she was dead. I don't know if she was dead or if she was in a coma, but he just took her by the hand and told her to get up. And she did, and he told them to give her something to eat. They were astonished, and we were too. And so were the others when we went out and told them what had happened. Well, that made us feel pretty special. Maybe that's where it started.

I: But he took the three of you off by yourselves at other times?

P: Several. Not so often that it made the others jealous. I guess the high point was when he went up on the mountain and something happened to him and his face got bright and his clothes were shiny and Moses and Elijah were up there talking to him. Just James and John and I were there to see that.

The other time was, of course, when he went to pray just before they arrested him. He asked us to go to the garden with him and pray. It was late. We were tired. He prayed. We slept. He was so disappointed. And he looked so weighed down. But I just couldn't keep my eyes open. I felt so badly that he'd picked us but we had let him down. I guess that was the down side of being one of the three. We had more privilege. But we had more responsibility. We had more opportunity to fail. Again, I guess he was teaching us something.

I: But why did he choose you?

P: I wondered. Some day, when I see him again, maybe that will be the first question I will ask him. Maybe it had something to do with the fact that the three of us had been with him the longest. But if that was so, why didn't he include my brother Andrew? He'd been there from the beginning. Was it because he needed a smaller group to be close to, or he felt we had some leadership potential? Were there some things he could only tell to the three of us and not the twelve, just as he could explain some things only to the twelve of us and not the crowds? Whatever. Whether it was our need or his or the movement, I learned that if you are going to be a leader you can't work just through the crowd or even the big group. You have got to find some others and bring them close to your life and your heart and share your mind with them so they can carry on.

Jesus had a knack for including, without anybody really feeling excluded. I don't do that as well as he did. I guess I'm not as secure in being a leader. I don't have that same special quality. But it rubbed off on me, and every day I pray that I can be like him in that.

I: Getting back again to the question of motivation, the sense of being included was an important part of that motivation?

He Confided in Me

P: Sure, and not just for the three of us, you know, but for all of us. He confided in us. The longer we were with him the more he'd tell us what he was thinking, where he was going, what he was planning. Especially when it was time for the last trip. As I look back, I realize he was taking us through two phases. The first was from the time he called us to the time when he asked us who he was and we recognized that he was the Christ. The second was from that point until he went to Jerusalem and died. During that whole time he was explaining why he had to die and why there would be suffering and conflict in God's work. He was also preparing us for the future.

As I think back now, there must have been half a dozen times when he told us what was going to happen. That he was going to be arrested and tried and flogged and that he'd die and that he'd rise again. I guess we must have been in shock, because we hardly heard it at first. We just couldn't grasp it. Again, our hearts hadn't grown big enough, deep enough. We didn't know the Scriptures well enough. We thought the Messiah was going to come riding on a white horse and overthrow the Romans and there would be peace and happiness forever. All that talk about a servant who was going to suffer went in one ear and out the other. But he told us again and again until a glimmer got in our minds and we began to realize what he was saying.

190

I: So it didn't take you by surprise?

P: Well, yes and no. We really weren't ready for it until it happened, but not because he hadn't told us. Over and over, he let us into his mind and his heart. He would teach us from the Scriptures. He would tell us what was going to happen. He would illustrate it with one of his stories, like the one about the landowner who sent for the rent. His tenants rejected his messengers, killed his son and tried to claim his vineyard for their own. And even if we didn't get it, we had the feeling he wasn't making it mysterious. He was letting us in on the secret. We were part of the inside.

I: When did it all begin to clear up?

P: I guess at the last supper. In that upper room. When he took off his coat and washed our feet. I got huffy and told him I didn't want him to wash my feet, and he told me if he didn't I couldn't have any part with him. That humbled me again. And when he broke some bread, poured out some wine and gave it to us, saying they were his body and his blood that would be shed for us, we all got sad. But as we looked around the room we knew we were part of one of the greatest moments in all history. The world didn't know it, but we knew it. The Son of God was going to die for them and us.

By the way, he said something that night that made such an impression I'll never forget it.

I: What was it?

P: Just one little thing. He'd been telling us how he was going to leave us and go back to the Father and send the Holy Spirit to be with us, and that we wouldn't be orphans but that he'd be with us and we should love one another. It was so quiet.

And he looked around at each one of us and said, "Greater love has no one than this, that he lay down his life for his friends." And he looked around that room, and he looked into the eyes of each of us, one by one. Thaddaeus, Philip, the other Simon, me.

He Made Me His Friend

And then he said this, "You are my friends if you do what I command. I no longer call you servants, because a servant does not know his master's business. Instead, I've called you friends, for everything that I learned from my Father I've made known to you. You didn't choose me, but I chose you to go and bear fruit—fruit that will last. Then the Father will give you whatever you ask in my name. This is my command: Love each other."

I thought to myself: He has called me his friend. I'm his friend. I'm the Lord's friend! I'm not an apprentice any more. He's taken me into his confidence. And if I do it the way he taught me to do it, we will be partners in the greatest work in the world.

I: So that's when it became clear?

P: That's when I saw what he was doing. You see, one thing he knew. Unless he could write himself and his message on our hearts, he would have failed. Any teacher can leave behind a set of ideas. He wanted to leave behind a band of people.

I: People who had those ideas?

P: No, who had him written in their minds and hearts. I realized then that for three years I'd been with him so long and so close that he believed he'd written his very life on my heart.

I: So now you thought of yourself as his friend?

P: Yes, for about nine or ten hours. That was the bitter pill. In one night I felt I had gone from being his closest friend to being his—his worst friend. I wouldn't have been surprised if he had treated me like an enemy.

He Warned Me

I: I know this is painful. What do you want to tell me about it?

P: Just the facts. We'd finished eating our last meal together, and we'd gone out to the Mount of Olives. We were feeling very sad because Jesus had told us again that he was going to die and that one of us would betray him. We hadn't noticed as we went out that Judas had already slipped away. It was then that Jesus told us we would all fall away because of him that night. In fact I can still remember the quote he used, "I will strike the shepherd, and the sheep of the flock will be scattered." I've often thought of that since and how dependent we are on keeping him at the center.

Well, I protested. Loudly. I looked around at the whole group and said, "Even if all the rest of them betray you, I won't." That's when Jesus told me that I would disown him three times that night, before the cock crowed at daybreak. But I told him again, "Never!" Everybody else said the same thing.

I should have realized that he knew me better than I knew myself. And I should have realized I was on my high horse and heading for a fall.

I: Then what?

P: That's when Jesus took James and John and me to the garden. Remember, I told you how we went to sleep three times while he was praying? I felt ashamed every time he had to wake me up, but then he was through and he said to get up and let's go. We heard some voices and saw some lights coming, and there was Judas with a large crowd and some of the police. They arrested him. One of us—in the confusion we never were clear about who it was—pulled out his sword and actually hacked the ear off the high priest's aide. In that moment we were all ready to die for him. But Jesus told us to put up the sword, that he could ask God for twelve legions of angels if he wanted to lead a rebellion, but that he had to go the way the Scripture said. You see, we still didn't have it straight. We still thought the leader had to be totally in control. Or else, how could he be the leader? Even at that late date we were still blind to the fact that sometimes we lead best through weakness, and not through strength.

I: Learning that didn't come easily.

P: I tell you honestly, that was hard on me. I had always felt that Jesus was grooming me for some kind of leadership. I was proud of that. I was sure I was strong enough. I learned my lessons from him. If there was anybody he could count on, it was me. I was in control.

That was the night my little house came tumbling down. He used to talk about the foundation being his words and about trusting him. I was still trusting in myself. And I wasn't big enough.

I: Coming back to your story . . .

P: Yes, well, when they took him off to the high priest's place I followed quite a distance back. I wanted to see what would happen. I was still shaken by the fact that he wouldn't let us fight.

I waited outside in the courtyard. While I was sitting there by the fire, warming myself, a servant girl came by. She looked at me strangely. "You're with him," she said. I saw a lot of heads turn and stare. That's when I blew it. "I don't know what you're talking about," I said.

I got up to walk out of the courtyard, and another girl saw me and pointed me out and said, "This fellow was with Jesus of Nazareth."

Again, I denied it. This time I cursed. I said, "I don't know the man." I could hardly believe my own voice.

Then several of them said my accent gave me away. They could tell I was from Galilee.

I started to curse and swear like I hadn't since I left my fishing boats. I remember I shouted, "Be quiet. I swear I don't know the man, I told you." And would you believe at that split second the cock crowed.

I glanced across the courtyard at that moment to where Jesus was standing, and he raised his head and looked me straight in the eye. His words echoed in my ears, "Before the cock crows you will disown me three times." And that is when I left . . .

I: Take your time. This is hard to talk about, isn't it?

P: Sorry, I still get choked up thinking about it. I don't cry very often, but that night I cried until I thought my eyes would come out.

I: What happened next?

P: I stayed by myself most of the time. That night and the next day were a blur. I was in a room with some of the other disciples, but I stayed by myself. I heard some of them talking, and I knew the mob had taken Jesus out and crucified him. Somebody came in and said he had died. I didn't care. What difference did it make? I felt as I had died and gone to hell myself. Three years wasted and down the drain. He'd picked me and trusted me, and I'd let him down when he needed me. I'd trusted him, and now he'd let us down. I'd left everything to follow him. My livelihood was gone. My family had suffered from my absence. My friends called me a fool. I'd given my best shot for what—a hoax? I didn't want to believe that, but what else could I believe? I tell you, looking back it may seem crazy, but we just couldn't believe that there could be a Messiah who would die.

He Gave Me Another Chance

I: So? What changed you back?

P: He did. I guess I must have been in that state for two or three days. No more tears. I was cried dry. Just depressed, bitter, angry. It was early on the sabbath when I heard a noise and some of the women came in. They'd gone out earlier, but I hadn't noticed them. I started to tell them to be quiet, but then I looked up and saw them. They were as white as a sheet. I could tell something had scared them. Then they said they'd been out to the tomb to anoint Jesus and he wasn't there. The tomb was empty. And they'd seen some young fellow sitting there who had told them that Jesus had risen.

The room fell silent. We couldn't believe them. We thought they were just silly women.

And then, I remember, Mary Magdalene turned and looked straight at me and said, "And do you know what he said? He said, 'Go tell his disciples and Peter. He is going ahead of you into Galilee. There you will see him, just as he told you.'"

I sat there stunned. It couldn't be true. But was it true? Was it my name that had been called?

We didn't believe them. It sounded like nonsense. But I had to see, so I got up and ran as fast as I could to the tomb. Sure enough, his clothes were there. Only Jesus wasn't.

I: What convinced you he was alive?

P: Two things. That night we were all gathered in the upper room, still wondering what had happened, and suddenly we looked up and he was there. The doors were bolted. We were still afraid that they might come to get us. The windows were barred too. And yet he was suddenly there. And he didn't rebuke us, he just said, "Peace." And when he held up his hands, I saw the nail prints. I knew. We all knew. It was Jesus.

I: And the second thing that convinced you?

P: It was back by the lake. The same place where he first called me. He'd told us to go back to Galilee. We still weren't sure what was going to happen. I thought maybe the whole thing was like a dream, and we had better get started fishing again. So we fished all night. It was just like the first time. We fished all night and caught nothing. Then early in the morning we saw someone on the shore. He called out and asked if we had caught anything. We said no. Then he told us to throw our net out on the right side, and we did that. We couldn't even pull it in, it was so heavy.

Then John said, "Peter, it's the Lord." When I heard him say that, I just knew I couldn't wait for the boat to get to shore. I jumped in the water, waded ashore, and there was Jesus. He had a fire going, with some fish on it, and he also had some bread. He told us to bring some more fish, so I went and hauled the net in—and would you believe it, we counted 153 big fish.

We could hardly believe our eyes, but when he said "Come and have breakfast" we knew it was Jesus. This was three times he had come to us after he was raised. The other was when he came and talked to Thomas.

I: So what did he say to you, Peter?

P: I'd been waiting for him to blast me. I deserved it. I wanted him to tear into me, ask me why I went to sleep when he was praying, why I'd denied him three times. If I'd been in his place, I would have taken a strip off me. I would have been rough. But do you know what he said to me?

I: What?

P: He asked me if I loved him. "Do you truly love me more than these?" he asked.

I said, "Yes. Lord, you know that I love you." Then he just said, "Feed my lambs."

The second time, the same thing.

The third time, he said, "Simon, son of John, do you love me?"

That really hurt. Because, you see, I denied him three times. And three times he was asking if I loved him.

I: That really hurt?

P: Of course it did. But that's how straight and real he was. He called me when I was going nowhere. He named me and changed me. He trusted me. He called me his friend. And he hurt me. He hurt me in the way I needed to be hurt. A way that took all of the pain and poison and shame that I felt. He didn't shove it under the rug. He brought it into the open. He wouldn't let it stand between us. He let me know that he was hurt. Really hurt. And I felt that hurt.

And I learned something then about rebuke and correction. I know that it can be the most loving thing in the world. It can be the most healthy thing. And it can make a relationship good again.

I learned from Jesus that love doesn't mean hiding the hurt, it means confronting the hurt and healing it.

I: What else did he say?

P: As I said. Three times he just said, "Feed my lambs. Take care of my sheep. Feed my sheep." Then I realized that he still trusted me. I remembered when we had our last meal together he had told me that the devil was trying to get me. He said then that he had prayed for me that my faith wouldn't fail and that when I turned back I would strengthen my brothers.

He Made Me Understand

From that moment it all came together. I saw it as I had never seen it before. He'd chosen me. Prayed for me. Died for me. And now he was trusting me. He said at the very beginning that he was calling me to leave fish and go for people. Now he was telling me that the greatest thing I could do for him was to take care of his people, his sheep.

I learned something else. He gave me one final little parable. He said that when you're a young man you get up in the morning, dress yourself and go wherever you want. When you get old and you're feeble, you're not in control. Someone else dresses you and picks you up and carries you or leads you around. Then I realized that he was telling me what real leadership in his kingdom involves. It's not being the one in control so you can do what you want. It's being the one who gives up the final control to God, just as Jesus did. If that means death, then that's OK. That's what Jesus meant when he said to me at the beginning to follow him.

That is what he meant at the end when he said, "Follow me." I was still concerned about the others, so I turned to John and said, "What about him?" Jesus said, "Forget about him. What's that to you? You follow me."

That is as simply as I can put it. He didn't call me to man his army, control his empire, juggle his programs.

I: So, what did Jesus teach you about leadership?

P: Simple. Follow him. Love him. Feed his sheep.

I: And that's what you meant when you wrote to the leaders in the early church?

P: Exactly. To be shepherds of God's flock. Not because you have to, but because you want to. Not because you're paid for it, but because you're eager for it. Not lording it, but being examples. He was the example, the Chief Shepherd.

And when we face him, those are the bottom-line questions he will ask. They are only ones that will matter: Did you love me? Did you follow me? Did you feed my sheep?

I: Thank you, Peter.

P: No, thank him.

11

THE LEADER AS SHEPHERD-MAKER (3)

•

"I have called you friends,
for everything that I have learned
from my Father I have made known
to you."
JESUS CHRIST

•

"Train a man and he will
become only what you are. Serve and develop a man
who is caught up with vision and is dedicated to God and the sky is the limit."
JIM KENNEDY

"The only way people will perform excellently over the long-term is if they fully
comprehend what they are doing."
FRED SMITH

Warren Benniss has described what he calls the "power reciprocal."[1]
He uses this to describe empowering leadership, leadership which uses power to empower others and which, by so doing, receives power back. Another way of putting this is that leaders who divest themselves of power and invest in others will find that the initial investment has grown.

This is the godly pattern of leadership. This is what God did when he created. Of his own free will without any necessity, he divested himself of his sovereign solitude and invested his powers in human beings whom he assigned as stewards—or to use modern terms, investment bankers or development agents—over his creation. He ran the risk (if that word can be used of God) of the enterprise backfiring, and in a sense it did. His stewards rebelled.

Again he divested himself by choosing one people of all the human peoples to be his representatives. Again the experiment backfired. But with divine patience—one might say with the positive self-regard that only the Deity can have—he divested himself again. This time he sent his only begotten Son into the world. Again, the result was rebellion, rejection, crucifixion. But God kept patiently on, knowing that in the long run—the eternal run—this was the only way to create a race of finite creatures who would ultimately be a reproduction of himself.

So Jesus the Son, doing only those things which his Father showed him, followed the same pattern. He could have healed everybody. He chose not to. He could have preached forgiveness to everybody. He chose not to. He could have fed everybody. Instead, when the crowd tried to get him to go into the bakery business and multiply enough bread to feed the whole nation, he withdrew. His purpose was not to preach all the sermons, do all the miracles, right all the wrongs or solve all the problems. His purpose was to reproduce the life he had in himself from his Father, to recreate his own leadership in his chosen people.

So he, too, divested himself, stood back patiently, invested himself in others, and waited for the final return on the investment.

Out of the crowds he picked twelve for a purpose. He trained them in a living classroom, first by their listening and watching, and then by their going and doing. He chose them to be with him, in order that he might later send them out. He entrusted them with a task and an authority. He explained and corrected. He provided resources and let them go and stepped into the shadows to watch over them until his final time came.

A Shared Life
Jesus' leadership development of his under-shepherds was not so much a course or a curriculum as it was a shared life. It was an experience of fellowship. The word *fellowship* has become trivial and superficial today.

We speak of fellowship as lighthearted camaraderie. Or of the church building as the "fellowship hall," meaning a gathering place for a meal, a program or a social occasion. But the Greek word used in the New Testament, _koinonia_ (fellowship), has a far deeper significance. It can imply a partnership, a common ownership of a business. In that sense, Peter and his brother Andrew, and James and his brother John, were partners with each other, each owning a share of their fishing boat and equipment. But true fellowship means much more than that. It means the common ownership and stewardship of all things. Dietrich Bonhoeffer, the German pastor martyred under Hitler, captured this fuller sense when he entitled one of his books _Life Together._[2] When it was said of the first followers of Jesus that they "had everything in common" (Acts 2:44), that was the ideal of fellowship lived out.

The short-lived communal experiment of the early church (an experience of community that has been idealized and repeated with only limited success in the centuries since) was a reflection, albeit a pale one, of God's own life. "In the beginning was the Word, and the Word was _with God,_" wrote John in the prologue of his Gospel (Jn 1:1). Within the reality of God there was an eternal community; Father, Son and Spirit shared Godness equally.

When the Word became flesh and lived among us human beings, Jesus quite naturally followed the same pattern. He divested himself of ownership and invested all he was and had in his close associates. With them—especially with his twelve, and most especially with his inner three—he shared all things. They ate and traveled, walked and slept together. If he had no place to lay his head, they shared in his deprivation. But if he had plenty, so did they. He did not hold back from them his deepest feelings, whether anger, joy, sadness or temptation. How could his biographers have written of his testings by the devil in the desert if he had not told them? How could they have known of his sweating tears of blood and agony in a garden as he faced crucifixion unless he had taken them along with him?

Think back over the case study of Jesus and Peter given in the last chapter. How did Jesus "deploy himself" in Peter and the other twelve? He did it by his shared life—shared vision and goals, shared partnership and time, shared learning and risks, a shared future, and shared power.

Let us pick up some of the things that Peter highlighted in our imaginary interview, and see what this says about Jesus as a shepherd-maker.

A Shared Goal

Peter's reminiscence: "He saw me."

Jesus' affirmation: "You are my vision and my goal."

Kingdom leadership, as we saw earlier, is both goal-oriented and person-oriented. Or, in contemporary terms, it is both market-driven and value-driven. Jesus' vision was for the establishing of his Father's rule in the entire world. The field, or the market, was the world. The means to carry out that goal was the spreading of the good news and the making of sons and daughters of the kingdom. That program was not something that could be separated from the value of the persons to whom the gospel came. Jesus made that clear in his first address (Lk 4:18-19). The Spirit of the Lord had anointed him, not to carry out a program, but to remove the binding forces which kept people from becoming all that God wanted them to be. So his call was for good news to the poor, sight to the blind, freedom to the oppressed. The kingdom had come to enable persons to be all that God dreamed they could be, living replicas of the heavenly Father. When he saw a fisherman or a tax collector, he did not see them as means to his ends. He saw they *were* his ends. In calling and transforming them, *they* were his product and *they* were his market! He wanted them to dream the same dreams he had for them. In turn, they would have the same vision for others as he had for them. Empowering leadership for Jesus meant not merely to get the job done, but *to help people to grow and get the job done*! In both areas he was results-oriented. Being and doing, experiencing the gospel and proclaiming the gospel, all were part of his vision for his people. His joy was in seeing others grow.

Here is an important difference between managing, as commonly understood, and leading. Of course, a good manager must be in some ways a leader, as a good leader must also be a manager. But where the manager is often primarily concerned with systems and physical resources, the leader is primarily concerned with the vision and the human and spiritual resources. When Jesus borrowed Peter's boat to preach to the crowd, he was more concerned with joining Peter than with using the boat. The fishing boat was handy for the moment; the fisherman was history-in-the-making.

It has been said that transformational leaders work themselves out of a job, as they turn subordinates into leaders. That was Jesus' vision: "Follow me and I will make you fishers of men"--and that is the vision he wanted them to share with him.

A Shared Partnership

Peter's reminiscence: "He picked me.... He called me.... He named me. ... He joined me with others."

Jesus' affirmation: "You are my partners."

Leadership in Jesus' style means we always keep our physical eyes and the eyes of our hearts open to see those that we might call some day. I once heard Peter Drucker relate the story of how symphony orchestras developed in the early 1800s. There was no place to turn for conductors. Individual musicians might be skilled in their particular instrument, but not in overall leadership. So schools for conductors developed. But along with that the best conductors were always keeping lists of young people and junior conductors whom they felt had great potential. The story interested me because for several years I have kept a file which I call GGTW—"Guys and gals to watch." Whenever I meet a young person who strikes me, or hear someone speak of him or her and find my attention drawn, I slip that name in a file with a note of who they are and why they caught my attention. Every once in a while I pull that file out and read through it to be reminded of these potential leaders. When we have a special project or assignment, I will take one of them along to be part of that particular effort.

If we are leaders, we need to pray that we may see people as God sees them, help them to see themselves in that way, and help them to see the world as God sees it.

Some years ago Dawson Trotman, who founded the Navigators organization, became very close with several young men who had recently committed their lives to Christ. One day he stood with them in the driveway outside their residence. He had them turn to the Gospel of Matthew and read the part where Jesus said, "Pray ye therefore the Lord of the harvest, that he will send forth laborers. . . ." (Mt 9:38, AV). Then he stretched out a big map of the world on the hood of a car, and he told one of the young men to take his finger and make a stab at some point on the globe. The young man's finger landed on Korea, a land that he had never really heard of at that time.

"Now," commanded Trotman, "pray that the Lord will raise up a laborer in Korea."

The young man was a bit nonplused, not being a public prayer. But he did as Trotman said, and in a few stumbling words asked God to raise up a laborer in Korea.

Over the weeks ahead, Trotman kept reminding them to pray for God to "raise up a laborer." They were young men. They were new believers. They hardly knew the world that existed outside their own neighborhood. But the seed of a great vision was passed on.

The young man who prayed for a laborer to be raised up was Douglas Coe, now the leader of what is sometimes known as the "Fellowship" or the "prayer breakfast movement." This international movement brings leaders together to build fellowship in the spirit of Jesus Christ. Doug Coe tells about a trip which he and several political leaders made to some forty islands in the South Atlantic and the South Pacific. In each case they went to say, "We want to be friends with you. We come from some large nations which haven't always been friends with the small nations. We want to have fellowship with you in the spirit of Jesus Christ. And we want to extend this fellowship to others." In almost every case someone caught a glimmer of the vision of a fellowship built around the person of Jesus Christ. As Coe told the remarkable story of this global journey, he traced it all back to that night when Dawson Trotman told a young man to put his finger on a map and pray that God would raise up a laborer.

Someone shared the vision and goal of Jesus with Dawson Trotman. He shared it with Doug Coe. Now Doug Coe shares it around the world.

A large part of leadership lies in "vision casting." Ordinarily people are drawn not so much to programs as to leaders who inspire.[3]

A shared partnership as well as a shared vision and goal was at the heart of Jesus' leadership process. Nothing is more important or more difficult for the leader than the choosing of a team and of other leaders. Jesus picked his select group early in his ministry, but he did it carefully, after some time to consider; he did it prayerfully, talking it over with his Father; and yet he did it unpredictably. The choosing of leadership is in itself a significant and powerful act. Who is included? Who is left out? The very choice is in a sense a self-fulfilling selection. Though done as carefully and as prayerfully and with as much wisdom as possible, the selection will not always be right. Jesus chose twelve, and one of them betrayed him. When Jesus chose them he knew he would have problems, but he did it with hope. He could look Peter straight in the eye and say, "You are Simon—I know all that you are and aren't—but you shall be called Peter. I see you with hope, and with that hope I bring you into partnership." For all their limitations, Jesus had obviously recognized in Peter and the others what my friend Fred Smith calls the "driving wheels," those who provide momentum to a movement, in contrast to those who are just along for the ride.

In his invitation to partnership, Jesus showed the wisdom of the out standing leader. He perfectly models the characteristics that Warren Benniss lists as making up "emotional wisdom":

1. The ability to accept people as they are, and not as you would like them to be.

2. The capacity to approach relationships and problems in terms of the present rather than the past.

3. The ability to treat those who are close to you with the same courteous attention you extend to strangers and casual acquaintances.

4. The ability to trust others, even if the risk seems great.

5. The ability to do without constant approval and recognition from others.[4]

When I look at Jesus' partnership with his twelve, I realize how much I have to learn about leadership. How many times do I want my teammates to live up to my unrealistic expectations, not seeing them as they are and I am, a mixture of strengths and weaknesses? How often do I hold their past mistakes against their present capacity and commitment? How many times do I find myself ignoring them or snapping at them or failing to compliment them while paying attention to a visitor? How often am I willing to trust people to do something they have never done, even though they may not do it as well as I would? How constantly am I able to consider them, whether or not they consider me? My answers will tell me whether I think of others as my staff, as my organization, as my subordinates, or as apprentices with me in the school of Christ and of life.

There are many myths about leadership abroad, and Jesus exposed them as just that, myths.

"Leaders are a rare breed." Perhaps great leaders may be. But Jesus saw that if a man could run a fishing crew he could lead part of Jesus' crew.

"Leaders are born, not made." Partially true, yet Jesus exposed the overlooked truth when he said, "Follow me and _I will make you._ . . ." And he made them from fishers of fish into fishers of people; from sand into rock; from sheep into shepherds. They learned to lead by following a good leader. How do we learn to be lovers or parents? By following good lovers and parents.

"Leaders are inspiring." Again, yes and no. Jesus was, but apparently some of the twelve were not. Peter was; Andrew was not. And even Peter was not at the beginning. I guess it was not until he rose to the occasion after Jesus' death and gave a great public talk in Jerusalem on the day of Pentecost that Peter became an inspirational leader. He certainly did not begin as such.

The transforming of ordinary people into apprentices and then into partners begins with the crucial choice, "I want you in this with me. You and I are going to be partners." It is a choice that does not guarantee results. It is a choice that must be made with hope and faith. It is a choice that must be made by the leader.

Shared Time

Peter's reminiscence: "He included me. . . . He joined me. . . . He took me along. . . . He spent time with me."

Jesus' affirmation: "You and I need to be together. . . . You deserve my time. . . . I want to be with you."

To have a vision and a goal is one thing; to share that goal and call others into partnership in striving for that goal is another; but to make that partnership a commitment and a priority is still another. The task of building a vehicle for a vision is essential to leadership. Jean Monet, a leader of the European Economic Community, has said, "Nothing is possible without men, nothing is lasting without institutions."[5]

For Jesus, that institution was not an organization but a team, a community, and quite clearly a priority. We see this priority in his initial choice of the twelve, with the stated purpose that they should "be with him" (Mk 3:14). "The primary purpose," notes Allen Cole,

> was that they should continually be in the company of their Rabbi, who was at once Teacher and Leader. . . . They would thus receive both formal and informal instruction, and treasure and lay to heart His casual sayings. . . . The secondary purpose was that He might send them out as His own personal representatives.[6]

This kind of association is not unusual. Socrates had disciples of this sort, as did Confucius, the Jewish rabbis, and, for that matter, John the Baptist.

To be "with him" meant more than the casual "hanging around together" that we speak of today. Being with Jesus involved being with him in the sharing of his purpose, his dream and eventually his suffering. But at the simplest and most practical level, Jesus chose his disciples simply to spend time with him. We have already noted that there are in the Gospels at least twice as many references to occasions when Jesus was with his disciples as there are to any of his other associations (see p. 164).

Quite clearly, then, his disciples were his priority. He wanted them to have access to him. True enough, at times he would withdraw from them for solitary prayer, or send them out on a project without him. But one gets the impression that in his three years of recorded ministry there were very few times when they were not around. Sometimes he was so busy and besieged by requests for help that "he and his disciples were not even able to eat" (Mk 3:20). But he did have time for long unhurried talks with his followers. Like a team of medical students following the chief resident on his rounds, they watched him heal, overheard his individual conversations, listened to his debates with religious leaders, sat next to him as they ate fish off the coals by the lake, saw him full of energy in the morning and weary at night. On at least one occasion we see him cooking breakfast for them. He was not a leader who held himself aloof from common chores of the family. Here was no mystic figure who hid himself in retreat and occasionally came out to dispense pearls of wisdom. Here was a leader who shared the flesh and blood, the sweat and tears and joys of those he called brothers as well as disciples.

While I was writing the above, the telephone rang. Answering, I immediately recognized the voice and accent of an Eastern European doctor whom I have known for several years. This young man and his wife have a tremendous ministry of service and witness in their country. He wanted to talk about a new opportunity and dream that he had.

I started to tell him I did not have time, that I was busy writing and would have to talk to him later. Then I thought, Would Jesus say he did not have time? So I assured him I had time, and I listened as he told me about his plans to build a Christ-centered medical center in his country which would deal with the whole person—body, mind and spirit—and would be the first of its kind in Eastern Europe. The authorities had given the go-ahead, and he was seeking to raise the funds and wanted both my good will and my guidance.

It was a wonderful vision, and when I hung up the phone I was thrilled that I could encourage him and open a few doors for him. Then I began to think that Jesus never regarded people who pushed into his life as interruptions of his ministry. Interruptions, in fact, made up a large chunk of his ministry! And I realized that if my time schedule and my work become more important to me than the interruptions God sends along the way, then I have lost the shepherd's vision, and I have forgotten that the bottom line is not the work but the people.

It has been said that truly transformational leaders use a "pull" rather than a "push" style of influence. President Dwight Eisenhower, when he was a general, pictured this kind of leadership by placing a long piece of string on the table. "Look what happens if I try to push this string," he would say. "It just bunches up. But look what happens if I pull it. That string will follow me wherever I go." Then he would challenge his officers to be the kind of leaders who would pull others along to follow.

Commitment to a "pull" style of leadership, one which really involves people, is costly, in terms of time, loss of privacy, vulnerability and exposure to others. But the rewards and results are worth it. Consider some of the likely outcomes of the "pull" style of leadership.

1. *A sense of significance.* Do you think Peter and the others ever forgot that Jesus knew them and liked them well enough to nickname them? Or that they ever got over the fact that out of all the crowds, "he chose us"?

Ajith Fernando, the gifted young leader of Youth for Christ in Sri Lanka, talks of team ministry. Ajith is an able speaker and writer. His public ministry is in demand throughout the world. He could travel constantly and have a rewarding career, but he has chosen to spend most of his time in his native Sri Lanka. There he struggles to find time for his family and for his passion—studying and writing. The bulk of his time he spends with his team, helping to develop their gifts and vision for bringing the gospel of reconciliation to their strife-torn country. "Leaders must make team life a primary commitment in ministry," Ajith says. "The primary ambition of a leader should be to enable his or her team members to achieve their fullest potential under God. We must dream about them, dream dreams for them. We must pray for them. As Paul said to Timothy, 'Night and day I constantly remember you in my prayers.' We may need to adjust our program according to their gifts."[7]

2. *An experience of equality.* "Great leaders have a passion for equality," writes Hugh Nibley, of Brigham Young University. "History defines examples, such as Alexander the Great, sharing his food with his men, calling them by their first names, marching along with them in the heat, and being the first over the wall in battle."[8] Nibley contrasts this kind of leadership with a management style which finds equality repugnant, "where promotion, perks, privilege and power are the name of the game [and] awe and reverence of rank is everything." While second-rate management shuns equality and feeds on mediocrity, leadership offers a way out. The true leader is never satisfied to leave his people where they are.

Jesus cut through the social roles of his day. He refused to be like Gentile kings who lorded it over others. He warned against the ego show of those who wanted to be recognized in the marketplace and be called by titles like "Rabbi." He himself accepted the title "Lord" from his followers, but he demonstrated his lordship by washing their feet. Without question he was Lord. He was also one with them. He was never satisfied to leave them there, but was always pulling them on.

3. *A contagious enthusiasm.* One gets the impression when reading about Jesus' disciples that, for all their blunders and shortcomings, they were with him for the long haul. Overconfident they may have been, but when Jesus asked James and John if they could share in his cup, they readily answered, "We can." The "pull style" in leadership is catching.

Warren Benniss interviewed Harold Williams shortly after his retirement as chairman of the U.S. Securities and Exchange Commission. Williams showed him a leather-bound volume of his speeches which his staff had presented to him. Their inscriptions were revealing, "You saw and understood us in a singular way." "You gave meaning and significance throughout our professional lives." "Working with you was a fine form of post-graduate education." "Always it was fun! Thanks!" The would-be leader in Jesus' style should ask not just "Am I getting the job done?" but "Am I fun to work with? Do I have a contagious enthusiasm?"

4. *Commitment to growth.* Jesus was constantly in the process of developing his people into confident fishers of men, or shepherds of the sheep. What better way than to be around the master fisherman and the chief shepherd and to watch him! In that sense the good leader is always a mentor who may simply let the student watch and see. Peter Drucker tells of one great piano teacher "who would let her students listen to her play and then say, 'Did you hear it? How should it sound? Why don't you play it like that?'

In my apprenticeship as a young evangelist, I learned by watching Billy Graham. Once, over a sixteen-and-a-half-week period, I sat six nights a week on the platform at Madison Square Garden listening, observing, taking notes on what he said and how he said it. Occasionally (though not as often as I wished!) he would invite me to sit in with him at a luncheon or a dinner where he was talking with a publisher or some business leader. I learned from him that witnessing to our faith can be oblique and need not always be direct. Instead of preaching to these people, he would tell them what he had told someone else. So in effect I was listening in on his conversation. The best way I know to grow in confidence is to be around a real "pro" who is so much better than I am that I realize how far I have to go, but who is so positive and caring that he makes me want to grow. Three years of the most intense postgraduate education, however worthwhile, cannot compare to three years by the side of a master!

5. *A unifying passion.* Note how Peter in our imaginary interview stressed that "he joined us together." Jesus' band of disciples was what sociologists call a "centered-set." Some relationships are defined by boundaries, formal memberships, and rules and regulations. Others are defined by their center. Jesus "centered" the twelve. He provided the balance wheel for the aggressive Peter and the contemplative John, the radical Simon and the conservative Matthew. In accountability to him they found a unity with each other. It did not come easily. Their bickering and ambition sometimes cut and hurt. But the depth of their commitment to Jesus finally brought a depth of commitment to each other that made the transformed group of recruits into a band of brothers. The corporate style of management may see people as replaceable parts of the organization; Jesus' style of "pull leadership," on the other hand, sees each one as the member of a family, whether he or she remains with the organization or not.

Several years ago, the Lausanne Committee for World Evangelization appointed a committee of younger leaders to arrange an international conference. The seventeen or eighteen members of the committee were strong-minded, visionary young men and women. When the committee met, each one had equally firm ideas of what should and should not be done. One of the earliest meetings took place in Stuttgart, Germany. Disagreements were sharp, passions ran deep, the leadership of the chairman was called into question, and the whole group was stymied. At one point it was suggested that they stop the business meeting and have prayer. Not one person prayed! The chairman called for a break, and they left the room in despair, some convinced that the conference would never be held.

When they came back together, however, one of them said, "We are brothers and sisters in Christ. We have a world to be won for him. If we can't come together, we don't deserve to be called leaders." Painfully they worked through the issues and committed themselves to stay together no matter what. The conference was held as "Singapore 87" and achieved most of its goals. But the chairman/leader told me that the most significant part of the conference for him was that he learned a new style of "pull leadership" (though he did not use exactly that term) in that high-powered group. Another committee member told me that for him the most important thing was that the committee had become a family. Still another suggested, in jest but sincerely, that perhaps the best thing they could do was not to hold the conference, but to step aside after they had finished their planning and appoint another group to go through the same process! What they had learned in being joined together meant more to them than the conference itself. Such is the centering, unifying passion which comes from the leadership of Jesus.

Shared Learning

Peter's reminiscence: "He taught me . . . explained to me . . . instructed me."

Jesus' affirmation: "You and I are growing together."

Jesus' commitment to spend time with his people made for an environment in which learning happened. So learning was not only something that casually happened; it was something that was intentionally focused.

Consider the following observations about the link between leadership and learning: "The most marked characteristic of . . . potential leaders . . . is their capacity to learn from others and the environment—the capacity to be taught."[9] "Leaders are perpetual learners. . . . learning is the essential fuel for the leader."[10] One way to recognize the true leader is this drive not only to learn, but to create what has been called "a commonwealth of learning," an attitude and environment in which learning takes place.

Suppose you had a serious problem and wanted to go to someone for some wise counsel. Where would you turn? I know where I would probably go. Immediately, there come to my mind two men, both older than me, both friends, both giants to me. One has been a leader in the military and the church, the other in business and the church. They have in common three characteristics. Both have *been through much.* Their experiences have been wide and varied across a lifetime of challenge and responsibility. Not only have they been through much, but they have *learned through much.* I see them both as curious men, men with probing minds who ask why, who are not satisfied with what seems to be, but who want to find what is the underlying reality. In the course of their learning they have both *prayed through much*. Often facing situations beyond their own expertise or experience, they have learned to ask God for wisdom—and they have received it.

Was Jesus that kind of learner? It almost seems heresy to suggest that. If he truly was the perfect Son of God, what did he have to learn that he did not already know? Here we are face to face with the mystery of the God-Man, the God of all wisdom who emptied himself, laid aside some of his powers, in order to be fully human. If he was fully human, how could he *not* learn?

At least the Bible writers are clear on this point. As a boy he "grew in wisdom," Luke tells us (Lk 2:52). He himself said, "The Son can do nothing by himself; he can do only what he sees his Father doing, because whatever the Father does the Son also does. For the Father loves the Son and shows him all he does" (Jn 5:19-20). The writer of Hebrews makes the amazing statement that "although he was a son, he learned obedience from what he suffered" (Heb 5:8).

True, he had uncanny, supranatural foresight and insights, and from time to time he knew what would happen to him in advance. But did he also know in advance all about fishing, family, flowers, animals—or did he learn about them in the normal way?

To me the answer seems obvious. Jesus was a learner. But he was the perfect learner, and since he was without sin he had no blocks to his learning. He was able to take in all that he read, heard, and saw, to absorb and process and include it in his vision of the kingdom. And being a learner himself, he created the ideal learning environment for his people.

He taught in so many ways. The sight of a harvest growing to ripeness was the occasion for teaching about the need for people to harvest the human crop of souls. There were times when he sat his disciples down for specific blocks of teaching to draw together the lesson they had learned and to prepare them for the next step. It is likely that he used repetition. Some scholars think that he may have repeated some of his favorite sayings scores or hundreds of times. Like Socrates, he knew the value of questions and dialog. His parables were little time bombs implanted in the minds of his disciples. They might be five days or five miles down the road when the truth embodied in those stories would explode in their minds and give them the insight or the challenge they needed. Always learning, Jesus was always teaching.

And that attitude must be central in those who are leaders in Christ. At a conference for young leaders, Dr. Roberta Hestenes, president of Eastern College, addressed the current idea that it is important for younger people to have mentors. "If you can find the right mentor," she said, "that's fine. But I have had some who could have directed me the wrong way. You may not always be able to find a mentor but you can always have a teachable spirit. And if you have a teachable spirit, God will provide for you to learn in his way and in his time."

I saw that kind of teachable spirit demonstrated at a conference for pastors in Yugoslavia. Halfway through the conference, a Pentecostal pastor from nearby Romania arrived unexpectedly. Someone pointed him out to me, a big, burly, wide-shouldered man, who looked as if he had been a manual laborer. I thought to myself, rather patronizingly, that I was so glad he was there and would be able to get the benefit of all of our teaching. During a break in the conference, one of my associates heard this man discussing Norwegian composers with a man from Scandinavia and German philosophers with an East German. It turned out that, like many pastors in his country, he is a professional man, a lawyer, and is highly educated. Although he has never been able to have formal seminary training, he spends several hours a day in theological and biblical studies and several hours improving his classical learning, and all of that along with the load of a preaching and counseling ministry! I was chastened when I realized that I had automatically assumed that we from the West would be better informed. And I wondered how many Western pastors have the hunger for learning, in order to be excellent servants of God and people, that this man demonstrated. Like Jesus, he was a learner.

Shared Risks

Peter's reminiscence: "He trusted me. . . . He challenged me."

Jesus' affirmation: "You and I are called to risk!"

An entrepreneur has been described by author and speaker Tom Peters as someone who "takes unreasonable risks based on inadequate evidence." When I suggested that definition to a group of entrepreneurial businessmen, they all smiled. They recognized themselves. Then one of them said, "It depends whether you are looking at a situation from the outside or the inside. To the outsider it may look as if the risk is too great to take. But from the entrepreneur's side it is a different situation. Even though he may not have all the evidence, as he sees it the risk is too small not to take." In a very real sense, faith is an attitude of risk—based on evidence, to be sure, but still with an element of uncertainty.

From the outsider's viewpoint, one might say that God took a risk when he created the human race and when he sent his Son into the world. He was risking rejection, and that rejection happened. Jesus took a risk when he chose Peter and the rest of the twelve, unlikely candidates as they were. He took a risk when he invested three years in those twelve and not in twelve others. He took a risk when he sent them out to represent him. He took a risk when he left them behind on earth to carry on his mission.

When he sent them out on their mission, Jesus asked them to take risks. "Go! I am sending you out like lambs among wolves" was his cheerful marching order (Lk 10:3). Frequently he put them into situations of uncertainty or anxiety to develop their confidence and their faith. In a swift-moving series of snapshots, Mark's Gospel shows Jesus leading his disciples through a storm that threatened to swamp their boat, into hostile territory to confront a near-madman possessed by a demon, and into the home of a synagogue ruler where they would have felt socially out of their depth (Mk 4:35—5:43). Only as they risked the unknown would they learn to trust.

Would they fall flat on their faces? Of course they would, and they did. But Jesus knew the difference between failure and learning. All learning involves some "failure," something from which we can continue to learn. I know a woman who learned to water ski in her early sixties! Since then she has taught thousands of young people to ski. "I am the world's best water ski instructor," she laughingly told me. "It took me eighteen months to learn to get up on those skis, and to trust the boat in the water to pull me. I know every way not to do it." When she kept falling down, she wasn't failing; she was learning.

Warren Benniss writes: "For a lot of people, the word 'failure' carries with it a finality . . . but for the successful leader, failure is a beginning, the springboard of hope."[11]

Tom Watson, founder of the corporate giant IBM, once assigned a young executive to carry out a risky venture. Ten million dollars were spent and lost in the gamble, which proved to be a disaster. After it was all over, Watson called the young man into his office. "I guess you want my resignation?" he asked. "Resignation?" said Watson, "You can't be serious. We've just spent ten million dollars educating you!"[12] So Jesus allowed for failure because he was looking not for perfection but for faith. When Peter saw Jesus walking on the water, he wanted to try it. Jesus told him to come, but Peter gave in to fear and began to sink. Jesus caught him and said, "You of little faith. Why did you doubt?" His rebuke was meant not to cow Peter but to challenge him. Without the risk and the lesson learned from failure, Peter's faith never would have grown.

A Shared Future

Peter's reminiscence: "He motivated me. . . . He warned me. . . . He stuck with me. . . . He promised me."

Jesus' affirmation: "You and I have a future to go for."

Closely allied to Jesus' risk-taking style was his focus on the future. True leaders are not pessimists; they are realists who believe in the future.

His master thought of the kingdom determined how Jesus looked at the future. The rule of God, he said, had already been initiated, but throughout history there would be an escalating process of conflict and crisis until he came again and God's kingdom arrived in all its fullness. But the kingdom was not some far-off event. It had already begun. With Jesus the future was already present! Salvation was something to be experienced now *and* something to reach for with anticipation. Jesus created a holy dissatisfaction with what was, and a longing for what would be.

So when he chose his disciples, he looked not at what they had been, but at what they could be with him redirecting their energies from the negative to the positive.

It was the same with their mission. With a tremendous mixture of realism and optimism, he forecast the future, preparing them for what was to come.

He warned:

Nation will rise against nation, and kingdom against kingdom. There will be earthquakes in various places, and famines. . . .

You must be on your guard. You will be handed over to the local councils and flogged. . . .

Brother will betray brother to death, and a father his child. Children will rebel against their parents and have them put to death. All men will hate you because of me. (Mk 13:8-9, 12)

He also promised:

On account of me you will stand before governors and kings as witnesses to them. And the gospel must first be preached to all nations. Whenever you are arrested and brought to trial, do not worry beforehand about what to say. Just say whatever is given you at the time, for it is not you speaking, but the Holy Spirit. . . . He who stands firm to the end will be saved. (Mk 13:9-11, 13)

Those words, spoken by Jesus to his disciples in the temple, shortly before his death, were part of his preparing them for the future. In reading them, one senses what a great understanding of motivation Jesus had.

"At the heart of sustained motivation," writes John Gardner, "lie two ingredients that appear contradictory: positive attitudes toward the future, and on the other hand, recognition that life is not easy enough that you are ever finally safe."[13]

Loss of confidence brings images of defeat and failure to our minds and incapacitates us for sustained effort. Lack of hope is a major ingredient in many of the great social and spiritual problems such as malnutrition, poverty, alcoholism and drug abuse. "Why bother? Nothing will ever change" is the ingrained thinking that often comes from failure.

On the other hand, writes Gardner:

Confidence is evident in the peak periods of great civilizations. . . .

A civilization rises to greatness when something happens in human minds.

Reflecting on Pericles, Socrates, Sophocles and the other great citizens of Athens in that most golden of golden ages, the fifth century B.C.; reflecting on figures so extraordinarily diverse as Shakespeare, Francis Drake, Thomas More, Francis Bacon and Queen Elizabeth in 16th century England; reflecting on Cortes, Santa Teresa, Cervantes, St. John of the Cross and others in 16th-17th century Spain, one is bound to believe that there occurs at breathtaking moments in history an exhilarating burst of energy and motivation, of hope and zest and imagination, and a severing of the bonds that normally hold in check the full release of human possibilities. A door is opened and the caged eagle soars.[14]

Such a moment—I would say the supreme moment—occurred when God became man, chose his people and gave them a vision of the kingdom, and sent them out to take his Word to the ends of the earth. Unlocking their hopes, channeling their fears, he gave them a positive view of the future tempered by tough-minded realism, and sent them on their way, uncertain of almost everything except that the future was his and they belonged to him.

Studying Jesus' focus on the future, I am reminded that it has been said that leaders need a new kind of competence in our complex, changing world, a competence which, acknowledging uncertainty, allows for mistakes and goes confidently into the future. If this is so, then who could be a better leader than Jesus?

In one of his final briefing sessions before his death and his return to the Father, Jesus told his disciples that he would be leaving them. Thomas said to him, "Lord, we don't know where you are going, so how can we know the way?" Jesus answered, "I am the way. . . ." (Jn 14:5-6). Of course, he meant that he is the way to salvation, to reconciliation with God, and to eternal life in heaven. But it is equally true that he was promising them, not a set of rules or a blueprint for the future, but his companionship. His whole life was characterized by "certain uncertainty"! Very little was predictable, except the knowledge of who he was, and why he had come, and where all things would lead. The faith to which he was constantly calling his followers was not an offer of predictability but a call for trust. He certainly allowed his followers to make mistakes. He knew that Peter was going to deny him. He told him, "I have prayed for you . . . that your faith may not fail. And when you have turned back, strengthen your brothers" (Lk 22:32). Whether in their personal successes and failures or in his prophecies of the great trends in history, Jesus was constantly responding to the future.

Another key concept that is emerging in leadership development studies is the distinction between *maintenance* learning and *innovative* learning. A publication by the Club of Rome draws the following distinction:

> Maintenance learning is the acquisition of fixed outlooks, methods and rules for dealing with known and recurring situations. It enhances our problem-solving ability for problems that are given. . . . But for long-term survival, particularly in times of turbulence, change, or discontinuity, another type of learning is even more essential. It is the type of learning that can bring change, renewal, restructuring, and problem reformulation—and which we have called innovative learning.[15]

What Jesus encouraged in his disciples was innovative learning, orienting them toward the future. He challenged them to unlearn bad habits and empty traditions which had grown up to cripple their lives in society. He called them back to basics, illustrating constantly how the great and lasting traditions, such as the sabbath, existed in God's creative and redemptive purpose to fulfill and liberate, not to squeeze and hound people. He walked them with him through situations that neither he nor they had ever seen, and he let them watch how he handled them. By innovation and participation he created anticipation and left them not with a well-oiled machine to run, but with a path to tread, a dream to pursue, a world to win and a pacesetter—himself—to follow.

Shared Power

Peter's reminiscence: "He breathed on me. . . . He gave me his Spirit."

Jesus' affirmation: "You have all you need to do what I send you to do."

At his final meal Jesus made this promise:

> If you love me, you will obey what I command. And I will ask the Father,

and he will give you another Counselor to be with you for ever—the Spirit of truth. The world cannot accept him, because it neither sees him nor knows him. But you know him, for he lives with you and will be in you.

Then he ended: "I will not leave you as orphans; I will come to you" (Jn 14:15-18).

The final step in Jesus' process of leadership development was to give his followers resources and responsibilities and let them go. The promise he gave at the Last Supper was repeated after the resurrection. He came to them in the same room, showed them his hands and feet, and told them that as his Father had sent him into the world so he was sending them. Then he breathed on them and said, "Receive the Holy Spirit" (Jn 20:22).

The apprentices had now graduated into senior partnership. He was willing not only to step back, but to return to heaven and leave his task in their hands. They would not be orphans, for he would be with them; but he would not be visibly present.

Peter Drucker explains the principle of shared power:

One cannot afford to hoard human resources. People either grow or turn rancid and sour. They can't be put on the shelf. The ablest always go out—the ones we would want to keep. Jesus sent the apostles. You who are church leaders must be sure your best people are not maintained. The innovators are the ones who will do the jobs that cannot be clearly defined.[16]

Warren Benniss puts the same thought in terms of the leader allowing for "creative space":

Where the intention is aesthetically and compellingly presented, the space within the vision can be ambiguous. The leader's intention is a playground, an arena surrounding an idea. . . . It's Robert Redford painting a verbal picture of the way he wanted the opening scene of _Ordinary People_ to look. Mr. Redford did not say, "Use an f/8 opening with 600 ASA Film and shoot from this angle." Within his rough but clear tapestry of intentions, the camera crew had all the freedom in the world to make decisions, be creative, and play.

People knock themselves out in that kind of setting. In the cases of really successful leaders whom I have studied they did create and express an overall set of intentions which was attractive enough both to involve people and empower them. The space generated by such visions makes transformative leadership genuinely participative and noncoercive.

When I began to realize that the expression of the intention is clear and simple while the space within is ambiguous and roomy, I then began to see that this is the art form of leadership.[17]

Was not "creative space" exactly what Jesus gave his disciples? He did not tell them how long to wait and pray until the Spirit would come. He did not give them small group exercises to do while they waited. He did not write Peter's sermon notes for the talk he would give, or even write the outline. He did not provide them with a map for their future missionary journeys, marking where to go first. However, he did make sure they understood his message of the kingdom; he did give them his commission to carry that message and embody it to the world; and he did promise that his Spirit would come and be in them—and that was all they would need, except to trust and obey.

As a good friend of mine says, "If all the fullness of God was in Christ, and if the fullness of Christ is in me, what more do I need to do what God calls me to do?"

And that, in a nutshell, is what Jesus did to develop his leaders: He gave them himself.

12

THE LEADER AS SPOKESPERSON

●

*Jesus knew the importance
of communication—he could
articulate his vision.*

●

"In the beginning was the Word."
JOHN THE APOSTLE

*"The word is one of the most precious moral choices
we individuals make, and if you really want to know what a man or
a woman believes, thinks, and how that person has made moral
choices, you want to look at the words they choose."*
BILL MOYERS

*I*n a fascinating article, newspaper columnist Joseph Sobran has raised the question: In the light of the skepticism modern scholarship has expressed about the accuracy of the Gospels, how can we be sure Jesus said the things attributed to him?

Sobran sets himself to answer the question, not as an expert on ancient texts, but as a writer. His argument is intriguing.

First, says Sobran, "every great writer has his own voice: an unmistakable style and tone." This voice makes us say, "Nobody else could have written this." Although we do not know of a word that Jesus ever wrote, his recorded sayings have a unique power. Sayings such as "Render to Caesar the things that are Caesar's" and "Unless you are converted, and become like little children, you shall not enter the kingdom of heaven" and "Let him among you who is without sin cast the first stone" are words that go right into the heart. "They are not the sort of thing that could be faked."

As a writer, Sobran is also impressed that Jesus' words do not date. "Even the work of a writer as great as Shakespeare ages after centuries." And Sobran admits that nearly everything he himself wrote at thirty-three (the age when Jesus died) seems "trivial to me now, or has been made irrelevant by the passing of time. . . . But nothing Jesus said has been superseded by modern science or human experience."

"Moreover," Sobran argues, "in Jesus' style there are no exaggerations or mannerisms which lend themselves to parody. Jesus can be denied and insulted and blasphemed, but he is still strangely immune to ridicule. After 2,000 years his words retain the power to convert."

Believers in Jesus' deity will not be surprised that his words should have such power, says Sobran. It is the atheists who believe Jesus to be a mere man.

Might the Gospels then be forgeries? Sobran concludes that, as Tennyson said, "Jesus' personality is his greatest miracle. Try making up a character who says things that men will die for, not just today but hundreds of years from now. Easy, is it? If this is just a forgery, maybe we should be worshipping the forgers."[1]

Sobran's critique makes me realize how much of so-called communication in our modern world lacks the depth, the inner power with which Jesus spoke.

We are communicating beings. Nothing distinguishes us from animals more than this ability. For this reason an effective leader must be an effective communicator. To mobilize followers and to ensure that they share a common mission is virtually impossible without the ability to communicate values and vision. In our modern world, leadership is increasingly seen as effective communication.

So important have the media become that an effective political leader today probably spends more time talking than thinking or reading. As much time or more must be given to thinking about how to sell a policy as to forming its substance. National leaders are learning that their communications managers may be even more important than their policy staff. With the advent of the television era, very few can aspire to high office who lack the skills to communicate before a camera.

This was brought home to me sharply during a trip to the Soviet Union and Eastern Europe. We happened to be in Moscow the same week that a summit conference took place between President Reagan and Secretary Gorbachev. From our hotel room we watched what was happening five miles away, picked up by satellite and relayed to CNN News in Atlanta, Georgia, then flashed back to our room. Would either of these leaders have been able to carry out his programs without a mastery of the media? I doubt it. Reagan was the consummate communicator, building on a generation of experience in the United States, while Gorbachev was the first leader of his country to establish himself as a media personality. A few days later in the German Democratic Republic, we discussed the influence of television with both religious and government officials. No "iron curtain" had been able to keep Western television signals out of that socialist nation, and both commercial and religious messages from the West, some positive and some not so beneficial, were reaching the masses of that country. Isolation is no longer possible in the information era.

While modern communications shrink the world, they also have the possibility of distorting reality and robbing us of the ability truly to communicate with one another. Modern secular urban experience chops life up into bits and pieces. Work, family and leisure become separate things. I work certain hours and places. Other times and places I am a parent. In still others I enjoy my leisure. If I happen to be religious, that takes place in still another sphere. The concept of a universal truth and reality gives way to a series of lifestyles, each with its own version of the "truth."

But humans are not able to live without some unifying reality. In the absence of truth, we must create at least its appearance. So while reality is disintegrating, we are "producing" reality on television and through other media. Ironically, the torrents of words and pictures which fall upon us are

225

at the same time the stuff of daily life, and yet they are hardly ever taken at face value.

This was illustrated in an almost frightening way in a program produced by social commentator Bill Moyers, a special called *Primetime President.* A few quotes (lifted in part from a British documentary on the use of television in American political campaigns) made the point:

Former president Jimmy Carter: "You even have the feeling that something is not happening unless it is recorded by the television camera and later rebroadcast."

Advertising writer Barbara Lippert: "The problem . . . is that there is no distinction between advertising and everything else. . . . Everything's blurred. . . . When you see everything is marketed and designed and positioned, then you begin to wonder, what is reality? And that becomes terrifying for people."

Communications professor Kathleen Jamieson: "We are now down to giving our average piece of political information in about 14.79 seconds if we hear it on the news, or 30 seconds in spot ads. Additionally, television has privileged visual argument, and as a result it's created a whole new grammar. Now politicians don't have to argue the old way, with evidence . . . they telegraph with pictures. When juxtaposed, pictures can create things that didn't actually happen in the real world."

Lippert: "What's happening to the video-fluent generation is that people can be on their car phones, watching television in their cars while they're talking to somebody else, and also listening to the radio. . . . What that really means is that they're not getting information. . . . They're getting little bits and pieces of things put together in a way that doesn't bore them."

Bill Moyers: "The other night, after the presidential campaign debate, David Brinkley asked his colleague Peter Jennings, who had been one of the questioners, for a reaction to the debate, and Peter said, 'It's very hard for me to react, I didn't see it on television.' Now, here was a man who was participating in the reality. He was one of the questioners in the hall where the debate was taking place, and yet he couldn't react to it because he hadn't seen it on television. What does that say about reality?"

Lippert: "Well, I think there is no reality on television. I think it depends how you like your reality."[2]

Suppose, however, that for the sake of argument we concede that television at its worst can twist and distort reality. And suppose we also concede that, at its best (as when it showed starving children in Ethiopia and generated world compassion), television can powerfully communicate reality. This still means, as in previous ages, that the challenge facing any leader is to help people to see realities that are, and to envision new realities that can be. In that communications challenge, what does Jesus' leadership have to say to us?

Jesus the Communicator

Jesus was the consummate leader; he was also a peerless communicator. The records of his career are an invaluable guide to communication with impact. It has been reckoned that Jesus' words approximately 20 per cent of the entire New Testament (36,450 of the total 181,253 words). This rich treasury is a communication model well worth the study.

The Gospels picture Jesus in a wide variety of situations, where he showed a striking ability to suit his words to the occasion and the audience. With cold and callous religious leaders he could be devastatingly harsh; with a woman caught in an adulterous liaison he could be both amazingly strong and tender. He taught his disciples simply and directly, yet mystified the multitudes with the puzzling elements of his parables. In the space of a few moments we see him drawing out of Peter thoughts that had never been expressed, and then calling him a voice of Satan. His style showed remarkable flexibility.

Jesus also appeared in a number of different speaking roles. Sometimes he spoke as a rabbi, the master teacher expounding his thoughts to a crowd sitting at his feet. When he debated with opponents he was like a skillful lawyer, deflecting their attacks and counterattacking with devastating thrusts of his own. On other occasions he was like a good counselor or physician, drawing out the inner thoughts and needs of the individuals who came to him. At such times he could be an excellent listener. The account of his talk with a Samaritan woman by a well indicates that she spoke twice as much as Jesus did. When he was conversing at a dinner party he spoke as an informal visitor and friend. Yet at other times he rose like a prophet in public to call down woes on those who failed to respond to God's challenge. He lamented like a lover when he wept over Jerusalem and said, "How often I have longed to gather your children together . . . but you were not willing" (Mt 23:37).

Yet whatever role Jesus took, the central thing that shone through was the very thing we most lack today, the sense of reality. So often we struggle to say what we mean and mean what we say. In him, word and reality were one. His person, vision and mission were all integrated in his speech.

John, one of his biographers and closest associates, expressed this when reflecting on his experiences with Jesus in the famous prolog to his Gospel:

In the beginning was the Word, and the Word was with God, and the Word was God. He was with God in the beginning. Through him all things were made; without him nothing was made that has been made. In him was life, and that life was the light of men. . . . The Word became flesh and made his dwelling among us. We have seen his glory, the glory of the One and Only, who came from the Father, full of grace and truth. (Jn 1:1-4, 14)

Later, John wrote in a letter to fellow believers:

That which was from the beginning, which we have heard, which we have seen with our eyes, which we have looked at and our hands have touched—this we proclaim concerning the Word of life. The life appeared; we have seen it and testify to it. . . . We proclaim to you what we have seen and heard, so that you also may have fellowship with us. And our fellowship is with the Father and with his Son, Jesus Christ. (1 Jn 1:1-3)

Although John wrote in Greek, to his Jewish mind *word* meant more than a symbol. The Semitic *dabar,* "word," also conveyed the idea of an event or action. To a Hebrew words had unique power; a word spoken was action. So for John to identify Jesus as "the Word" was to say that Jesus did more than cast light on reality. He was both the creator and the communicator of that reality. Jesus was light not only in dispelling darkness, but also in actually imparting new life and enabling people to see a whole new reality.

As Word he was active, living and powerful. He not only discussed life, he was the life; and he appeared in order to give life. He not only held up the ideal of a new fellowship, he made that fellowship happen.

John's inspired description of Jesus as a communicator is in philosophical language to appeal to a Greek-speaking readership. But the impact of Jesus' speech can also be sensed in the exclamations of ordinary people. Jewish people expected that their leader would be able to move their hearts and minds by his speech. Otherwise, how could he be like Moses, who as the great lawgiver was described as "mighty in words and in deeds" (Acts 7:22 AV)? Or like David, man of song and man of action, writer of the Jewish hymnbook and also military commander?

A quick run through the Gospels shows the impact of Jesus' words. When he was twelve years old his parents took him to Jerusalem for the Feast of Passover, and then by mistake left him behind in the temple. Three days later, after a frantic search, they found him in the temple court, sitting among the teachers, listening to them and asking them questions. Luke records that "everyone who heard him was amazed at his understanding and his answers" (Lk 2:47). When he began his public career eighteen years later, the Gospel writers noted the immediate power of his words. He exorcised an evil spirit from a man, and a few days later in the same city he told a paralytic to stand up and go home. In both instances his words were immediately obeyed, and the people were amazed at his word and teaching (Mk 1:27; 2:7).

The potential of his words was tremendous. To a man with leprosy, he said simply "Be clean," and it happened (Mt 8:3). Knowing his reputation, a Roman centurion with a sick servant came to Jesus and asked for healing. "Just say the word," he asked Jesus, "and my servant will be healed. For I myself am a man under authority, with soldiers under me. I tell this one, 'Go' and he goes; and that one, 'Come' and he comes" (Mt 8:8-9). That same compelling authority showed in the two little words "Follow me." He had only to say them and the fishermen and tax collectors would leave their families and their livelihoods.

Not only in his actions, but also in his teaching, there was this astonishing power. "Where did this man get this wisdom?" his hearers asked after he had finished a teaching session at his hometown synagogue (Mt 13:54). They marveled at his "gracious words" (Lk 4:22). So did those who listened all the way through his Sermon on the Mount. They drew in their breath, looked at each other, and were "amazed at this teaching, because he taught as one who had authority, and not as their teachers of the law" (Mt 7:28-29). Later, even his enemies reacted with that same amazement when they tried to trap him in a debate in the temple precincts in Jerusalem (Mt 22:22).

The impact of his speech was inescapable. He communicated with an immediacy and an incisiveness that unerringly found its mark. Luke's Gospel records a conversation between Jesus and some of his followers. Afterwards they said to each other, "Were not our hearts burning within us while he talked with us?" (Lk 24:32). Those who resisted his word found their hearts became colder; those who received his word found their hearts burning. Only a few could remain neutral for long.

Jesus' Model of Communication

The available means of communication have multiplied so fantastically in the twentieth century that we may be tempted to think our age invented communication skills! In fact, the underlying principles go back centuries. In his *Rhetoric,* the great philosopher Aristotle set forth enduring principles of effective persuasion. He taught the importance of combining *logos* (the essence of the message), *ethos* (the credibility of the messenger) and *pathos* (the appeal to the inner motives of the hearer).[3]

If we go to Jesus expecting to find a conscious philosophy of communication or specific speaking techniques, we will be disappointed. If, however, we see communication not as a technique, but as the expression of all that we are, then we find in Jesus the model of a master communicator. Both what he said about words and the way in which he spoke are a living demonstration.

Let us pick out the key lessons we can learn about communication from Jesus. Each one will be summed up in a "Communication Imperative."

1. *Clarity of speech comes from clarity of purpose.* Some speakers remind us of a marksman shooting a rifle without a target. They aim at nothing

and they hit it! Not so with Jesus. From the beginning he knew why he had come, and his speech reflected this. "Simply let your 'Yes' be 'Yes,' and your 'No,' 'No' " (Mt 5:37). His warning was specifically against careless oaths, but the rule applies to every aspect of speech. Frequently Jesus prefaced his words with "Verily, verily," or "I tell you the truth." As the Word of God, he had come to communicate truth which could set people free. The theme runs through all the Gospels, especially John's.

Toward the end of his ministry, Jesus was brought before the Roman governor Pilate, on trial for his life. Pilate asked Jesus if he actually claimed to be King of the Jews, as his accusers alleged. When Jesus said, "My kingdom is not of this world . . . ," Pilate blurted out, "You are a king, then!" Jesus replied, "You are right. . . . In fact, for this reason I was born, and for this I came into the world, to testify to the truth. Everyone on the side of truth listens to me." "What is truth?" countered Pilate, speaking not as a lofty philosopher, but as a man of affairs who had to keep public order and meet the payroll (Jn 18:29-38). What did truth matter in such a pragmatic world? But Jesus was king in the kingdom of God's truth. To neglect that truth is to perish. To know it is to live for ever. And his passion was to communicate truth. He knew why he had come, and that gave a sharp cutting edge to all that he said.

Dwight Eisenhower and Ulysses S. Grant were military and political leaders, and both were renowned for their consistent calmness, whether in triumph or in difficulty. Russell F. Weigley compares them: In both Ike and Grant, this quality sprang from a complete self-confidence that underlay apparent modesty.

> In both, furthermore, self-confidence sprang in turn from a consistency and fixity of purpose that would not let them be diverted from their goals. In both, clarity of purpose also expressed itself in crystal clear use of the English language (a quality of Ike the soldier that memories of the later Ike sometimes cause us to forget).[4]

Without a clear picture of our goal, our train of thought will wander away on sidetracks. The best writers, whether of editorials or of mystery stories, have thought through the conclusion before they write their first sentence. Everything leads up to the last page.

And everything Jesus did and said led up to his cross and resurrection. Clarity of speech, Jesus shows us, comes from clarity of purpose. Therefore, COMMUNICATION IMPERATIVE 1: KNOW WHERE YOU ARE HEADING.

2. *Believability comes in direct proportion to a quiet sense of confidence.* By confidence I mean a combination of true humility and genuine authority. Some leaders impose their ideas and their will on others by the brilliance of their ideas or the bombast of their personality. But those traits do not make for long-haul trust. Significantly, Matthew applied to Jesus the words of Isaiah the prophet: "He will not quarrel or cry out; no one will hear his voice in the streets" (Mt 12:19). In Jesus we see neither blustering nor faltering.

His confidence sprang from an innate sense of knowing that he was the Son of God. He could send his followers out with authority and tell them, "He who listens to you listens to me; he who rejects you rejects me; but he who rejects me rejects him who sent me" (Lk 10:16). Repeatedly he used the formula, "You have heard that it was said to the people long ago . . . but *I tell you.*" Moses, for example, said not to commit adultery, "*but I tell you* that anyone who looks at a woman lustfully has already committed adultery with her in his heart" (Mt 5:27-28). With quiet confidence he could tell his would-be followers: "The words I have spoken to you are spirit and they are life," and, "I am telling you what I have seen in the Father's presence," and, "He who belongs to God hears what God says" (Jn 6:63; 8:38, 47). Such authority came in tandem with his deep humility. Clearly he was not operating on his own. When some who were amazed at his teaching asked, "How did this man get such learning without having studied?" Jesus answered:

My teaching is not my own. It comes from him who sent me. If anyone chooses to do God's will, he will find out whether my teaching comes from God or whether I speak on my own. He who speaks on his own does so to gain honor for himself, but he who works for the honor of the one who sent him is a man of truth; there is nothing false about him. (Jn 7:15-18)

The authority of Jesus' speech was in fact a kind of ambassador's credential. Behind him was all the power of his Father; verbal manipulation was unnecessary, for the truth would speak for itself.

232

People sense instinctively when a speaker is trying to intimidate, or is intimidated, that the pressure comes from a lack of inner authority. In Jesus we see authority and humility wonderfully coupled together. In him we see that humility is not denying that one possesses a gift; it is recognizing the source of that gift. It would not be humility for a great speaker like Billy Graham to say in false modesty, "I can't speak." That would be an untruth! Humility, rather, is recognizing that our gift comes *through* us and not *from* us.

"Humility," explained John Baillie, "is the obverse side of confidence in God, whereas pride is the obverse side of confidence in self."[5] Such humility does not rob us of aspirations or of a strong desire to achieve our goals. Rather, it heightens those aspirations, grounding them in the certainty that God runs the universe and channeling them in productive, healthy and God honoring ways. Humility based on confidence in God gives us both an acceptance of those things we cannot change and an aspiration to change what we can. We can see this clearly in Jesus.

With everything that was within him, he wanted to finish the task his Father had given to him (see Jn 17:4).Yet when the time came he accepted the end that came to him on the cross, and saying, "It is finished," he bowed his head and gave up his spirit (Jn 19:30). Surely it was his own special restlessness and rest that made people heed when Jesus said, "Come to me . . . and I will give you rest" (Mt 11:28).

Believability, Jesus teaches us, comes in direct proportion to a quiet sense of confidence. Therefore,

COMMUNICATION IMPERATIVE 2: KNOW YOUR SOURCE AND YOUR IDENTITY.

3. *Words live for ever; therefore, they must be handled with care.* There is a power in language, a power far greater than our careless use of words often allows for.

Jesus saw words as the revealer of the true person: "Out of the overflow of the heart the mouth speaks" (Mt 12:34). Just as a tree is recognized by its fruit, evil words disclose an evil heart, and good words, a good heart. A jug that is knocked over will spill out its contents, and the words that come out of the mouth of a person who is jarred will show what that person's spirit is like. So, said Jesus, "men will have to give account on the day of judgment for every careless word they have spoken. For by your words you will be acquitted, and by your words you will be condemned" (Mt 12:36-37). Our words are the evidence that shows what we really are, the measure of our hearts on the day of judgment.

But Jesus also knew the power of words to save. His words nourished the souls of those who believed, as bread sustains the body (Jn 6:35, 63). He had only to say the word and the blind would see, the lame walk, and the sinners be forgiven. There was a creative, liberating power to his words.

To those who have been the victims of dull sermons, "preaching" is the driest sort of communication. It conjures up the sound of droning voices and pious phrases. For Jesus, however, preaching was the most powerful of all activities. He was "anointed to . . . proclaim," he told the townspeople in the Nazareth synagogue (Lk 4:18). And for him proclaiming was not just *saying* something; it was *doing* something. He had been sent "to *proclaim freedom* for the prisoners," to *proclaim "recovery of sight* for the blind." Proclaiming was not discussing liberation or sight or forgiveness, it was *making them come true.* Consider the difference between a report that *says* something has happened and an announcement that *makes* something happen. When Abraham Lincoln issued his famous Emancipation Proclamation, ending slavery in America, he was not saying it would be nice if it would happen, he was saying it was *happening.* For Jesus, the preaching of the gospel was not talk about God; it was God talking. So when "the good news of the kingdom of God is being preached," the preaching actually opens a door so that "everyone is forcing his way into it," jostling to get in while the door is open (Lk 16:16).

In still another sense, Jesus spoke of the dynamic power of faith expressed in words of prayer: "I tell you the truth, if you have faith as small as a mustard seed, you can say to this mountain, 'Move from here to there' and it will move. Nothing will be impossible for you" (Mt 17:20).

Words, as Jesus weighed them, are powerful. They reveal our hearts. They judge our motives. They are used by God to create faith and life, hope and healing—truly to move mountains! We are told by scientists that every sound we utter goes on indefinitely through the atmosphere. Jesus taught that the effects of our words—good or evil, believing or unbelieving—go on eternally.

Words live forever, so use them with faith, but use them with care. Therefore,

COMMUNICATION IMPERATIVE 3: KNOW THE POWER OF LANGUAGE.

4. *How they hear is as important as what you say.*

The late Senator Robert Kennedy never earned the reputation that his brother President John Kennedy did as a persuasive orator. Yet there was an immediacy and a directness about him that was appealing. He knew how to go to people where they were and to reach them as they were. After his assassination, some of his aides were reminiscing about how he reached people. "Why," said one of them, "the thing about Bobby Kennedy was that he would go down to the people in the ghetto, and he would get up on a truck and tell it to them just like it was." His former press secretary, Frank Mankiewicz, interrupted, "No, you don't understand. It wasn't what Bobby was saying, it was what they were hearing that made the difference."

We can have the greatest message in the world, but if people are not hearing it, it is not going to do them any good. The great communicators know this instinctively.

Clearly Jesus was a student both of his message and of his audience. He listened carefully to what his Father wanted him to say. But he also looked at the people he wanted to reach—their fears, their preconceptions, their longings. Think of his parable of the seed and the soils as modeling a philosophy of communication. In every crowd, he knew there would be people like the hard unplowed ground where the seed bounced off and was picked up by the birds. Those hardened by gross sin or self-righteousness would not be interested in what he had to say. With that kind of person he would either say nothing ("Do not throw your pearls to pigs. If you do, they may . . . turn and tear you to pieces," Mt 7:6), or he would give them a stern warning ("Those eighteen who died when the tower in Siloam fell on them—do you think they were more guilty than all the others living in Jerusalem? I tell you, no! But unless you repent, you too will all perish," Lk 13:4-5).

There would be people like the shallow soil, who would respond quickly and emotionally, then fade away under pressure. They needed a caution

("Count the cost—if a man starts to build a building and doesn't have enough money to finish it, everybody will laugh at him," Lk 14:28-30).

There would be those with open hearts to respond in positive faith to his message. They needed encouragement ("I am the vine; you are the branches. If a man remains in me and I in him, he will bear much fruit; apart from me you can do nothing," Jn 15:5).

Because he was a student of people, Jesus had no one pattern for dealing with them. He had a consistent message of salvation and God's kingdom. He also repeated a number of his sayings and parables. But a quick survey of the way he talked to individuals shows a communicator who tailored his approach to each person. To Nicodemus, the ruler who came to him by night, he said, "You must be born again" (Jn 3:3, 7). As far as we know, he never said exactly those words to anyone else. When he met the Samaritan woman by the well, he promised her "living water" (Jn 4:10). She was the only one to receive that promise. When a rich young man came asking how he could inherit eternal life, Jesus did not offer him living water. He told him to sell all that he had and give it to the poor and follow him (Mk 10:17-23). Zacchaeus, the little man who climbed a tree to see Jesus, was also rich. But his lust for money must have come out of a deep sense of inferiority, so Jesus did not tell him to sell everything. Instead, he invited himself to Zacchaeus' house. Zacchaeus was so overwhelmed that Jesus would come to his house that he spontaneously gave 50 per cent of his capital to the poor (Lk 19:1-10). New birth. Living water. Eternal life. Salvation. That is the message Jesus wanted to get across. But just as a sailor rows around an island until he spots the best place to beach his boat, so Jesus studied people until he knew the best way to deliver that message to them.

If you attend a management seminar these days, you will likely hear a discussion of "management by walking around." Business leaders are learning that the best management does not take place by writing tidy organization charts or carefully constructed memos. It takes place by walking around and seeing and listening to the people who are doing the work— knowing their problems and frustrations, listening to their ideas and solutions. Jesus was the greatest example of *"communication by walking around."* As he walked around on the dusty paths, through the cornfields, and by the boats at the lake, he had open eyes and open ears. He knew how people talked. He knew what they thought about.

Jesus was both message-oriented and market-oriented. He knew the message clearly. But he also knew what was in people.

It seems strange that those of us who are concerned to communicate the message of Christ in today's world do not pay more attention to how Jesus did it. We are often very message-centered, concerned that the message gets across exactly right. But we have not sufficiently learned the other half of the communication equation: the orientation toward the market, those we need to reach. "Market-orientation" may sound too commercial, but perhaps we have something to learn from those who understand marketing.

Mary Crowley was a magnificent lady who formed an immensely successful business called "Home Interiors." She was also a devoted follower of Christ who taught a weekly Bible class in her church and served on Billy Graham's board. I once heard Mary sum up her philosophy in a little bit of verse:

To sell Jane Doe what Jane Doe buys you must see Jane Doe through
Jane Doe's eyes.

Mary Crowley tried to see people through their own eyes. If we are to be effective in presenting the Christian message to people who are uninformed or indifferent, then we must see them both through God's eyes and their own. Jesus never changed the heart of his message. He was committed to bear witness to the truth. Yet if we fail to address our communication to people as they are, it will be a serious mistake.

How they hear is as important as *what you say,* Jesus tells us. Therefore, COMMUNICATION IMPERATIVE 4: KNOW YOUR AUDIENCE.

5. *Having the truth is only half the battle.* It does not release us from the responsibility to think about how we can best get the truth across. A corollary of our last point, the importance of knowing our audience as well as our message, is that we must learn to be skilled in the presentation of that message.

When I study Jesus I have the distinct impression that he was a skilled craftsman. Perhaps he picked up this skill in the carpenter's shop as a youngster, helping his father to fashion homemade implements. When they made a yoke for oxen, they would have to shape and smooth the yoke carefully so that it would fit the beast's neck with no friction. Perhaps this trained him to allow for sensitivity and variety and flexibility in the presentation of his message.

Yokes had a common purpose; yet each one had a distinct contour. So, too, given a constant truth, Jesus had great freedom in the way he shaped that truth to his audience. One gets the impression that he was not "scripted" in the modern sense of an actor or a politician who simply reads off what some scriptwriter has designed for a situation. Of course, he and his Father had worked out a "master script," a plan of new life for all people. But Jesus was free to draw from many sources in setting forth this master plan. As needed, he could quote a proverb, tell a parable, use an analogy or make a very blunt statement.

Ralph Lewis has written a fascinating study of Jesus' skill as a communicator. He points out, for example, that Jesus used two distinct styles of communication. When he spoke to those who were already committed to his cause, he would use a deductive approach. Often he would begin by quoting Scripture or an authority, or by giving his major premise. Then he would apply it. But when he was speaking to those who were not yet committed, he would use a different approach. Here he would begin inductively with some common everyday experience, and then he would move to the truth he wanted to get across.

"Time and time again," writes Lewis, "Jesus trips the memory banks of his hearers. . . . He digs into life. He ferrets out feelings. He probes into his hearers' deepest relationships. Life and experience—normal, healthy, common life and experience—seem to dominate his talks with the people."[6] His subjects ranged from anger and anxiety to marriage and money, to sex and slander.

The common ingredients in Jesus' communication were narrative, analogy, dialog and questions. His parables were little stories tied to big ideas. His analogies were rich, varied and concrete. The everyday becomes "a lesson in trust." The ideal of service is symbolized by a cup of water. Commitment is pictured as entering through a narrow gate.

Jesus also knew how to use questions to draw out his listeners. A quick look at Mark's Gospel shows that Jesus used questions more than any other form of address, with teaching and explaining coming in a close second. The four Gospels record more than 150 questions that Jesus asked of his listeners. As Ralph Lewis puts it:

God didn't start his great Incarnation sermon to the waiting world by spelling out his thesis. He didn't say, "This is what I am going to do when I send my Son into the world," and lay out the details about mangers, rejection and crosses. No, instead God allowed the concrete to come before the abstract. . . . It seems Jesus recognized in his preaching what God understood when he dreamed up the incarnation concept: Experience carries the persuasive authority inductive human beings need to comprehend and believe the truth.[7]

Having the truth, Jesus tells us, is only half the battle. It does not release us from our responsibility to speak wisely. Therefore,

COMMUNICATION IMPERATIVE 5: KNOW YOUR CRAFT.

6. *Knowing when is as important as knowing what to say.* One of the chief ways in which leaders stand head and shoulders above other people is in their sense of timing. To be able to grasp the moment, to seize the initiative, to do the right thing at the right time is part of the genius of leadership.

What makes the star athlete? Timing . . . being able to meet the ball at exactly the right moment. What makes the great politician? Timing . . . instinctively knowing when to act. What is the mark of a master comedian? Timing . . . knowing just when to deliver the punch line. For example, Bob Hope has great material. But a lesser comedian would not get nearly the same number of laughs with the same material because he lacks Hope's timing.

God's perfect timing is beautifully illustrated in the coming of Jesus. As Paul wrote, "When the time had fully come, God sent his Son" (Gal 4:4). Why was Jesus born in 4 B.C.? The answer is that the timing was perfect. Politically, one power (Rome) controlled the entire known world. The Romans kept the peace so the people could wake and sleep without fear. The international system of Roman-built roads facilitated the movement of troops and trade. The first followers of Christ used that road system to spread Christ's message swiftly. A half century earlier, that would not have been possible. Culturally, Greek had become an almost universal common language. The missionaries of Christ did not have to go to language school to communicate the gospel. As at no other time, they could move freely, preaching to everyone in a common language. Psychologically and spiritually, also, it was the perfect time. Belief in the ancient pagan gods was dying. Thoughtful people were searching for the one true God. On the international scene, the cultural scene, the religious scene, it was the "fullness of time," the right moment for Christ to come.

Jesus had a superb sense of place and timing. Like any gifted communicator, he knew that you do not have to say everything at once to make your point, that the strongest impressions are often created by what is left out. For those who were spiritually ready to receive his truth, his parables were a path to follow for further illumination. For those who were not ready, his parables were mysterious stories which took them no further. In using parables, Jesus was protecting the truth from those who might attack it, and protecting unready hearers from truths that they were not yet ready to act upon.

His acute sense of timing is found throughout his story. There was a time when he stayed in Galilee, purposely not going to Jerusalem because he knew there were enemies waiting to take his life. His brothers, who did not yet believe in him, urged him to go to Jerusalem for one of the annual feasts. "You ought to leave here and go to Judea," they told him. "No one who wants to become a public figure acts in secret. . . . Show yourself to the world." But Jesus replied, "The right time for me has not yet come. . . . I am not yet going up to this Feast" (Jn 7:1-9).

Halfway through the festival time, however, he did go up to the temple courts and begin to teach. Still later, when some foreigners requested an interview with him, Jesus told his followers, "The hour has come for the Son of Man to be glorified. . . . For this very reason I came to this hour. . . . I, when I am lifted up from the earth, will draw all men to myself" (Jn 12:23, 27, 32). He was referring here to his death.

Throughout his career there was this instinctive sense of choosing the time, the place and the occasion when he would speak. Everything was leading up to the event of his death on the cross. He would not be forced into acting and speaking when he was not ready. And he would not be forced into saying things to people when they were not ready.

This skill in timing and communication is not easy to acquire. But it is the kind of wisdom a leader should seek through prayer, through the study of times and seasons, through the observation of people, through the guidance of listening to God's inner voice. A leader will seek to know not only what to say and how to say it, but also when to speak and when to be silent, when to reveal and when to conceal, when to hold back, and when to speak boldly and decisively. Therefore,

COMMUNICATION IMPERATIVE 6: KNOW YOUR TIMING.

7. *Simplicity means to say one thing well.* Winston Churchill once remarked that one of his political opponents had the ability to compress "the minimum amount of thought into the maximum number of words." That criticism could never be leveled at Jesus. Rather, the marvel is that he could focus such profound truth in such simple ways. If, as Kierkegaard said, purity (or simplicity) of heart is "to *will* one thing," then simplicity of speech might mean to *say* one thing. Jesus held one supreme ambition before his disciples: "Seek first the kingdom of God." He was always aware of his kingdom purposes, and the incisiveness of his speech reflected that simplicity of purpose.

His conversation included no wasted words, no useless patronizing and no shallow platitudes. His words were as sharp as a surgeon's scalpel, cutting through confusion, pretension and delusion, and penetrating the very hearts of the men and women he encountered. When he used metaphors and graphic images, as he frequently did, they were never mere rhetorical flourishes. It helped that Jesus spoke in Aramaic, which linguists tell us was a simple and direct language. But aside from that, it is clear that he chose his words carefully for maximum impact.

A few illustrations make the point. When Satan tempted him in the desert, Jesus' reply to each attack was incredibly brief. He did not lecture Satan or engage in verbal sparring, but simply quoted Scriptures that went right to the heart of the temptation: "Man does not live on bread alone. . . ." "Do not put the Lord your God to the test," and "Worship the Lord your

God, and serve him only" (Mt 4:4, 7, 10). Consider Jesus' encounter with the rich young man who came seeking eternal life. Jesus did not compliment him on his search; rather, cutting straight to his glaring area of weakness, he told him the one thing he lacked was to sell his possessions and give to the poor (Mk 10:17-23). This directness shows in his encounter with the tax collector Zacchaeus. When he passed the tree where Zacchaeus was perching, he looked up and said, "Zacchaeus, come down immediately. I must stay at your house today" (Lk 19:5). Over the objections of the "righteous," he went and dined at the house of this "sinner," making no grandiose statements about God's acceptance of everyone or his own open-mindedness. Perhaps the clearest example of Jesus' incisive communication was the encounter with the community leader Nicodemus. He came to Jesus with flattery, "Rabbi, we know you are a teacher who has come from God." It is difficult not to smile at the abruptness of Jesus' reply, "I tell you the truth, no one can see the kingdom of God unless he is born again" (Jn 3:2-3). Jesus completely dispensed with social convention and formality. In each of these encounters we are struck by how much more Jesus could have said. His simplicity made his words penetrate like arrows, cutting right through verbal smokescreens and barriers.

So, too, Jesus' parables are a model of simplicity. Some later Christian commentators constructed elaborate interpretations of Jesus' parables, treating them as allegories in which each detail had a meaning. But that is to miss the point that each parable generally has only one point. Often he ended a parable with one summing-up statement. For example, when the teachers of the law criticized Jesus for welcoming sinners, he told his stories of the lost sheep, the lost coin and the lost son, to make the point that "there is rejoicing in the presence of the angels of God over one sinner who repents" (Lk 15:10). To some who were so self-righteous that they looked down on others, Jesus told a story about the Pharisee who went to the temple and congratulated himself in his prayers, while the tax collector asked God to have mercy. "Everyone who exalts himself will be humbled, and he who humbles himself will be exalted" was Jesus' blunt conclusion (Lk 18:9-14).

There is a simple-mindedness which cannot handle complexity and retreats into superficiality. But there is also a simplicity which can get to the heart of complexity. It was the latter which marked Jesus. His simplicity was like the Japanese art of flower arranging, where beauty comes perhaps through one flower which focuses all together and commands attention. Perhaps the notable Black preachers have learned that artistry as well as anyone. They know how to take one phrase and repeat it scores of times, coming at it from many different directions but never leaving their hearers in doubt as to what they have heard. Their concern is not to make ten points, but to make one point in ten or a hundred different ways.

So it was with Jesus. He taught us that simplicity means to say one thing well. Therefore,

COMMUNICATION IMPERATIVE 7: KNOW YOUR POINT.

8. _Take your calling seriously, but do not be anxious for yourself._ In all of Jesus' communication there is an almost overwhelming sense of urgency. He continually reminded his listeners that now was the time for decision, that delay was dangerous, that the times demanded disciples willing to forsake all for his sake and for the sake of the gospel. He knew that he had been sent into the world at the appointed time, that the kingdom was near, that the rules of the game had irrevocably changed, and that nothing would ever be the same. The sense of immediacy and urgency surfaces again and again:

"Why do you call me, 'Lord, Lord,' and do not do what I say?" (Lk 6:46).

"Enter through the narrow gate. For wide is the gate and broad is the road that leads to destruction" (Mt 7:13).

"Do not suppose that I have come to bring peace to the earth. I did not come to bring peace, but a sword" (Mt 10:34).

"If anyone would come after me, he must deny himself and take up his cross and follow me" (Mk 8:34).

"For many are invited, but few are chosen" (Mt 22:14).

These words almost tremble with urgency.

Yet coupled with urgency there is also a sense of calmness in Jesus. He knows that the destiny of people and nations is decided by the actions they take in response to his truth. But he does not have to rise to a feverish pitch, and there is no record of his coercing others. When the rich young ruler turns and goes away sadly, Jesus does not run after him. He lets him make his decision and go. He tells his disciples that the kingdom of heaven is like a farmer who sows the seed and then goes to sleep while it grows (Mt 13:24-30). While he can spend sleepless nights in prayer, he can also quietly withdraw and let the word he has spoken do its work.

How could Jesus have such urgency and yet be so calm? The secret is perhaps to be found in John's description of Jesus, coming as a light into the world. Inevitably that light would cause a crisis, a separation. Those who loved darkness would not come to the light. Those who sought truth would come to the light. Jesus put it this way:

> I have come into the world as a light, so that no one who believes in me should stay in darkness. As for the person who hears my words but does not keep them, I do not judge him. For I did not come to judge the world, but to save it. There is a judge for the one who rejects me and does not accept my words; that very word which I spoke will condemn him at the last day. For I did not speak of my own accord, but the Father who sent me commanded me what to say and how to say it. I know that his command leads to eternal life. (Jn 12:46-50)

Perhaps we could paraphrase it this way:

> My responsibility is to be the light and let the light shine. How people respond is not my concern at this point. I am a witness and not (as yet) the judge. My Father sent me to give his word. Those who follow will be led to life. If they refuse, they will be judging themselves. I care deeply what happens. With all that is within me, I want those who hear me to come to the light. But my responsibility is to let the light shine. The results are in the hands of my Father.

Most of us are put off by communicators who oversell, in whom we sense strain and anxiety. We can learn from Jesus that anxiety comes when we take God's responsibility on ourselves. Our task is to give one hundred per cent, to communicate well, and then to leave it up to God.

A few years ago I was asked to speak to an open-air gathering at Victoria University in Wellington, New Zealand. That university community has been known for its negative attitude to religion and for not being hospitable to visiting evangelists. When the sponsoring groups announced our rally, a tiny but very vocal and highly organized group of gays and lesbians staged a protest. When the time arrived, we found that the demonstrators had placed themselves immediately in front of the platform, with signs proclaiming, "Leighton Ford is a bigot." I asked one of the women if she had ever heard me speak or read anything that I had said. When she said no, I asked, "Who is the bigot?" In spite of this they kept up a noisy demonstration and almost drowned out the singer who preceded me.

Frankly, I wanted to be anywhere but there. I kept wishing that Billy Graham would materialize and take my place on the platform! But I also knew that I had been called to speak at that moment. To our amazement, no doubt having been attracted by the protesters, close to a thousand students had gathered, far more than the fifty or seventy-five that usually showed up for any kind of gathering, religious or political. It was an opportunity that could not be lost.

I stepped nervously to the platform and prayed for grace and strength. As I talked, the hullabaloo kept up. One of the protestors stood three feet in front of me with a loud megaphone in his hand, heckling me. They were throwing eggs, and one of them hit my shoes. Concentrating was difficult, but somehow I was able to complete my talk and to disregard the opposition, trying to bear in mind the hundreds of students listening to a message that otherwise they would not have heard. Before, during and after, we sought to treat the demonstrators with courtesy.

When it was all over, I felt drained. Yet our team knew that we had carried out our responsibility. The next Saturday night, at a large youth rally, the headmaster of a local school spotted one of his former students in the crowd. Knowing the young man had not been at all interested in spiritual things, he said, "What are you doing here?" And the young man replied, "Sir, last week I went with my friends to hear Leighton Ford at the university. We saw grace and love and a courage in the Christians that attracted us. We want to know what they have." A year later Tony Campolo, another Christian speaker, was at the same university to lecture to a sociology class. He discovered that the earlier meeting had had a profound and lasting effect, opening up a dialog between the Christian students on the campus and the gay/lesbian groups, exploding the stereotype of Christians as bigots, and opening new doors for communication.

245

For me, it was a chance to learn again from Jesus the lesson that we ought to take our task with the utmost seriousness, but not to be anxious about ourselves. Which leads to

COMMUNICATION IMPERATIVE 8: KNOW WHERE YOUR RESPONSIBILITY BEGINS AND ENDS.

9. *Never underestimate your opposition; but always count on your hidden resource.* We tend to exaggerate the power of reason in our interpersonal communication. And we underestimate the power of what is unreasonable and hidden below the surface. "Be reasonable," a spouse says, not sensing that hurt or fear has shoved reason aside. "If only Dad would listen to reason," a teenager storms to his mother, not knowing that his dad is reacting the way he is because of a forgotten incident in his own teen years. The inexperienced persuader marshals all his reasons logically and cannot understand why it is not working. The more seasoned communicator understands from experience that if the heart and imagination and feelings are not moved, reason probably will not persuade.

But more lies under the surface of communication than emotions and past experiences. Jesus was always conscious of a dark element which opposed the truth. At the outset of his ministry, in the synagogue at Capernaum, he confronted a man possessed by an evil spirit who cried out, "What do you want with us, Jesus of Nazareth? Have you come to destroy us?" Jesus commanded the spirit sternly, "Be quiet! Come out of him!" And the spirit left with a shriek (Mk 1:21-6). This story represents all kinds of forces which bind people—the sense of being driven, the fear of the future, the tyranny of death, the inability to express love, the need to dominate other people.

Perhaps the power of evil was most dramatically evident in the case of the man who lived "in the tombs," shunned by society, with fetters hanging from his wrists where he had broken them. When Jesus and his disciples beached their boat near the lakeside caves where he lived, he came running out of the tombs, frightening the disciples and falling in front of Jesus. He was a terrible picture of the way evil makes people less than human.

Demon possession was a shocking and awesome but very real part of Jesus' experience.

Sophisticated modern people tend to scoff at the idea of demons, treating them as simply incredible. Yet Scott Peck, in his book *People of the Lie,* tells how as a psychiatrist he came across instances of destructive human behavior which he could only call evil.[8] The behaviors he describes are more than sick. They became so destructive that they could only be described as evil. Whatever the things are that make people live "in the tombs"—mental illness, alcohol or drug addiction, criminal behavior, sexual kinks, personality cults, fanatic ideologies, or the will to control others—may become beachheads which can be the dwelling-places for evil powers. The demon-possessed man who met Jesus was an awful example of this, separated from his family, not knowing his own name, cutting himself until he bled. Here is a picture of evil which isolates persons or groups from normal relations, which binds them with a strength that neither therapy nor constraint can subdue, and which leads to increasingly self-destructive behavior.

These extreme cases of demon possession are only dramatic illustrations of a more subtle darkness which seeks to overcome the light. So Jesus told a cultured, sophisticated and well-educated Jewish leader, "No one can see the kingdom of God unless he is born again" (Jn 3:3). A deep, radical, inner change is necessary for the truth to be communicated.

In one of his parables Jesus described the spreading of the good Word of God as being like a farmer who sows his seed. At night, when everyone is sleeping, an enemy comes along and sows weeds in the same field. To the sower's amazement, wheat and weeds spring up together (Mt 13:24-30, 36-43). "Don't just look on the surface," Jesus is saying in effect. "Underneath human personality and behind human history there is an enemy who is opposing what God is doing, who doesn't want people to see the light and to live free."

Jesus put this in another vivid figure of speech. There was a man who was mute because he was possessed by a demon. When Jesus freed him, he spoke and the crowd was amazed. Some reacted by attributing Jesus' miraculous power to the devil. Jesus answered them with his well-known saying about "a kingdom divided against itself" which will surely fall. Then comes his vivid illustration:

If I drive out demons by the finger of God, then the kingdom of God has come to you. When a strong man, fully armed, guards his own house, his possessions are safe. But when someone stronger attacks and overpowers him, he takes away the armor in which the man trusted and divides up the spoils. (Lk 11:20-22)

The comparison is clear. Human personality is like a house guarded by a strong man. The house cannot be opened up and its goods revealed (true communication cannot take place) unless someone stronger first overcomes the "strong man." Jesus paints his own self-portrait as the leader of shock troops against the powers of evil. By the power of God's strong finger—which in another place he calls "God's Spirit" (Mt 12:28)—he frees the captives.

He then depicts human personality as a house which is vacated, swept clean and put in order (Lk 11:24-26). But no new tenant occupies it. So seven ruffians come, rattle the lock, peer in the windows, break open the door, throw a wild party and ruin the place. That happens, says Jesus, when there is a vacuum in the human spirit. One evil spirit may leave, but seven worse will come. Human personality cannot be an empty house. If it is not occupied by the power of good, it will be taken over by the power of evil. And then it takes more than "reasonable communication." It takes a powerful spiritual battle to bring home the truth.

In our modern world many people will scorn the biblical stories of demons and the devil as hopelessly old-fashioned. And yet, evil has shown its wicked face in spite of better education, technology and communications than ever before. Many counselors are now beginning to recognize that deep-seated human problems, for example, drug or alcohol addiction, pornography, sexual aberrations, or racial hatred, can only be overcome by a deep, powerful experience of religious conversion. The various twelve-step programs such as Alcoholics Anonymous have all emphasized that release from addiction must involve surrender "to a Higher Power." We are just beginning to catch up with what Jesus said about communication nearly twenty-one centuries ago! Jesus taught out of his own deep and powerful experience. When he sent his followers out on their first mission, he told them to expect opposition, "I am sending you out like sheep among wolves. Therefore be as shrewd as snakes and as innocent as doves. Be on your guard. . . . They will hand you over to the local councils and flog you. . . . On my account you will be brought before governors and kings" (Mt 10:16-18). He repeated the same teaching again before his death and resurrection and final marching orders. But he also told them to expect a good response, "He who receives you receives me, and he who receives me receives the one who sent me" (Mt 10:40). And he promised them hidden resources, "When they arrest you, do not worry about what to say or how to say it. At that time you will be given what to say, for it will not be you speaking, but the Spirit of your Father speaking through you" (Mt 10:19-20; cf. Mk 13:11).

They would face the same enemy that he had faced. They would experience the same opposition. But they could also count on the same resource. The Holy Spirit who had been Jesus' hidden ally was also to be his gift to them:

Unless I go away, the Counselor will not come to you; but if I go, I will send him to you. When he comes, he will convict the world of guilt in regard to sin and righteousness and judgment. . . . When he, the Spirit of truth, comes, he will guide you into all truth. (Jn 16:7, 8, 13)

With that calm confidence and with the repeated encouragement "Do not be afraid" (Mt 10:26-31), Jesus sent them into the world as his Father had sent him—to bear witness to the truth, to face opposition and rejection and dullness. But they knew that they had only to ask and they would receive the power and wisdom to open closed minds and stubborn hearts to the light of God himself.

"Do not underrate your enemy, your opposition. And do not forget about your resource," was Jesus' message to his disciples. Therefore,

COMMUNICATION IMPERATIVE 9: KNOW YOUR ENEMY AND KNOW YOUR ALLY.

There is a prayer written by my friend Lloyd Ogilvie that I often use, praying it quietly just before I speak. It sums up what we have been saying in this chapter, recognizing that when we ask and trust him Jesus Christ will indeed communicate through us:

Lord, here's my mind, think your thoughts in me. Be my wisdom, knowledge, and insight. Here is my voice. You told me not to worry about what I am to say, but that it would be given me what to say and how to say it. Free me to speak with silence or with words, whichever is needed. Give me your timing and tenderness. Now Lord, here is my body. Release creative affection in my face, my touch, my embrace. And Christ, if there is something I am to do by your indwelling presence, however menial or tough, control my will to do it.

Lord, I am ready now to be your manifest intervention in situations to infuse joy, affirm growth, or absorb pain and aching anguish. I plan to live this day and the rest of my life in the reality of you in me. Thank you for making it so![9]

13

THE LEADER AS
STRUGGLER

●

*Jesus was prepared to
face conflict—he was gracious,
courageous and wise.*

●

*"Blessed are the peacemakers,
for they will be called sons of God."*
JESUS CHRIST

*"Do you think I came to bring peace on earth?
No, I tell you, but division."*
JESUS CHRIST

"As weather shapes mountains, so problems make leaders."
WARREN BENNISS

*T*o lead is to struggle. In a world such as ours, in history as we know it, to choose the path of leadership is to be on a collision course with conflict.

Why? The reason is quite clear. Leadership always involves change, moving people from one point to another, from the old way of doing things to the new, from the security in the past to the insecurity in the future. Within us there is a built-in resistance to change which seems to threaten our stability and challenge our power. Even if our current situation is unhappy, we still dig in our feet. As a young woman with severe problems ironically responded, when challenged to undergo a spiritual conversion, "I think I prefer the security of my misery!"

The degree of resistance depends on how critical the change is. *Crisis* is a word which comes from the Greek *krisis.* It implies a separating or dividing. Every crisis brings about a polarization and reveals what is truly inside people. During the First World War, a munitions ship blew up in the harbor in Halifax, Canada, causing terrible devastation. Much of the city was knocked flat, and thousands were killed or injured. That crisis brought out the best and the worst in people. One man with half his face blasted refused treatment in order to rescue those who were buried under the rubble. But others prowled the wreckage, stealing rings and money from the corpses.

Since leadership involves change, and change precipitates crisis, a leader must expect that there will be those who resist as well as those who follow. "One could argue," writes John W. Gardner, "that willingness to engage in battle when necessary is a *sine qua non* of leadership."[1]

Some of the greatest leaders portrayed in the Bible actually came to the point of praying for death because of conflict. Moses led the people of Israel across the Red Sea from slavery in Egypt. That was easy compared to the task of *forming* a crew of slaves into an organized community. Their discontent and criticism became so strong that in anguish Moses said to God, ". . . The burden is too heavy for me. If this is how you are going to treat me, put me to death right now" (Num 11:14-15). Elijah the prophet also came to despair, not in forming but in *reforming* the people and calling them back to God. Under pressure he wilted, fled from a wicked queen named Jezebel, and prayed, "Take my life" (1 Kings 19:4). A third leader, Jonah, was God's instrument for *informing* the Jewish people about their mission to the Gentile world. Jonah ran away from his responsibility at first. But when he finally delivered God's message to the wicked city of Nineveh and saw to his amazement that its people repented, he moaned in self-pity, "O Lord, take away my life" (Jon 4:3).

So we are not surprised that Jesus, the *transforming* leader, faced conflict from his birth—when King Herod tried to locate and murder the newborn baby whom he saw as a threat—to his death, which was provoked by religious leaders and carried out by a Roman leader who wanted to wash his hands of trouble. The conflict motif runs through Jesus' life and ministry, leading Gustav Aulen to see in the New Testament "a doctrine of atonement whose central theme . . . is divine conflict and victory: Jesus Christ—Christus Victor—fights against and triumphs over the evil powers of the world."[2]

A major theme in the story of Jesus is that of a deep ongoing struggle with evil. Like a gigantic volcano, the struggle rumbled and churned under the surface and regularly erupted into conflict and misunderstanding with the devil, with Jesus' family and neighbors, with religious and government leaders, with the occasional stranger, and even with his followers. It would have hardly been an ordinary day for Jesus without conflict.

Nice People Don't Fight?

In recent years conflict resolution has become a major field of study and a big industry. Read through the catalog at the library or glance at the brochure advertising seminars on leadership, and it quickly becomes apparent that skills in conflict resolution are regarded as very important for leaders and managers. Clearly, leaders must know how to cope with the divisions within modern society, how to tone down the rhetoric, how to search for acceptable compromises, how to help opposing parties understand how the other perceives the problems, and how to open the way for creative solutions. John Gardner emphasizes that leaders must "go to the root of the communication breakdown, whether it is anger, fear, mistrust or differing assumptions and definitions."[3]

All this is important and helpful. But we commonly assume that the problems of conflict are problems of culture, style and lack of communication. "If we can just tackle these," we think, "we can resolve the conflict." Yet this in a sense is to evade the central problem. _Communication_ implies a _community_ of interests; but if there is no common ground, how can there be communication? Much depends on the issues and dynamics that underlie the conflict.

The modern world generally, assumes that there is no "truth" which is objectively true. Rather, there are only "values" which we supposedly hold because of our personality or background or culture. These values need to be "clarified." In an age like ours, the number one virtue is not to be valiant for truth, but to be tolerant of values. And perhaps the most important value is to be nice to everyone—except those who are not tolerant enough for our liking!

Malcolm Muggeridge writes of an experience which brought him into conflict when tolerance broke down. He had been elected by the students at Edinburgh University as their rector, and he had a wonderful reception at his installation. Some months later the Students' Union requested the governing body of the university to make contraception available through the university infirmary. Muggeridge refused to do this, and a conflict ensued:

> I was subjected to abuse, to the point that I found it necessary to resign. In a farewell sermon in St Giles' Cathedral, I explained why I had done what I had and received some private thanks, but none publicly. The conclusion I came to was that in a Libertine society any attack on Libertinism is anathema.[4]

Some conflicts are so deep and fundamental that they simply cannot be resolved. In this light, we must understand Jesus' seemingly contradictory statements, "Blessed are the peacemakers" (Mt 5:9) and "I did not come to bring peace, but a sword" (Mt 10:34).

Discerning Conflict

Jesus was uniquely free of inner conflict, although he still felt the pain of the costly struggles in which he was involved. But that very lack of inner conflict freed him to deal creatively and flexibly with various conflict situations:

> When the less-than-friendly hometown people of Nazareth rejected his message of confronting love, he chose to withdraw. . . . He cut off conversation and debate with the Pharisees when the point of clear rejection had arrived. . . . He confronted the hustlers in the Temple on win-lose terms. . . . At his arrest . . . Jesus chose to submit to the anger of others, absorb it, and speak back the word of forgiveness, grace and acceptance.[5]

In the Gospels we see Jesus in conflict with four parties—the devil, the

254

religious leaders, his own followers, and certain outsiders or bystanders. In all of these conflicts Jesus' weapons were grace and truth, but he employed these weapons somewhat differently depending on the nature of the conflict. We might dub these conflicts *supra, contra, intra* and *extra.*

Supra-conflict. This conflict was with the devil, was supernatural and was sometimes direct and sometimes indirect. But it pervaded Jesus' ministry from the beginning to the end: Jesus cast out evil spirits (Mk 1:21-26; 9:14-29); the devil tried to deflect Jesus from the cross by speaking through his close friend Peter (Mk 8:32-33); when his disciples returned from a preaching mission and said that the demons had submitted in his name, he replied, "I saw Satan fall like lightning from heaven" (Lk 10:18); and he even described his work as a battle in which he overpowered the "strong man," that is, Satan (Lk 11:18-22).

This supra conflict was *fundamental* in its nature. At issue were ultimate loyalties, values and beliefs; obedience or disobedience to the mission on which Jesus had been sent; and the choice of whether he would go by way of the cross or some less demanding way.

Contra-conflict. Here the conflict was with the religious leaders, especially the Pharisees. This conflict, too, began early in Jesus' ministry and involved accusations that he committed blasphemy, associated with notorious sinners and led people to break sacred traditions such as the sabbath. Mark's terse account compresses the Pharisees' growing opposition into several vivid incidents. When Jesus forgives a paralytic man they say, "Why does this fellow talk like that? He's blaspheming! Who can forgive sins but God alone?" (Mk 2:7). When he associates with a tax collector named Levi, they ask, "Why does he eat with tax collectors and 'sinners'?" (Mk 2:16). When he allows his disciples to pick grain as they walk through the fields on the sabbath, and on the same day heals a man with a shriveled hand in the synagogue, they accuse him of doing what is "unlawful" on the sabbath (Mk 3:2, 4). Soon they are even accusing him of being in alliance with the devil himself (Mk 3:22)!

This contra-conflict we may designate as *unavoidable.* At stake here are the issues of tradition, power and control, of ritual versus reality.

Intra-conflict. The inner group of twelve that Jesus chose to be with him

255

was made up of such diverse personalities and loyalties that it is utterly remarkable that they could be kept together. Yet it is the mark of leadership to bring partial loyalties and lesser talents together in a unifying passion for a higher cause. That Jesus did this is astonishing. That he still had problems with them, and they with each other, is understandable! As David McKenna comments in his fine book *Power to Follow, Grace to Lead,* "Especially in the development of diverse and dissimilar disciples interpersonal conflict is part and parcel of the nurturing and norming process."[6]

McKenna suggests that three kinds of conflict between the disciples are revealed in the Gospel of Mark: public conflict over the failure of the disciples to heal a sick boy; interpersonal conflict over who would be the greatest in the kingdom; intergroup conflict over who had the right to belong to their group (Mk 9:14-41).[7] To these I would add spiritual conflict over their frequent lack of faith and understanding.

This intra-conflict was *essential* in nature. If they were going to become all that Jesus wanted them to be, it was crucial that the disciples were able to work through these conflicts. The issues here revolved more around matters of faith, relationships and position and around the basic value of status versus service.

Extra-conflict. Like the "extras" or bit players in a drama or movie, there were bystanders, people on the fringe of Jesus' work, who proved to be difficult. These included his family members, his neighbors and certain Samaritans. On one occasion Jesus' mother and brothers thought he was out of his mind and went to take charge of him, presumably to guard him until he came to his sanity (Mk 3:20, 31-32). They could not believe that one of their own family was making the claims he did and causing such a public stir. Overfamiliarity also led some of the people from his hometown to dismiss him. "Where did this man get this wisdom and these miraculous powers?" they derided when he came to teach in their synagogue. "Isn't this the carpenter's son?" (Mt 13:54-55). On another occasion, he set out for Jerusalem and was going through a Samaritan village. The people there did not welcome him, because he was going to Jerusalem. So in this case Jesus merely bypassed their village, and went to another instead (Lk 9:51-56). Here it was not familiarity, but strangeness, which brought the resistance.

In these cases the conflict was *incidental.* Jesus chose not to make relatively minor events into major incidents. The issues at stake—whether jealousy, or culture and style, or the fear of foreigners—did not yet strike at the heart of his mission.

Transforming Conflict

Austrian psychiatrist Viktor Frankl wrote about the ways in which Jewish inmates of Hitler's concentration camps met their suffering.[8] He felt passionately that persons could bring meaning to some of the most inhumane circumstances by the ways in which they chose to react to them. While they could not control their captors or change their circumstances, they could control the way in which they faced those circumstances. So, too, transforming leaders will learn to transform conflict by the way they deal with it. Such leaders will discern the nature, the issues, and the seriousness of the conflict; they will then choose a stance and make the most of it. They will understand, as William Barclay has said, that endurance is the ability not just to bear a hard thing, but to turn "the hardest trial into glory."[9]

For a leader in conflict *not* to see the issue and *not* to choose a response is the worst thing one can do. On the other hand, to choose deliberately, and with good reason, *not to act* is quite different.

Too often a leader will prolong or worsen the conflict by reacting instead of acting. The reaction may be to fight or to flee, our two most common responses to fear or anxiety, but these responses are neither creative nor transforming. When we succumb to our "fight or flight" reactions (either to bulldoze our opponents or to run), it is usually because our own inner conflicts have not been resolved. Some of us tend to be constitutional belligerents because we have a deep need to dominate. Others of us tend to be constitutional pushovers because of a need to please and be accepted. Either case shows a lack of inner strength and the presence of unresolved conflicts. Unresolved conflicts in a spiritual leader often give rise to the worst form of sectarianism. Sectarianism is a coupling together of a deeply held religious conviction with an extreme political ideology, such as has been seen in Northern Ireland, Lebanon and South Africa. Often the sectarian spirit becomes the vehicle to express the personal conflicts of the

257

leader. A friend of mine once commented that in some cases conversion is "just a switch of hostilities."

Jesus was able to transform conflict because he himself was so free of conflict. From the beginning, his relationship to his Father as Son and servant was pure and full of integrity. With total honesty he could say, "The one who sent me is with me; he has not left me alone, for I always do what pleases him" (Jn 8:29). And in his turn, the Father gave his stamp of complete approval: "This is my Son, whom I love; with him I am well pleased" (Mt 17:5).

Not for a moment did this mean that Jesus was free from struggle. The temptations in the wilderness were very real. So was the agony on his last night when, facing arrest and execution, he prayed in the garden, "Father, if you are willing, take this cup from me" (Lk 22:42). But his basic identity and calling were clear and without conflict.

Leaders who want to transform conflict need to face their own inner wars; to know what it is to find acceptance with God through the sacrifice of Jesus Christ; to understand that integrity comes in seeking as a priority the rule of God; and to draw on the power of God's Spirit to overcome the ongoing conflict between the sinful nature and the new life in Christ (Rom 8:5-6). We have considered the different kinds of conflict which Jesus faced. To understand the stance which he took in each is both instructive and inspiring.

In Fundamental Conflict: Stand and Fight!

When Peter wrote to some of his compatriots in the early Christian movement who were undergoing great persecution, he counseled them: "Be self-controlled and alert. Your enemy the devil prowls around like a roaring lion looking for someone to devour. Resist him, standing firm in the faith. . . ." (1 Pet 5:8-9).

Peter's counsel was lifted straight from the model of Jesus, an example of total resistance. When in the desert Jesus was tempted by the devil to turn stones into bread, to make a spectacular leap off the top of the temple so that the angels would catch him, and to worship the devil in order to gain sovereignty over the world, there was no argument, no debate. In each case he countered the devil firmly and immediately by quoting appropriate Scriptures. As Son and servant he was loyal to his Father, his God. Later, when the devil came speaking through the voice of Peter and telling him not to go to the cross, there was an abrupt rejection: "Get behind me, Satan!" (Mk 8:33). And when in the Garden of Gethsemane he wrestled in sweat, blood and agony over his impending crucifixion, there was both an agonizing plea to be released and an unconditional affirmation, "Yet not what I will, but what you will" (Mk 14:36).

Conflict always takes an emotional toll, and Jesus was not immune to this cost. After the weakness of a forty-day fast in the desert he faced supernatural assault. In the garden he went through an intense struggle, felt agony and actually sweated blood. These times of struggle must have been intensely lonely, for in the desert he had no companion, and in the garden Peter, James and John, whom he had asked to pray with him, went to sleep.

In the most crucial times of testing, Jesus had no one but his Father. Yet that was enough. His strategy was to face unconditional opposition with unconditional resistance, and his weapons were prayer and the words of Scripture.

The Leader and Spiritual Warfare

Leaders need to recognize the power of evil to cause conflict in people and among groups. Through the Spirit and mind of Christ, they will seek to discern prayerfully whether the opposition is indeed from the evil one, Satan. Then they need to know that the battle is on a spiritual level and that the weapons to use are spiritual and stem from the Lord's victorious battle. Evil is not to be feared, ignored or shrunk from, but to be exposed, confronted, overcome and used for God's glory.

One thinks of the martyrs who like their Lord resisted to the point of death. There is the story of Blandina, who in A.D. 177 was martyred for her steadfast and clear testimony to her faith. Eusebius the church historian described how Blandina was taken to the amphitheater, hung on a stake and exposed to wild beasts. Eventually she was killed by a bull. As Eusebius narrates:

For while we were all afraid . . . Blandina was filled with such power that she was released and rescued from those who took turns in torturing her in every way from morning until evening . . . but the blessed woman, like a noble athlete, kept gaining in vigor in her confession and found comfort and rest and freedom from pain from what was done to her by saying, "I am a Christian woman and nothing wicked happens among us."

Like Blandina, some resist and die, while others resist and live. At the time of writing, we have in our home a guest, a pastor from Romania, a country which until recently was ruled by one of the most oppressive communist governments. Several times this man was threatened with death. Often he was harassed. On one occasion the authorities told him not to accept a call to serve a church in a university town, because they feared the influence he would have on the students. When he persisted in going, they arranged an "accident" in which a bus deliberately hit his car and almost killed him and his wife. When the revolution came to Romania in December 1989, a few churches locked their doors and refused to offer the protesters sanctuary from the armies that had orders to shoot them. In contrast, when the protest leaders wanted someone to speak in the name of God, this brave Baptist pastor indicated his willingness. He stood on a balcony overlooking the town square and told the people that after forty-five years of state atheism he had come to speak in the name of God. Two hundred thousand people began to chant in unison, "There is a God! There is a God!" That same day the Romanian dictator Ceausescu fled, and on Christmas Day he was executed.

Charles Olcott was a successful businessman and a conventional churchgoer when God seemed to speak to him one night and say, "All this 'stuff' you own is not yours. It is mine. I have a purpose for you to use these things for me." This led to a new commitment to Christ. Shortly after, he was appointed as the chief executive officer of a large franchise fast-food chain. He was able to turn the company around and improve its financial condition. "For the first time I took my hand off the steering wheel and turned it over to God," he says. But then he faced his own crisis. The chairman of the corporation which owned his company asked him to doctor some figures, to build a mathematical model which would project a level of future earnings which had no relationship to reality. The idea was to increase the value of their shares so they could sell the business at a handsome profit but at the expense of the company, its employees and shareholders. Charles said he could not do it. "Then you are off the team," said the chairman. It was a harsh sentence. Twenty years on the corporate ladder were gone. When he told me this story, I asked him what difference it would have made if this episode had happened before he made a commitment to Christ. "I would still be at that company," he said. "I would have found a way to bend the figures, because then I was living by earthly values." Now in a new business, he is a wounded but contented man who knows he did what was right but at significant cost.

Blandina resisted and was killed by wild animals. The Romanian pastor resisted and became a hero of the revolution. Charles Olcott resisted and was fired. In each case they followed the leadership of Jesus, who went through total resistance, met death by crucifixion, and conquered. Here was a transforming leader who never promised those who followed his lead that it would be easy.

So we see in Jesus that when the issue is ultimate loyalty to God against evil, the leader is to stand and resist; and that whether the immediate result seems to be triumph or loss, the ultimate promise is conquest and a crown of life.

In Unavoidable Conflict: Face and Seize!

It has been said that the Pharisees in the New Testament get a lot of bad press. Certainly the wholesale condemnation of all Pharisees as hypocrites and bigots is unfair. We must remember that they cared deeply about God. And not a few of the Pharisees (like Nicodemus) were drawn to Jesus. But the religious leaders in Jesus' time had built up a system which, however good its initial intentions, had become unreal and oppressive. So a clash between them and Jesus was inevitable.

They tangled with Jesus over three major issues: over the meaning of religious traditions such as sabbath-keeping, and whether their original purpose had been forgotten; over the importance of ceremonial rituals such as hand-washing before eating, and whether the "heart of the matter" had been forgotten; and over the implicit claims of Jesus to have authority to teach and forgive, and whether he was truly the Christ who had been prophesied.

Two sequences in Mark's account highlight the development of Jesus' conflict with the Pharisees, one at the beginning of his career, the other at the end.

Mark 2—3 tells of how Jesus healed a paralytic, but only after first forgiving him his sins; of how he called a tax collector named Levi to follow him, and went to his house for a meal; of how he did not require his disciples to fast; and of how on the sabbath he let his disciples pick grain as they walked through a field, and in the synagogue he healed a man with a shriveled hand.

The thrust and counter-thrust between the religious leaders and Jesus is fascinating. When Jesus heals the paralytic, the teachers of the law do not voice their criticisms. They simply think, "Why does this fellow talk like that? He's blaspheming! Who can forgive sins but God alone?" (Mk 2:6-7). Jesus, knowing intuitively what they are thinking, asks them very directly, "Why are you thinking these things?" Is it easier, he asks, to say "Be forgiven" or "Get up and walk"? Then, to show what authority he has, he heals the man (Mk 2:8-12).

When he goes to eat at Levi's house, the teachers are a little bolder. This time they go up to his disciples and ask, "Why does he eat with tax collectors and 'sinners'?" (Mk 2:16). Overhearing again, Jesus replies with an analogy, "It is not the healthy who need a doctor, but the sick. I have not come to call the righteous, but sinners" (Mk 2:17).

A little later, when his disciples pick the grain, the Pharisees are bold enough to come directly to him and say, "Look, why are they doing what is unlawful on the Sabbath?" (Mk 2:24). His answer is to draw a historical precedent from King David, who when he was in need ate some consecrated bread. Then he makes a fundamental point: "The Sabbath was made for man, not man for the Sabbath" (Mk 2:27). In the synagogue that same day, it is Jesus who takes the initiative. Knowing the Pharisees want to accuse him, he stands by a man with a shriveled hand and asks, "Which is lawful on the Sabbath: to do good or to do evil, to save life or to kill?" They remain silent (Mk 3:4).

Up to this point, Jesus has dealt with them patiently, directly and courteously. He has tried to reason with them, to deal with issues and principles, not with personalities. He does not allow himself to be caught up in details, but looks at the core of the issues. He knows that institutions are to serve people, and not vice versa. As a leader he must keep his main purpose before him—to show the kingdom.

But these leaders are refusing God's purpose to heal, to forgive, to serve. So now comes a remarkable insight into Jesus' deep feelings. He has compassion for the man with the shriveled hand. He shows high courage when he knows that to persist will bring certain opposition. And, Mark tells us, he looks around at the Pharisees in anger; and, deeply distressed at their stubborn hearts, he says to the man, "Stretch out your hand." And the man's hand is healed (Mk 3:5). It is then that "the Pharisees went out and began to plot with the Herodians how they might kill Jesus" (Mk 3:4).

When Jesus faced unavoidable conflict, his stance was to face it directly and seize it as an opportunity. His attitude was a combination of patient long-suffering, of challenge, and, eventually, of anger.

As we noted in an earlier chapter, Stephen Neill, in _A Genuinely Human Existence,_ has described Jesus' relationship to the Jewish traditions as that of a "courteous rebel." As a loyal Jew, he criticized the actions of his people but did not separate himself from them. He never took the view that tradition was a bad thing in itself. Traditions in a community are like habits in our personal lives. If we had to think through the details every time we took a walk or tied our shoes or fed ourselves, we would be exhausted. As Neill says, if tradition is used in the right way it sets "energies free for new discoveries and new adventures of living."[11]

Jesus enthusiastically accepted the traditions of the Old Testament, though at points he went beyond it. He accepted without objection those traditions, such as paying the temple tax, which conflicted with no deep personal or moral principle (Mt 17:24-7). But he came into violent conflict with the Jewish traditions as interpreted by the leaders, traditions which had become a system of legalism run riot. When legalism and tradition were limiting proper human freedom, making a supreme virtue of outward ritual, and becoming positively cruel, Jesus stood against them as a "courteous rebel." When accused of breaking the law by healing on the sabbath day, he asked the radical question: What is the sabbath for? And he showed that to heal on the sabbath was the best possible way of keeping God's purpose.[12]

Toward the end of his ministry, Jesus engaged in a drawn-out debate with religious leaders over a number of matters.[13] At this time he made his final visit to Jerusalem and caused a stir by throwing the money-changers out of the temple and by causing the fig tree to wither (both actions being acted-out parables of the fate of the nation).

On his arrival in Jerusalem, the chief priests, the teachers of the law and the elders came and asked him, "By what authority are you doing these things?" He answered with a question: "Answer me, and I will tell you by what authority I am doing these things. John's baptism—was it from heaven, or from men? Tell me!" This put them in a dilemma. If they said John's authority came from heaven, the people would ask why they did not believe John. On the other hand, if they said that John was operating on his own initiative, then the crowd, which revered John as a prophet, might turn on them. So they waffled: "We don't know." And Jesus then said, "Neither will I tell you by what authority I am doing these things" (Mk 11:27-33). After that, he told the story of a man who had planted a vineyard, rented it out and then at harvest time sent a servant to collect his rent. The tenants beat him up and sent him away empty-handed. Other servants were rejected and beaten up, and some were even killed. Finally, he sent his beloved son, believing they would respect him. But the tenants killed the heir in order to get the vineyard for themselves. The point of Jesus' parable was obvious. The leaders knew he had spoken it against them, and they therefore began looking for a way to arrest him (Mk 12:1-12).

The Leader's Rejection

The parable of the tenants in the vineyard is really Jesus' autobiography, and it gives us an insight into what it means to be a leader who is rejected. God's servants may find their authority not only questioned, but actually resisted—painfully, shamefully, even fatally.

But when we are rejected, we must ask whether we have in some measure created our own problems. When we face painful opposition, it would be wise to ask:

1. Am I really on God's business? Or how much of my own need am I fulfilling under the guise of representing God?

2. Can I live with my insecurities by resting in God's love?

3. Can I accept the hardship and even rejoice in sharing God's pain, and thus have it transformed?

4. Can I patiently wait God's vindication, and put aside my hostility?

Peter clearly picked up his model from Jesus:

Do not repay evil with evil or insult with insult, but with blessing, because to this you were called so that you may inherit a blessing. . . . But even if you should suffer for what is right, you are blessed. . . . It is better, if it is God's will, to suffer for doing good than for doing evil. . . . Rejoice that you participate in the sufferings of Christ. . . . Those who suffer according to God's will should commit themselves to their faithful Creator and continue to do good. (1 Pet 3:9, 14, 17; 4:13, 19)

The Leader's Discretion and Discernment

If part of effective leadership is having the wit to "answer on your feet" and to think under pressure, then Jesus' giftedness is evident in the debate recorded in Mark 12. He debated with the Pharisees over politics ("Should we pay taxes to Caesar?"), theology ("Will we be married at the resurrection?"), and ethics ("Which is the most important commandment?").

Mark's account of the parrying between these leaders and Jesus over the question of taxes provides a good example of his wit and wisdom. "Teacher," they said, "we know you are a man of integrity. You aren't swayed by men, because you pay no attention to who they are; but you teach the way of God in accordance with the truth. Is it right to pay taxes to Caesar or not? Should we pay or shouldn't we?" (Mk 12:14-15). Jesus' response is a splendid example of his ability:

1. To discern motives. "Jesus knew their hypocrisy" (Mk 12:15).

2. To sense ill will and danger. "Why are you trying to trap me?" he asked (Mk 12:15).

3. To deflect the attack. He did this by asking them to produce a coin (making generalities specific), and then by asking a question in return. "Whose portrait is this? And whose inscription?" (Mk 12:16). To answer a question with a question was his usual ploy.

4. To see the heart of the matter. When they said it was Caesar's picture, he replied, "Give to Caesar what is Caesar's and to God what is God's" (Mk 12:17). He discerned the basic point at issue—not taxes, but conflicting loyalties.

5. To challenge the questioners' consciences. He was, in fact, going back to the issue of whether they were obeying God's authority when they rejected him and John the Baptist.

6. By knowing when to stop. He stated the principle, but let the Pharisees draw out the implications and apply it (Mk 12:13-17). Jesus' consistent response to this kind of criticism was to face the question, detect prejudice, expose the issue in depth and at its heart, and then to return it as a challenge to the questioner.

Mark notes that Jesus' opponents were amazed at him and finally did not dare to ask him any more questions (Mk 12:34). Then Jesus himself went on the offensive and asked the Pharisees how the Messiah could be David's son when David himself in the Psalms had called him "Lord" (Mk 12:35-37).

The whole narrative of Jesus' conflict with the Pharisees is a powerful example of how the transforming leader can be positive, using even controversy as a great opportunity for communication. Jesus did not back off from these encounters. With tremendous faith and security, he made use of them to clarify issues; to appeal to the consciences of his hearers; to win over some of the Pharisees, like Nicodemus and others; and to get across his point to those who were looking on, both his disciples and potential converts.

In my own experience, I have often found that controversy provides an outstanding opportunity for communication. I have frequently been involved in hostile debate or questioning, whether before a group of university students or on a television interview or a radio call-in show. At such times, while I am dealing directly with a questioner or an opponent, scores or even thousands of others are listening but not saying anything. I always try to keep in mind that silent majority, realizing that even if I do not win over the person whom I am directly confronting, I may be able to influence those others who are listening. People sometimes say, "I listened to your answers. And I really appreciated the way you kept your cool, didn't lose your temper, and treated your questioners with respect." Under pressure, God's grace can stand out clearly. That was something Jesus taught us when dealing with the Pharisees.

In summary, Jesus dealt with unavoidable conflict by facing it and seizing the opportunity. His strategy was one of timed confrontation and withdrawal. In the Gospels, we see him move from patient explanation, through debate, to exposure of wrong motives and hearts, and finally to outright denunciation. The series of "woes" which he delivers in Matthew 23 against the Pharisees is an announcement that they and their system will be overthrown. Even so, the truth is still tempered with grace and a longing for them to change, as he concludes, "I tell you the truth, all this will come upon this generation. O Jerusalem, Jerusalem . . . how often I have longed to gather your children together, as a hen gathers her chicks under her wings, but you were not willing" (Mt 23:36-37). From Jesus we learn that the transforming leader who follows him will meet unavoidable conflict with patience, with ingenuity and, where necessary, with purposeful anger.

In Essential Conflict: Sit and Teach

Jesus is the ultimate model of the transformational leader who motivates us to be and to do more than we had expected.

Bernard Bass, in *Leadership and Performance beyond Expectations,* has contrasted the style of transactional and transformational leaders.[14] The transactional leader talks about *payoffs;* the transformational leader talks about *goals.* The transactional leader bargains about *exchanges;* the transformational leader provides *symbols.* The transactional leader consults about what *followers want;* the transformational leader talks to them about *higher objectives.*

The track record of Jesus' inner core of disciples was certainly mixed. In

almost equal proportions they showed great promise and marked insensi-
tivity. Jesus' attitude toward this intra-conflict was a combination of both
patience and exasperation. More than once he sighed over their failure to
understand or put into practice what he taught. But as a transforming
leader he saw that disagreement among the disciples was an essential conflict that had to be faced and one he could use to make truth live.

Out of many examples, we pick two. Shortly after Jesus announced to
his disciples his coming arrest and death, an argument broke out among
them concerning which of them was the greatest. Sitting down, Jesus called
the twelve and said, "If anyone wants to be first, he must be the very last,
and the servant of all" (Mk 9:35). Rather than rebuking their ambition, he
played the part of the transforming leader and linked greatness with servanthood.

But the subsurface power play among the disciples did not go away. A
day or two later, it surfaced a second time, when James and John approached him and asked to be awarded the favored places on his right and
left hand in his coming kingdom (Mk 10:37).

When the root of conflict is in the drive of our human nature for power,
it tends to rise again and again. As David McKenna has said, "The hatchet
has been buried, but the handle is close to the surface."[15]

But once again Jesus the transforming leader turned conflict into a
chance to make truth live creatively. The other disciples were indignant at
James and John's ambition. Jesus brought them to common ground by
reminding them how the rulers of the Gentiles "lorded it" over others (Mk
10:42). All of them shared a distaste for the Roman exercise of power. Jesus
then presented himself as the symbol and model: "The Son of Man did not
come to be served, but to serve, and to give his life as a ransom for many"
(Mk 10:45).

In his book _Power to Follow, Grace to Lead,_ David McKenna admirably
sums up Jesus' stance of sitting and teaching when conflict arose among
his inner core:

First, Jesus accepted conflict as another opportunity of developing His
disciples. Second, He confronted the conflicting parties immediately.
Third, He diagnosed the root of the problem in human nature. Fourth,

He moved the conflict to common ground where the protagonists agreed. Fifth, He found a common symbol with which the parties could affirmatively identify. Sixth, He used the occasion to refocus His vision and reinforce His mission in the minds of His "storming" disciples. Seventh and finally, He patiently and positively dealt with conflict even when the problems surfaced repeatedly in different guises.[16]

In Incidental Conflict: Walk and Wait

From time to time Jesus faced conflict from those who were the "extras" or the bystanders, whether in the form of misunderstanding from his family or of jealousy from his former neighbors.

Perhaps the best example of how he faced incidental conflicts is recorded by Luke. Jesus knew the time had come to finish his work on earth. He had resolutely set his face for Jerusalem, knowing the end that was ahead. When they came to a Samaritan village, he sent messengers on ahead to get things ready. But the people of the village did not welcome him, because they recognized him as a Jew heading for Jerusalem and the Samaritans at that time would have no dealings with Jews. Two of the disciples (interestingly, James and John, the "Sons of Thunder" who also wanted the top positions) asked him, "Lord, do you want us to call fire down from heaven to destroy them?" But Jesus turned and rebuked them, and he passed by the village, going to another instead (Lk 9:51-55).

In this case, Jesus' attitude was one of tolerance. This is not to say that he approved of the Samaritans' intolerance or that he put his stamp of approval on their somewhat distorted understanding of God (see, for example, his conversation with a Samaritan woman in John 4), but that he saw no need to pick a fight.

Unlike James and John, Jesus did not flare up in rage at the personal discourtesy. His emotions were disciplined by understanding and compassion. Once again, he used conflict to teach his disciples, and it is quite likely that he left a lasting impression on the Samaritans. Be that as it may, what Jesus' tactic suggests is that if we give time to every incidental conflict, we will wear ourselves out and miss our mission. There is therefore a time to "walk by" conflict, or perhaps to wait and deal with it later if necessary.

Meeting Conflict with Truth and Grace

When the angels heralded Jesus' birth, they announced and promised "glory to God in the highest, and on earth peace to men on whom his favor rests" (Lk 2:13). Shortly after he was born, Mary, his mother, was told, "This child is destined to cause the falling and rising of many in Israel" (Lk 2:34). Jesus the peacemaker himself said he had "not come to bring peace, but a sword" (Mt 10:34).

To understand this seeming paradox, we must remember that his ultimate goal was to establish the peace, the *shalom,* of his kingdom, a kingdom where justice and righteousness would prevail.

What did this kingdom peace mean when his kingdom faced conflict? Where it was possible, Jesus sought peace and resolution. Where it was tolerable, he allowed for sidestepping. Where it was inevitable, he did not avoid separation.

It has been said that some people are so full of grace they have no room for truth, and that others are so full of truth they have no room for grace; but Jesus was "full of grace *and* truth" (Jn 1:14). He faced the various dimensions of conflict he encountered with a wonderfully creative combination of grace and truth, deciding when to increase the pressure and to probe, and when not to.

As people were moved to decide about Jesus and his kingdom, the polarization increased. Some followed him and some fought him and some tried to ignore him. So the conflict deepened; and as it did, Jesus administered grace and truth in various degrees of strength and intensity, as he knew the situation called for.

With the devil, from the beginning there was truth but no grace, no possibility of reconciliation.

Those of the Pharisees who responded to his message Jesus welcomed and warmly commended, like the teacher of whom he said, "You are not far from the kingdom of God" (Mk 12:34). But from those Pharisees who became hard and bitterly hostile he eventually withdrew, as they resisted both grace and truth.

As his disciples committed themselves and grew, he gave them both more truth and more grace—not always in ways that they enjoyed, but in ways that enhanced their stature.

With the crowds and the bystanders, he gave only *enough* grace and only *enough* truth to test their response. If they were not responsive, he did not force the issue. If they were open, they came along with him.

Finally, in his judicial pronouncements of doom on Jerusalem and the temple, he indicated that there is a time when grace and truth can run out, both for people and for institutions.

Those of us who as leaders must deal with conflict in our families, our businesses and our relationships will look at Jesus' balance of grace and truth with a mixture of admiration and awe. We can learn from him, but can we ever be like him?

If the Spirit of Jesus truly lives in us, then we can seek and learn from him answers to such questions as these:

Is my inner security firm in Christ, so that my own inner conflicts are being resolved?

In situations of conflict, do I embody grace and truth, caring both for principles and for people?

Can I learn to discern the nature of specific types of conflict and choose the best strategy for dealing with them?

Do I, like Jesus, trust in my heavenly Father and in the spiritual weapons of prayer, the Word of God, and the Spirit which he promises?

Conflict is never comfortable, but God is more concerned for our character than our comfort. After we have passed through struggle, and bear as Jesus did the scars of conflict, we can affirm with J. Wallace Hamilton:

I am sure that most of us, looking back, will admit that whatever we have achieved in character we have achieved in conflict; it has come to us through powers hidden deep within us, so deep that we didn't know we had them, called into action by the challenge of opposition and frustration. The weights of life keep us going.[17]

271

14

THE LEADER AS
SUSTAINER

●

*Jesus made provision to
keep the movement going—he was
committed to the future.*

●

*"The art of leadership
dwells a good deal in the future."*
MAX DEPREE

"It is for your good that I am going away."
JESUS CHRIST

*"By the very nature of their role, incarnate leaders
must plan to make an exit."*
DAVID MCKENNA

A parable:

Once upon a time there was a dangerous seacoast where shipwrecks often occurred. On that coast was a little lifesaving hut, very crude and with only one boat. But there were a few devoted members who gave themselves day and night, at the risk of their own lives, to rescue those who had been shipwrecked.

Soon this little station became famous because so many were saved. Others wanted to become associated with this very famous enterprise and gave time and money and effort to buy new boats and to train more crews. After a while some members were unhappy with such a poorly equipped center, so they enlarged the building and put in better furniture. The lifesaving station became a popular gathering place and the members used it as a club.

As time went on, fewer members were interested in the dangerous lifesaving missions and instead hired crews to do the work. But lifesaving motifs were prominent in the decorations and there was even a liturgical lifeboat in the room where they had initiations!

About this time there was a large shipwreck. The hired crews brought in the cold half-drowned and dirty people—some with dark skins—and the club was messed up. The property committee had a shower house built outside, where victims could be cleaned up.

A split developed among the members at the next meeting. Most of them wanted to stop the lifesaving activities which were a hindrance to their social life. Some members insisted that lifesaving was their priority. The majority prevailed and the minority was told they could begin their own lifesaving station down the coast. They did. As the years went by the new station went through exactly the same changes as the old. It evolved into a club, and yet another lifesaving station was founded. History repeated itself, and on that coast today visitors find a number of exclusive clubs along the shore.

Shipwrecks are still frequent. But most of the victims drown.[1] Unfortunately, the parable is an all-too-vivid satire of the cycle by which missions become movements, movements evolve into machines, and machines end up as monuments.

It is a dramatic portrayal of the need for the transforming leader to be not only an initiator but also a finisher, and not only a finisher but also a sustainer.

We see this in Jesus' prayer towards the end of his career. Looking back in review, he said to his Father, "I have brought you glory on earth by completing the work you gave me to do" (Jn 17:4). Then he focused on his disciples, "those whom you gave me out of the world," as he described them (Jn 17:6). And looking forward, he prayed for them: for their protection from the evil one; that they might be set apart in a lifestyle that reflected Jesus; that they might be sent into the world to continue his work; that they might have a deep unity, reflecting the unity that existed between the Father and Jesus (Jn 17:9-23). Jesus realized that a transforming leader must provide not only a legacy but also a way of sustaining and renewing momentum.

History is full of instances where powerful leaders have failed to meet the challenge of the future.

The L-Principle

An American professor, Dr. Eugene Jennings, after a lifelong study of the problem of success and succession in world history since the time of the pharaohs, has formulated what he calls the L-principle (where L stands for leadership).[?]

Jennings believes the L-principle holds the key to the future leadership of the world's superpowers. His study of history has led him to conclude that only rarely is a powerful and charismatic leader succeeded by another of comparable stature. Oliver Cromwell was succeeded by his son Richard, whom history knows as "Tumble-down Dick." Anthony Eden lived in the shadow of Churchill. The article which I read about the L-principle did not say whether Jennings simply gives this as an observation or he speculates on the reasons the powerful leader is followed by lesser ones. One sensible reason would appear to be that few leaders of giant caliber appear on the stage of history. But a clue may also be found in the Indian proverb, "Nothing grows under the giant banyan tree." Powerful leaders often will not let the light filter through to nurture seedlings and will cut off challenging colleagues who may arise as rivals.

The Moses and Mao Malady

The influence of great leaders may also be cut short by their inability to adjust their leadership style to changing situations. Moses and Mao both illustrate this malady.

Moses was preeminently equipped to lead the children of Israel out of slavery in Egypt. He boldly faced up to and faced down the tyrannical

Pharaoh, withstood his ground against threats, drove a hard bargain, and under the providence of God led the Jewish people through a series of miraculous events to their freedom. Life in the wilderness of the Sinai Peninsula was far different. Moses found it difficult to delegate authority, though he eventually did so. The long-drawn-out journey required patience with a grumbling crowd that Moses found difficult. To be sure, the people were to blame for their whining. But Moses had his own problems, and though eventually he brought them to the brink of the Promised Land, God moved him aside, and it was his protégé, the younger Joshua, who led them into the next phase.

Mao Tse-tung, the leader of the Chinese communists, faced a similar situation. Mao's intrepid leadership brought 100,000 of his troops on the famous Long March from the south to the north of China, through mountains and marshes and bitter weather in one of history's memorable treks. Only 10,000 of the original army survived as a remnant to join with other communist forces. Mao's sheer brilliance and force of personality was crucial to the Long March. But as the communists consolidated power in the years ahead, that same force of personality turned into a cult of personality, and his egotism grew increasingly paranoid. The so-called Great Leap Forward (which actually took China back many years), the Cultural Revolution (which destroyed much of the nation's best human potential), and finally the scheming of Mao's cronies, the infamous Gang of Four, were due not only to the corruption of his ideology, but also to the malady of a leader who could not transform himself.

The Spurgeon Syndrome

The great English preacher Charles Spurgeon illustrates something of the same phenomenon. In the middle of the nineteenth century, Spurgeon began to preach in London as a lad of nineteen. Huge crowds came to hear this eloquent young man expound the message of God. Spurgeon was very successful in reaching the children and grandchildren of those who had immigrated to London early in the 1800s. But by 1880 urban change was making its impact. Spurgeon said at that time, in lectures to his students, "I used to believe that if a man preached the gospel anointed by the Spirit, people would flock to him. But I have changed my mind, for society has changed and hardened." He ministered on, and there was no significant change in membership numbers while he was the pastor of the great Metropolitan Tabernacle. But after his death in 1892 the number of baptisms began to drop and attendance at the huge sanctuary dwindled. Dr. Timothy McCoy has commented that Spurgeon was shrewd enough to see the problems that were coming, but neither versatile nor flexible enough to make the changes that the times demanded.[3]

Intercepting Entropy
Max DePree was the highly regarded chief executive officer of the Herman Miller furniture manufacturing company. A 1988 *Fortune* poll picked Herman Miller as one of the USA's ten most admired companies. In his book *Leadership Is an Art,* DePree tells how his team was in Boston to put on a "dog and pony show," a presentation of the value of their company to financial analysts. During the question-and-answer period an analyst asked DePree to name one of the most difficult things that he personally had to work on. The man was surprised when DePree answered, "The interception of entropy." DePree explains that from a management standpoint, everything has a tendency to deteriorate, and a leader must learn the signals of impending deterioration. DePree includes among the signs of entropy

a tendency toward superficiality;

a "dark tension" among key people;

no longer having time for celebration;

problem-makers outnumbering problem-solvers;

the pressures of day-to-day operations pushing aside the concern for vision and risk.[4]

DePree's striking phrase, "the interception of entropy," underlines the need for transforming leaders who are sustainers.

To maintain continuity with the best of the past and still change with the times: That is the challenge. And leaders have no choice except to meet the challenge. Change is constant and nothing remains the same. Strategies are needed, but the future is uncertain. Important events usually cannot be forecast. For example, in early 1990 I heard the former American secretary of state Henry Kissinger tell how he had advised the newly elected President Bush that political changes in Eastern Europe would not take place before the late 1990s!

Not only do circumstances change, but values decay. People age and get fatigued. Systems become rigid. Purposes get lost.

Movements and organizations also change. As John Gardner has said, new organizations are "like eight small boys chasing a chipmunk, lots of noise and confusion, lots of wasted energy, but great flexibility and motivation." As the organization matures, the challenge to the leader is to keep youthful zest without youthful disorder and to grow into mature order without taking on an aging rigidity.[5]

Leaders under stress themselves need renewal. Someone has said that the world is run by tired men and women. Not only do systems deteriorate, but there is also a spiritual entropy faced by leaders who want to serve God, but who get tired of fighting the world, the flesh and the devil.

Strategies for the Sustaining Leader

What can we learn from Jesus about letting go and leading into the future?

He showed his way.

It was not accidental that the early followers of Jesus were called people who belonged "to the Way" (see, for example, Acts 9:2). Jesus had defined reality by saying, "*I am the way* and the truth and the life" (Jn 14:6). In so doing, he had set the direction. His successors' mission was not primarily to implement a program but to pursue the reality of Jesus.

If Jesus had tried to ensure future directions by issuing a policy manual, a program guidebook or a set of rules (a procedure that has been tried, though not very successfully, by many groups using Jesus' name in subsequent centuries), it would soon have been out-of-date and codified into some sort of rigid and not very helpful principles. Instead, Jesus showed "the Way" as he embodied the reality of his kingdom.

How he did this has been the subject of this book. There was the sharing of himself by means of his daily life, his teachings, his healings—the kingdom reality focused in one solitary life. Then there was the revealing of his mission. After his closest followers identified him as "the Christ," he began to speak of his death, suffering and resurrection, of his redemptive mission, and of his return at the end of history. Then there was the commissioning of his followers to go to all nations, to preach, to make disciples, and to teach others what he had taught them.

The wisdom of Jesus' direction-setting is clear when we understand how often means triumph over ends and people lose sight of the goals and forget what they set out to do in the first place. Someone has said that the last act of a dying organization is to produce its new edition of the rule book.

No doubt Jesus' followers wished he had given them a detailed road map instead of just saying, "Go into all the world and preach the gospel." But Jesus knew the importance of giving direction rather than details. He set the guidelines: the truth of his teaching, the good news of the gospel, the power of the kingdom, the mission into the world. Then he allowed them creative space to operate. This he knew was the best way to interweave continuity and change.

He shaped his people.

It has been said that "without a successor there is no success." From the beginning Jesus had succession in mind. The preparation of future leaders was at the top of his agenda, for he knew that people empowered by God are the key to renewal.

Management consultant Robert Waterman has observed that "renewing companies treat everyone as a source of creative input. Their managers define the boundaries and their people find out the best way to do the job within those boundaries. . . . All the renewing companies are busy taking out layers of management . . . , leaner organizations set the stage for renewal."[6]

Long before modern managers, Jesus was busy preparing people for the future. He was not aiming to pick out a crown prince, but to create a successor generation.

We have seen how carefully he picked, named and developed his inner core and let them share the center of his life. When the time came for him to leave, he did not need to put in place a crash program of leadership development—the curriculum had been taught for three years in a living classroom.

But it is worth noting several distinctive ways in which he shaped his successors for the future. For one thing, he allowed them to fail, and then he reinstated them.

Warren Benniss, when considering how leaders deploy themselves, cites the "Wallenda Factor."[7] The "Great Wallenda" was the famous tightrope walker who fell to his death from a wire stretched between buildings in San Juan, Puerto Rico. Afterward, his wife recalled that in the weeks leading up to that fatal walk Wallenda had become obsessed with the possibility of falling, insisting on checking all the wires and attachments himself. The fear of falling itself became a factor in his fall. Future leaders, Benniss is saying, need to overcome the fear of failure by being allowed to go through failure without fear of losing their positions.

Jesus let his chosen people go through a process of trial-and-error many times. At the end, he gave them one more chance, and they failed. He asked his inner three, Peter, James and John, to stand by him in his hour of trial, and to stay awake with him in an agonizing period of midnight prayer before he was arrested. Instead, they went to sleep and later denied they knew him. His strategy was not to cast them off, but to confront them, reinstate them, and entrust them with an even bigger task.

The most dramatic example came after his death and resurrection. Jesus kindly, but firmly, asked Peter three times, "Do you love me?" Three times Peter had denied him; three times he was offered the chance for a comeback. Then Jesus said, "Feed my sheep" (Jn 21:17). Jesus was the living embodiment of Max DePree's principle: "Today's trust enables the future. We also enable the future by forgiving the mistakes we all make while growing up. We free each other to perform in the future through the medium of trust."[8]

It was not only through trusting them, but also in praying for them that Jesus shaped his successors. When he initially selected them, he prayed for wisdom, knowing the testings they would face. He told his would-be leader, "Simon, Simon, Satan has asked to sift you as wheat. But I have prayed for you, Simon, that your faith may not fail. And when you have turned back, strengthen your brothers" (Lk 22:31-32). When he looked forward to the work they would do long after he was gone, he previewed the future and as a priestly leader prayed to his Father for the safety, the security, the sanctity, and the unity of those God had given him (Jn 17:6).

It is a commonplace to say that Jesus selected his seventy, then his twelve, then his inner three, and *de facto* seemed to name Peter as his primary back-up, the first among equals. What we often fail to note, however, is that Jesus seemingly planned to allow for dissent among his successor/leaders. John Gardner has pointed out that effective leaders change the constellations of key players, shifting people into new responsibilities, to be assured of new blood and fresh ideas. The transforming leader also provides an environment that is open and hospitable for what Gardner calls "the pathfinders," those who will be the "seed beds of new solutions."[9]

After one of the original twelve, Judas, had betrayed Jesus and then committed suicide, the other eleven cast lots to pick his successor. They chose a man well known to them, who had been around for many years and who met the qualifications of an apostle. But the Lord had another "apostle extraordinary" in mind to come into major leadership: a brilliant, difficult, somewhat irascible rabbi named Saul of Tarsus. Highly trained, strongly opinionated, Saul was a sworn enemy of Jesus and the people of "the Way." He was a determined opponent of Jesus and his followers. One day, at high noon, the risen Jesus appeared to Saul in a vision while Saul was on the way to Damascus to arrest the disciples of Jesus. In a blinding light he revealed himself stunningly, so that Saul asked the question, "Who are you, Lord?" and learned that the Lord was Jesus. Jesus told him that he was a chosen vessel to witness to kings and to the world (Acts 2:15-18). Paul was destined to take his place along with Peter among the leaders of the movement. Later he referred to himself as one chosen late, "abnormally born" he put it (1 Cor 15:8), not one who had known Jesus in his earthly life as the other apostles had.

Paul was singled out by the Lord to take the gospel crossculturally to Gentiles. As a Jew of the Diaspora, who had been born and lived outside the Jewish homeland, Paul was ideally equipped for this task. With his sharp intellect and the Spirit's guidance, he cut through cultural side issues to the transcultural truth of God's new reality. So when the other leaders wanted to rule that Gentiles must, in effect, become Jews by circumcision to be accepted as followers of Christ (and even Peter fudged on this issue), it was Paul who upheld the truth of God's acceptance by grace and not by race and who, after extended hard debate, won the day (Gal 2:11-21). Christianity could never have become the missionary movement and the world faith it has been if it had not been for this one "abnormally born," the dissenter, the pathfinder whom Jesus chose to be the "seed bed of a new solution."

As a sustaining leader, Jesus showed the direction and shaped his people. Both are essential. Without direction the best people can wander aimlessly. Without prepared people, direction will not be pursued. This, too, we learn from Jesus.

He symbolized his values

Effective leaders must know the importance of symbolizing their cause. When Jimmy Carter became president of the United States, he deliberately set his style to contrast with Richard Nixon's so-called imperial presidency. Rather than riding in a limousine, Carter walked to his own inaugural ceremonies and often carried his own briefcase. When Ronald Reagan came to power, he in turn tried to reestablish the image of a strong presidency, even to the point of being photographed flexing his muscles as he split wood with his shirt off!

Business leaders, too, have their own symbols of power. "Rented limousines are less prestigious than ones that are owned," writes Michael Korda; "a Rolls Royce carries more prestige than Cadillacs and nothing equals a Mercedes 600, with the chrome painted black and the rear windows tinted to make the occupant invisible."[10]

Effective leaders use symbols which show they are in command. So it is no surprise to find that in Jesus' final week he used far more symbolism than in all the previous three years. What is surprising is the kind of symbolism that Jesus used.

Take for example his so-called triumphal entry into Jerusalem recorded in Mark 11. As he approached Jerusalem, Jesus sent two of his disciples to commandeer a colt which had never been ridden. The disciples threw their cloaks over the colt, and Jesus sat on it as he went into the city. Many people spread their cloaks on the road in front of him, others spread branches, and those going ahead shouted, "Hosanna! Blessed is he who comes in the name of the Lord!" (Mk 11:9). When Jesus entered Jerusalem, he went to the temple and "looked around at everything" (Mk 11:11), then went out to Bethany to sleep. The next day Jesus was hungry, and seeing in the distance a fig tree in leaf, he went out to find if it had any fruit. When he reached it, he found nothing but leaves, because it was not the season for figs. Then he said to the tree, "May no one ever eat fruit from you again" (Mk 11:14). The next day the tree had withered from the roots (Mk 11:20).

On reaching Jerusalem, "Jesus entered the temple area and began driving out those who were buying and selling," overturning the tables of the money-changers and not allowing anyone to carry merchandise through the temple courts (Mk 11:15-16). He accused them of turning God's "house of prayer" into a "den of robbers" (Mk 11:17). And later he summed up this series of incidents by reminding his disciples of the need for genuine prayer, based on faith in God and forgiveness toward others (Mk 11:22-25).

Here, then, are three examples of a leader's need to symbolize his or her cause. Each is significant and each strange. After many months of making people be quiet about him, and seeking privacy, Jesus went public and seemingly provoked an outcry of acclaim. And yet his "publicity" was deliberately staged and timed to show the nature of his leadership. It was a saving leadership, one exercised in meekness and service, as demonstrated by his riding on a colt, the "march of the meek one"—a new kind of king. Yet at the same time it was a strong leadership. The withering of the fig tree seems out of character, the only miracle of destruction that Jesus enacted. But he was not showing his disciples how to destroy fig trees. He was driving home the need to live in such a way that they would not be destroyed as the fig tree was withered. The fig tree with leaves but no fruit was like the temple with money-making ritual but no reality of faith. Without that reality both the temple and the nation would be judged.

Jesus' strange symbols were designed to reveal clearly the essentials of true leadership and true faith. Genuine faith results not in empty ceremony but in vital prayer and renewed relationships. Jesus' symbolic acts were chosen to reveal this truth in startling, unexpected ways. Mere statement could not have set forth the contrast so vividly symbolized, of the servant king on the donkey, of the strong Lord who can either empower or destroy.

The images Jesus chose heightened reality. In this, his symbolism was different from that which is often used in our image-conscious age, where symbols frequently obscure reality. It should make us ask: Do we as leaders know how to use publicity and symbolism in a way which serves the mission rather than undermining it? Does the mission control the media, or vice versa? In today's media information era, this is a crucial question.

Other symbols also crowd into Jesus' final days and hours. A piece of bread is broken and a cup of wine is poured out at the Last Supper, symbols of a broken body and poured out blood. At the same meal Jesus rises from the table, strips himself of his outer clothes, girds himself with a towel and washes the feet of his startled disciples. Here is an act of courtesy usually carried out by a slave and one which none of his status-conscious disciples thinks of doing. When it is Peter's turn, he protests, "You shall never wash my feet," and Jesus tells him that unless he washes them he will have no fellowship with Peter (Jn 13:2-8). Here is a picture not only of humility, but also of the cleansing Jesus' death will bring. "Do you understand what I have done for you?" he asks them. "You call me 'Teacher' and 'Lord,' and rightly so, for that is what I am. Now that I, your Lord and Teacher, have washed your feet, you also should wash one another's feet. I have set you an example that you should do as I have done for you" (Jn 13:12-15).

Each symbolic act is chosen to set forth the leader's mission statement: "The Son of Man did not come to be served, but to serve, and to give his life as a ransom for many" (Mk 10:45).

Above all, the cross itself was Jesus' chosen and freely accepted symbol. As John Stott has pointed out, every religion has its visual symbol—the lotus flower of Buddhism, the crescent of Islam, the Jewish star of David. And there were many possibilities for a "universally acceptable Christian emblem":

> Christians might have chosen the crib or manger in which the baby Jesus was laid, or the carpenter's bench at which he worked as a young man in Nazareth, dignifying manual labor, or the boat from which he

taught the crowds in Galilee, or the apron he wore when washing the apostles' feet, which would have spoken of his spirit of humble service. Other possible choices might have been the stone which was rolled away from his tomb, or the dove which was a symbol of the Holy Spirit. Instead, the chosen symbol came to be a simple cross. . . . [Christians] wished to commemorate as central to their understanding of Jesus neither his birth nor his youth, neither his teaching nor his service, neither his resurrection nor his reign, nor his gift of the Spirit, but his death, his crucifixion.[11]

If Jesus' symbols spoke of saving, sacrificial love, then his last symbolic act left that same legacy. After his resurrection Jesus went in to a locked room where the disciples were gathered in fear. He wished them peace, showed them his hands and his side with the marks of the cross, and said to them, 'As the Father has sent me, I am sending you.' With that he breathed on them and said, 'Receive the Holy Spirit' (Jn 20:21-22). His breathing was a prophetic parable, symbolizing that his Spirit would be poured out on them, and that they in turn, empowered by his Spirit, were to live out lives of sacrificial love. One way in which we pass on our values from generation to generation is tribal tales. Every family has them. Every organization tells them. They help to weave continuity between our core values and the changes which inevitably come. Jesus' symbolic actions were the stuff of tribal tales. When rivalries arose among the early followers of Jesus, they must have told again the story of Jesus' picking up a little child and saying, "Whoever humbles himself like this child is the greatest in the kingdom of heaven" (Mt 18:4). When they argued over whether preaching the gospel or helping the poor had priority, someone must have brought up the story of the woman who brought a jar of very expensive perfume and poured it on Jesus. When she was criticized Jesus said, "Leave her alone. . . . She has done a beautiful thing to me. The poor you will always have with you, and you can help them any time you want. But you will not always have me. . . . She poured perfume on my body beforehand to prepare for my burial" (Mk 14:6-8).

A true leader's words will express reality. Jesus shows us that symbolic action helps to make the words come alive and the impressions be lasting.

He Set His Stage

The time came for Jesus to remove himself from the scene. As the symbols he used show, he had the power and the security to let go. But he also had the wisdom and trust to prepare his followers to carry on.

Recently I have had the pleasure of getting to know Kenneth Blanchard, the author of *Leadership and the One Minute Manager*.[12] Blanchard has developed and teaches what he calls "situational leadership." Leaders, he believes, have to be flexible and to change their style according to the situations and people they work with. "Enthusiastic beginners," for example, need directions about how to get started in a new activity. After a while they become "disillusioned learners," finding the task more difficult than they thought it would be. Then the leader needs to be a coach, offering both direction and support. Later, learners become "reluctant performers," knowing what they are supposed to do but not feeling very confident about their ability. Then the leader's task is to encourage them to act on what they know. Finally, Blanchard believes, every person has the potential to become a "peak performer," someone to whom a task can be delegated and who can move with competence and commitment.

Jesus used a kind of "situational leadership." At first he directed his disciples to listen and watch what he did. Then he put them in some situations—like the storm on the sea—where they were clearly beyond themselves. At that point he became a coach, offering continued direction and support. Later he sent them out to teach, preach and heal as his representatives. They went out somewhat timidly, but came back with great joy when they saw powerful results. Finally, after months of development—and of success and failure—he prepared to go away and to delegate the ongoing task to them.

In order to get them ready for full responsibility, we see him "setting the stage." He has an extended conversation with them over a last supper in a private room (see Jn 13—16). Over and over, in many different ways, he repeats his message: "I will be with you only a little longer," "Where I am going, you cannot follow now," "I am going to . . . prepare a place for you" (Jn 13:33, 36; 14:2).

His words fill them with consternation. "Why can't I follow you?" asks

Peter (Jn 13:37). "We don't understand what he is saying," say others (Jn 16:18).

But Jesus knows what he is doing. His worldwide mission could not be carried out if he did not leave them.

A striking approach to preparing future leadership comes from Japan. The president of Misawa Homes, the largest home builder in Japan, "dies" at least once every decade in order to arrest the momentum of the past. He sends to his company a memo that announces "The Death of Your President." It is his way of forcing the company to rethink out-of-date assumptions. If the employees resist, he declares, "That was the way things were done under Mr. Misawa. He is now dead. Now, how shall we proceed?"[13]

Jesus knows that for his disciples to be motivated and committed to carry on, they will need a strong dose of realism and of hope.

In his final dialog he matches reality with promise. They need to know four realities. First, he is going away (Jn 14:28). Second, the "prince of this world"—that is, the devil—is coming (Jn 14:30). Not only that, but the "world" will hate them just as it hated Jesus (Jn 15:18ff). Finally, some of them will be not only persecuted but killed by religious leaders (Jn 16:2).

Does that sound like a bleak kind of motivation? John Gardner reminds us that "at the heart of sustained morale and motivation lie two ingredients that appear somewhat contradictory: On the one hand, positive attitudes toward the future . . . and on the other hand, recognition that life is not easy and that nothing is ever finally safe."[14] We need to believe in the future but not to think that life is easy.

Jesus' masterly understanding of motivation joined hard realities with strong promises. Was he going away? Yes, but he was going to prepare a place for them (Jn 14:2). Was he leaving them? Yes, but he would continue to be present with them through the Holy Spirit, "another Counselor" who would be with them forever (Jn 14:16). Would the world hate them? Yes, but he promised to answer their prayers: "You may ask me for anything in my name, and I will do it" (Jn 14:14). Might they be persecuted and killed? Again the answer was yes, but the promise was peace: "I have told you these things, so that in me you may have peace. In this world you will have trouble. But take heart! I have overcome the world" (Jn 16:33).

This setting of the stage over his final meal was a strong reminder of what Jesus had done a few days earlier. When the disciples were overwhelmed with the beauty of the temple buildings, Jesus had said quite bluntly, "Do you see all these great buildings? Not one stone here will be left on another; every one will be thrown down" (Mk 13:2). Then he gave them a forecast of the future which was a mixture of grim realism and powerful optimism. History, he told them, would be unstable. There would be wars and persecutions, earthquakes and turbulence. They would be hated and hunted down. False "Christs" would appear. But the Holy Spirit would strengthen them. Those who stood firm would be saved. The gospel would be preached in all the world. The days of hardship would be cut short, the Son of Man would come with great power and glory and his chosen ones would be with him for ever (Mk 13:5-27). Once again reality was matched with hope. Jesus motivated by holding together the most tough-minded realism and the most positive outlook on the future.

Here was a leader who had finished his task. He had set the stage. He had prepared his people. He had made them "touch the earth" and come into firsthand contact with reality—a mark of all renewing leaders. Yet, he had also opened the doors and the windows and let hope come in. His vision had become theirs. They saw what he saw. They hoped for what he hoped for.

Jesus' stage-setting is a challenge to me, and it should be to every senior leader: Am I prepared to let go? Have I found the security that enables me to prepare others and turn the task over to them? Or do I have an inner drive to grasp the power, the salary, the recognition, the perks that go with leadership, so that I pretend to myself and others that I am indispensable and no one could possibly take my place? Can I face the reality of decreasing strength and changing times? Can I trust God to raise up others who will carry on the work, not only as I have, but perhaps much more effectively? If Jesus, the absolutely unique Son of God, the peerless leader, could leave his work to men and women he knew were imperfect and had often failed, can I not do the same?

There is an old story about Jesus returning to heaven. One of the angels welcoming him back asked, "Master, what plans have you made to carry on the work that you began?" Jesus answered, "I have chosen twelve and left them to carry on." Puzzled, because he knew how frail humans are, the angel ventured to ask again, "But Master, what if they fail? What is your plan then?" And Jesus gave a smile and a nod and said, "I have no other plans. They will not fail."

And with that confidence Jesus set the stage; and then he did the one more thing that was necessary.

He Sent His Spirit

Many years ago, in a hotel in California, I was suddenly awakened early in the morning by a shaking. The whole room was trembling and felt as if a train were passing through the floor below. Finally my befuddled mind realized I was experiencing a major earthquake. The hotel was quickly evacuated, and I stood outside, looking up at the eleventh floor where my room was.

"How in the world do they build these high-rise buildings to withstand such a shaking?" I asked a man nearby. His reply gave me a memorable insight into life itself.

"Two things are necessary," he told me. "First, they have to go way down with the foundations, until they are actually based on bedrock. And then they have to design the buildings with give-and-take in the joints, so that the building can sway and not crack. In fact, the top of this hotel was probably swaying several feet at the height of that earthquake!"

Foundations and flexibility. Both are necessary not only to high-rise buildings, but also to us as persons and to our communities. Without foundations there is no stability. But without prestressed give-and-take, an absolutely rigid building would crack and fall apart, even with the best foundations.

That prestressed high-rise building has become for me a parable of the need for continuity and change. "The only stability possible is stability in motion," writes John Gardner.[15] For the leader of a movement, that poses a very interesting challenge: How does one provide for "stability in motion" in an unknown future?

Suppose that you are the leader of a little colony in some new world. You

289

have established a beachhead, started a new way of life, picked and trained the colonists, devised plans to explore and develop the uncharted wilderness. Now it is time for you to return to the home country and to turn the little colony over to those who would remain. You have sought to teach and embody the values of the homeland. New challenges and new dangers will come after you have gone. These colonists will have children and grandchildren, they will die and other generations will come. How do you ensure "stability in motion"?

Jesus must surely have mused on this. What were his options? Should he leave behind a detailed plan? Produce an expanded and revised book of rules? Generate a detailed set of orders to cover every possible situation, as many of the religious leaders had done in his day? Should he write his autobiography as a last inspiration? Or put his philosophy into a manuscript to be studied by coming generations? Some of these options might have been attractive.

But Jesus had another and much greater possibility. He could go back to first principles. What was his mission? It was to remove obstacles so people might become all that his Father had created them to be. And what did his Father want? To create a race of creatures like himself. To populate the world with people in whom his own image was reproduced. Jesus' kingdom strategy was a people strategy, a radical strategy of transforming people so that he and his kingdom would live in them. So his plan for continuity was not something that would prod their memories from the outside, but something that would penetrate them powerfully from inside. It was a matter not of a rule book or a philosophy or a plan, but of a spirit. His legacy to his people would be the "new spirit."

Dr. Paul Brand, one of the world's leading hand surgeons, says that the genetic code contained in DNA (the main constituent of the chromosomes in each cell of our body) gives us some insight into the new spirit or "new birth" by which Jesus transforms people.[16] The order in which the four bases of DNA are arranged makes each of us unique and gives us our physical identity. If we knew a person's full genetic code, in theory that individual could be rebuilt from the information contained in a single cell!

Now, suggests Dr. Brand, the designer who gave us our unique physical

290

identity has another design: to give us a spiritual identity as well, to make us a part of his spiritual body, the body of Christ. If this world is to be the kind of place God wanted it to be—a place of authentic love and concern in relation with God and others—he had to begin a new spiritual creation. So the same God who called matter into existence out of nothing took a young woman named Mary and put within her, not the seed of her husband, but the seed of God's own Spirit.

The child that was born to her had, so to speak, a new spiritual DNA. Fully human, he was also fully divine. Neither sin nor death had a grip on him.

Because of this new spiritual DNA code, Jesus was and is unique. For people to be transformed into his likeness, they needed to be "born again," to receive a spiritual exchange of DNA—a replacement for their own sinful egocentric self. It would take the death of an old identity and the resurrection of a new one.

So as Jesus prepared to leave his "colonists" he knew very clearly what his option was. The old human identity (*flesh* is a New Testament word used to describe it) had to die—and would die with Jesus on the cross. His death was to be more than physical death. He died also a spiritual death, the end result of the human race's old sinful DNA. He would become sin by taking human sin on the cross. He would rise to release a new life available to those who would say: "God, I want to die to the old life and live to a new life." Those who turned to God like children would know what it means to be "born again," not of the physical seed that gives the physical identity or DNA, but by the Word and Spirit of God himself.

Jesus would leave behind not simply persons who had adopted a new code of ethics or who had joined an institution. He would leave behind people who had become part of a new life. They would have not just a new philosophy, but a new spirit living within them, creating a new life which would go on deepening and extending forever.

True, this new life would not come without death. It required a painful separation and an agonizing death for Jesus. There would be painful times for his people, and even martyrdom for some of them. But grief would turn to joy, like that of a woman going through the pain of childbirth to the joy

291

of a new life. The cross would lead to resurrection. The suffering would produce glory. The death would be the seed of a new life.

On the eve of his death, Jesus sat with his closest people, sharing a final meal and telling them that he would leave. "Because I have said these things, you are filled with grief," he told them. "But I tell you the truth: It is for your good that I am going away. Unless I go away, the Counselor will not come to you; but if I go, I will send him to you" (Jn 16:6-7). The Counselor, of course, refers to the Holy Spirit. Maybe an even more apt description of this Spirit is that he would be "another Strengthener." For that, perhaps, is the root meaning of the Greek term *paraclete* which Jesus used to describe the Spirit. This "Strengthener" would be another person like Jesus, not just an abstract force or inspiration. This Strengthener whom the Father and Jesus would send had been the third person of the three-personal God from the beginning. Jesus promised that this Strengthener who had been *with* the disciples invisibly throughout Jesus' days would be *in* them in the future (Jn 14:17). He would teach them all things. He would remind them of what Jesus had said. He would work with them as they testified to others about Jesus. He would convict the world of sin and guilt and the need of Christ's transforming power. He would guide the followers of Jesus into all the truth that they would need to know. He would bring glory to Christ (Jn 14:26; 15:26; 16:8-11, 13-14).

At that point, what Jesus was saying seemed to be so many words, a puzzling mystery to his followers.

But after he had died and risen Jesus came back and met them again in that same upper room where they had eaten their last meal together. His followers had gathered there behind locked doors, for fear of those who had crucified Jesus. Jesus came and stood among them, wished them peace, and showed them the marks of his crucifixion in his hands and side. He said again, "Peace be with you! As the Father has sent me, I am sending you." And with that he breathed on them and said, "Receive the Holy Spirit. If you forgive anyone his sins, they are forgiven; if you do not forgive them, they are not forgiven" (Jn 20:19-23).

His breathing was his last prophetic symbol. It was his promise that after he had left, his Spirit would come to live in them. His Spirit would be his successor. And they in turn, empowered by his Spirit, would not stay hidden in a locked room, nor would they be absorbed in building monuments to the past. Rather, through the Spirit, they would be enabled to live lives of powerful, sacrificial love, to witness to the reality of Jesus, and to weave a "web of witness" which would begin in Jerusalem and reach out into a worldwide network that would carry the goodness of Jesus to the ends of the earth.

Would it work? Time would tell. But what would work better? In the early centuries of the church, when a convert from paganism to Christ was asked what new thing Jesus had brought, he responded: "Why, he brought us himself." And it is himself, his never-ending life through his Spirit, which has been and always will be the secret of his sustaining power.

EPILOG

The historian Arnold Toynbee concluded his *A Study of History* with a discussion of the types of "saviors" who have appeared on the stage of history. Some saviors have tried to restore past glories, while others have tried to pull us forward into future possibilities. There have been political and military leaders—saviors "with a sword"—and philosophers seeking to save by their ideas. Toynbee's final assessment was that all saviors had fallen out of the race; none had been able to halt the disintegration of people and civilizations. All had failed the final ordeal of death—all, that is, except one. Toynbee concludes:

> And now, as we stand and gaze with our eyes fixed upon the farther shore, a single figure rises from the flood and straightway fills the whole horizon. There is the Savior; "and the pleasure of the Lord shall prosper in his hands; he shall see of the travail of his soul and shall be satisfied."[1]

As we have thought about the meaning of Jesus' leadership for our own lives, our reactions may have ranged from admiration (What a leader!), to naive idealism (I'll try to lead like Jesus), to despair (How can I ever be like him?). In the end, who can feel adequate to understand, let alone to emulate, the leadership of Jesus? How much we need the assurance that he is not only a leader to follow, but also a Savior to forgive and a Sovereign to empower! And that just as he once said, "Follow me, and I will make you fishers of men" (Mk 1:17), so he can say again, "Follow me, and I will make you my servant-leaders."

Questions of a Young Leader

I can imagine a young man or woman who aspires to leadership being full of questions to Jesus about himself or herself, about the world and the church, full of hopes and fears. Can we guess what Jesus might answer?

A question of motivation

Dear Lord,

I see a lot of leaders who seem to be acting out of insecurity or a need to control. I want to lead, but how can I be secure enough to be sure my motivation is right?

Uncertain

Dear Uncertain,

"Come to me, all you who are weary and burdened, and I will give you rest. Take my yoke upon you and learn from me, for I am gentle and humble in heart, and you will find rest for your souls" (Mt 11:28-29).

Jesus, the Son

A question of mission

Dear Lord,

So far as I can see, most organizations, including the church, are concerned mainly with maintaining their traditions and programs. Honestly, I'm a little disillusioned about the possibility of changing anything. How shall I start?

Disillusioned

Dear Disillusioned,

"This is how you should pray: 'Our Father in heaven, hallowed be your name, your kingdom come, your will be done on earth as it is in heaven' " (Mt 6:9-10).

Jesus, the Strategist

A question of values
Dear Lord,

Aren't we supposed to be concerned about the poor and the hungry and the people who have lost their way? Then why does the church put so much emphasis on budgets and buildings? Haven't we been caught up in a lot of empire-building? And how do I deal with ambition in my own life?

Confused

Dear Confused,

"The pagans run after all these things, and your heavenly Father knows that you need them. But seek first his kingdom and his righteousness, and all these things will be given to you as well" (Mt 6:32-33).

Jesus, the Kingdom-Seeker

A question of vision
Dear Lord,

Someone told me a leader is supposed to be a visionary. Well, I guess that leaves me out. Lots of times I can't even see what I'm doing today clearly. We don't need any more blind leaders of the blind. Any advice?

Clouded

Dear Clouded,

"Blessed are the pure in heart, for they will see God" (Mt 5:8).

Jesus, the Seer

A question of character
Dear Lord,

I have dreamed of changing the world. But I've seen so many so-called leaders who have been shown to be bankrupt. On the outside they look good, but something sucks the character from their insides. How can I keep from letting that happen to me?

Genuinely Concerned

Dear Genuinely Concerned,

"I am the vine; you are the branches. If a man remains in me and I in him, he will bear much fruit; apart from me you can do nothing. If anyone does not remain in me, he is like a branch that is thrown away and withers" (Jn 15:5-6).

Jesus, the Strong One

297

A question of power

Dear Lord,

I have been asked to head up a project that could do a lot of good, and I'd have some staff and a good-sized budget. But they say power corrupts and absolute power corrupts absolutely. If this is true, wouldn't it be better for me to turn down this responsibility?

Perplexed

Dear Perplexed,

"You know that those who are regarded as rulers of the Gentiles lord it over them, and their high officials exercise authority over them. Not so with you. Instead, whoever wants to become great among you must be your servant, and whoever wants to be first must be slave of all. For even the Son of Man did not come to be served, but to serve, and to give his life as a ransom for many" (Mk 10:42-45).

Jesus, the Servant

A question of priorities

Dear Lord,

I'm frustrated because there is never enough time. If I keep up with the deadlines on my work, I don't focus on people. If I take time for people, I get behind. Either way, I feel guilty. Any advice?

Stressed Out

Dear Stressed Out,

"Do you truly love me? . . . Take care of my sheep" (Jn 21:16).

Jesus, the Shepherd-Maker

A question of speech

Dear Lord,

I get uneasy with the idea of speaking about you in public. I have been so turned off by the way some preachers and politicians use the media to manipulate the facts, not to communicate. Can you help me?

Inhibited

Dear Inhibited,

"Simply let your 'Yes' be 'Yes,' and your 'No,' 'No' " (Mt 5:37).

Jesus

Dear Lord,

May I ask one more follow-up question? How do I know the difference?

Still Puzzled

Dear Still Puzzled,

"If you hold to my teaching, you are really my disciples. Then you will know the truth, and the truth will set you free" (Jn 8:31-32).

Jesus, the Spokesperson

A question of conflict

Dear Lord,

I am trying to do your work the best I can, but I've been teamed up with someone who is a constitutional pessimist. He thinks everything could have been done differently or better. We have talked, but nothing changes. Should I accept a call to go somewhere else?

Fed Up

Dear Fed Up,

"If your brother sins, rebuke him, and if he repents, forgive him. If he sins against you seven times in a day, and seven times comes back to you and says, 'I repent,' forgive him" (Lk 17:3-4).

Jesus, the Struggler

A question of endurance

Dear Lord,

You've really inspired me. I want to be like you. I want to follow you to the ends of the earth. The problem is me, not you. Sometimes my spirit burns high and sometimes it's so low. I don't want to make promises I can't fulfill.

Fearful

Dear Fearful,

"All authority in heaven and on earth has been given to me. Therefore go and make disciples of all nations. . . . And surely I am with you always, to the very end of the age" (Mt 28:18, 20).

Jesus, the Sustainer

The Lion and the Lamb

Years after he first met Jesus, John was in lonely exile on the island of Patmos. He saw a vision in which a door was standing open into heaven itself. In God's right hand was a scroll that was sealed and seemed to speak of unfulfilled destinies. An angel asked, "Who is worthy to break the seals and open the scroll?" (Rev 5:2). When no one was found worthy John wept, until another voice said, "Do not weep! See, the Lion of the tribe of Judah, the Root of David, has triumphed. He is able to open the scroll" (Rev 5:5).

John looked up, expecting to see this great triumphant figure, and instead saw "a Lamb, looking as if it had been slain" (Rev 5:6). When the Lamb took the scroll, the citizens of heaven sang:

You are worthy to take the scroll
    and to open its seals
because you were slain,
    and with your blood you purchased men for God
from every tribe and language and people
    and nation.
You have made them to be a kingdom and priests
    to serve our God,
and they will reign on the earth. (Rev 5:9-10)

In his vision, John saw the essence of the leadership of Jesus. Human destiny can be fulfilled, and our most powerful enemies overcome, only by the power of God's rule. And that power is made available through the Lion who acts as a Lamb, and through leaders who behave like servants.

One day, a day that only God knows, his rule will be complete and his process of leadership development will be finished. Then the leadership of Jesus will be reproduced in every segment of the human race, in every aspect of human life, to the fullest extent that is possible in a fallen world. Then God will bring his drama to its final act. The Lion/Lamb will reappear. The final curtain will go down and up again. The cast of all the centuries will appear on the stage, and cosmic applause will go up from all creation. The leaders of all nations will acknowledge the power and glory of God and of his appointed leader, Jesus Christ. Then the leader for all times and all peoples will have finished his task, and he will reign forever.

NOTES

1 Leadership: Why Now?

[1]Arthur Levine, *When Dreams and Heroes Died* (San Francisco/London: Jossey Bass Publishers, 1981), p. 26.

[2]Ibid.

[3]John R. Mott, *The Future Leadership of the Church* (London: Hodder & Stoughton, 1909).

[4]James McGregor Burns, *Leadership* (New York: Harper & Row, 1978).

[5]Bernard M. Bass, *Leadership and Performance Beyond Exectations* (New York: The Free Press, 1985), chs. 1 and 2.

[6]John W. Gardner, *Leadership Development, Leadership Papers 17* (Washington, DC: Leadership Studies Programs, Independent Sector, 1987), p. 24.

[7]Ibid., pp. 5ff.

[8]Warren Benniss and Burt Nanus, *Leaders: The Strategies for Taking Charge* (New York: Harper & Row, 1986).

[9]Ibid., p. 44

2 Jesus and Leadership

[1]*The Willowbank Report* (Wheaton, IL: Lausanne Committee for World Evangelization, 1978), pp. 17-18.

[2]Charles Colson, *Kingdoms in Conflict* (Grand Rapids, MI: Zondervan; London: Hodder & Stoughton, 1987), p. 128.

3 The Leader as Son

[1]G. W. Barker, W. L. Lane, J. Ramsey Michaels, *The New Testament Speaks* (New York: Harper & Row, 1969), p. 101.

[2]G. B. Caird, quoted in Norman Anderson, *The Teaching of Jesus* (Downers Grove, IL: InterVarsity Press; London: Hodder & Stoughton, 1983), p. 158.

[3]J. Ramsey Michaels, *Servant and Son: Jesus in Parable and Gospel* (Atlanta, GA: John Knox Press, 1981), ch. 2.

[4]Paul Tournier, *Creative Suffering* (London: SCM Press, 1982).

[5]Richard Foster, *Money, Sex and Power* (San Francisco: Harper & Row; London: Hodder & Stoughton, 1985), pp. 216-17.

[6]Henri Nouwen, *The Way of the Heart* (New York: Seabury Press, 1981), p. 25.

[7]Malcolm Muggeridge, *Christ and the Media* (Grand Rapids, MI: Wm B. Eerdmans, 1977).

4 The Leader as Strategist

[1]Paul Johnson, *Modern Times* (New York: Harper & Row, 1983), pp. 128ff.

[2]Shakespeare, *Macbeth*, act 5, sc. 5, lines 25ff.

[3]David Wenham, *The Parables of Jesus* (Downers Grove, IL: InterVarsity Press; London: Hodder & Stoughton, 1989), pp. 22-23.

[4]Ibid., p. 23.

[5]Alexander Solzhenitsyn, *A World Split Apart* (New York: Harper & Row, 1978).

[6]Quoted in Robert Slocum, *Ordinary Christians in a High-Tech World* (Waco, TX: Word Books, 1986), p. 56.

[7]Wenham, *The Parables of Jesus,* pp. 45-46.

[8]Richard C. Halverson, *How I Changed My Thinking about the Church* (Grand Rapids, MI: Zondervan, 1972), p. 104.

[9]Robert Bellah, Richard Madsen, William M. Sullivan, Ann Swidler, Steven M. Tipton, *Habits of the Heart: Middle America Observed* (Berkeley: Univ. of California Press, 1985; London: Century Hutchinson, 1988).

[10]Charles Colson, *Kingdoms in Conflict* (Grand Rapids, MI: Zondervan; London: Hodder & Stoughton, 1987), p. 85.

[11]Wenham, *The Parables of Jesus,* p. 25.

[12]See, e.g., Jacques Ellul, *The Technological Society* (New York: Alfred A. Knopf, 1970); *Money and Power* (Downers Grove, IL: InterVarsity Press, 1984).

5 The Leader as Seeker

[1]Quoted in Basil Matthews, *John R. Mott, World Citizen* (London: World Christian Movement Press, 1934), pp. 49-50.

[2]J. Oswald Sanders, *Problems of Christian Discipleship* (London: The China Inland Mission, n.d.), p. 86.

[3]Ibid., p. 88.

[4]Arnold A. Dallimore, *George Whitefield* (Edinburgh: Banner of Truth, 1979), p. 31.

[5]Ibid.

[6]Ibid., pp. 263-64.

[7]Ibid., p. 32, quoting J. R. Green, *A Short History of the English People* (New York: Harper, 1899), pp. 736-37.

[8]Quoted in J. Oswald Sanders, *Spiritual Leadership* (Chicago, IL: Moody Press, 1980), p. 32.

[9]Charles Blair, *The Man Who Could Do No Wrong* (Wheaton, IL: Tyndale House, 1984), pp. 210, 221.

6 The Leader as Seer
[1]Warren Benniss and Burt Nanus, *Leaders: The Strategies for Taking Charge* (New York: Harper & Row, 1986), p. 32.

[2]Ibid., p. 102.

[3]Ibid., p. 88.

[4]Ibid., p. 96.

[5]Charles Swindoll, *Quest for Character* (Portland, OR: Multnomah Press, 1987), p. 98.

[6]J. Ramsey Michaels, *Servant and Son: Jesus in Parable and Gospel* (Atlanta, GA: John Knox Press, 1981).

[7]Ibid., p. xii.

[8]Ibid., p. 102.

[9]Terry Fullam, *Leadership,* Winter, 1984, p. 13.

[10]Ruth A. Tucker and Walter L. Liefeld, eds., *Daughters of the Church: Women and Ministry from New Testament Times to the Present* (Grand Rapids, MI: Zondervan, 1987), p. 320.

[11]Douglas Hyde, *Dedication and Leadership* (Notre Dame, IN: University of Notre Dame Press, 1966), p. 31.

[12]Thomas Sowell, *A Conflict of Visions* (New York: William Morrow & Co., 1987).

[13]See Stephen Neil, *A Genuinely Human Existence* (London: Constable, 1959), ch. 6.

[14]Ibid., p. 159.

[15]Ibid., p. 149.

[16]Ibid., p. 150.

[17]Ibid., p. 149.

[18]Quoted in John Piper, *Desiring God* (Portland, OR: Multnomah; Leicester: IVP, 1986), p. 203.

[19]Hugh T. Kerr and John M. Mulder, eds., *Conversions* (Grand Rapids, MI: Wm. B. Eerdmans, 1983), p. 182.

7 The Leader as Strong One
[1]Tony Campolo, *The Power Delusion* (Wheaton, IL: Victor Books, 1983), p. 159.

[2]Stephen Neill, *A Genuinely Human Existence* (London: Constable, 1959), p. 50. Bishop Neill's book is a remarkable and penetrating attempt to describe a Christian psychology, "a genuinely human existence" as the title puts it, in the light of Jesus and faith. I am indebted to his stimulating observations and insights into the character of Jesus.

[3]Virginia Woolf, *Three Guineas* (San Diego, CA: Harcourt Brace Jovanovich, 1963), p. 72.

[4]Neill, *A Genuinely Human Existence,* p. 51.

⁵Ibid., p. 56.

⁶Ibid., p. 66.

⁷Ibid., p. 59.

⁸Robert Coles, *Harvard Diary: Reflections on the Sacred and the Secular* (New York: Crossroad, 1988), pp. 17-18.

8 The Leader as Servant

¹Thomas McCann, *An American Company: The Tragedy of United Fruit* (New York: Crown Publishers, 1976), pp. 125-27.

²John W. Gardner, *Leadership and Power,* Leadership Papers 4 (Washington, DC: Leadership Studies Program, Independent Sector, 1986), p. 3.

³Hedrick Smith, *The Power Game: How Washington Works* (New York: Random House, 1988), p. 42.

⁴Richard Foster, *Money, Sex and Power* (San Francisco: Harper & Row; London: Hodder & Stoughton, 1985), pp. 178.

⁵Quoted in "I Made Mistakes," interview with Richard Dortch, *Christianity Today,* 18 March 1988, pp. 46-47.

⁶Foster, *Money, Sex and Power,* pp. 205-6.

⁷John R. W. Stott, *The Cross of Christ* (Downers Grove, IL/Leicester: InterVarsity Press, 1986), p. 67.

⁸*A Chance to Die* is the title of the American edition of Elisabeth Elliott's biography of Amy Carmichael (Old Tappan, NJ: Fleming H. Revell, 1987), published in Great Britain as *Amy Carmichael: Her Life, Her Legacy* (Eastbourne: Kingsway, 1988).

9 The Leader as Shepherd-Maker (1)

¹Peter Drucker, *Managing in Turbulent Times* (New York: Harper & Row, 1980).

²Warren Benniss and Burt Nanus, *Leaders: The Strategies for Taking Charge* (New York: Harper & Row, 1986), pp. 224-25.

³Klaus Bockmuehl, *Living by the Gospel* (Colorado Springs: Helmers & Howard, 1986).

11 The Leader as Shepherd-Maker (3)

¹Warren Benniss and Burt Nanus, *Leaders: The Strategies for Taking Charge* (New York: Harper & Row, 1986), p. 80.

²Dietrich Bonhoeffer, *Life Together* (New York: Harper & Row; London: SCM Press, 1954).

³John White, *Excellence in Leadership: The Pattern of Nehemiah* (Downers Grove, IL/Leicester: InterVarsity Press, 1986).

⁴Benniss and Nanus, *Leaders,* pp. 66-67.

⁵Quoted in John W. Gardner, *The Tasks of Leadership,* Leadership Papers 2 (Washington, DC: Leadership Studies Program, Independent Sector, 1986), p. 14.

⁶R. A. Cole, *The Gospel According to Mark,* Tyndale New Testament Commentaries (Grand Rapids, MI: Eerdmans; Leicester: InterVarsity Press, 1961), p. 78.

[7]Ajith Fernando, notes from an unpublished talk.

[8]Hugh Nibley, *Executive Exellence,* December 1987, p. 9.

[9]James MacGregor Burns, quoted in Benniss and Nanus, *Leaders,* p. 205.

[10]Benniss and Nanus, *Leaders,* p. 188.

[11]Ibid., p. 71.

[12]Ibid., p. 76.

[13]Gardner, *The Tasks of Leadership,* p. 10.

[14]John W. Gardner, *The Task of Motivating,* Leadership Papers 9 (Washington, DC: Leadership Studies Program, Independent Sector, 1988), p. 7.

[15]Benniss and Nanus, *Leaders,* p. 193.

[16]Peter Drucker, *Managing in Turbulent Times* (New York: Harper & Row, 1980).

[17]Warren Benniss, "Leadership Transforms Vision into Action," *Industry Week,* 31 May 1982, p. 56.

12 The Leader as Spokesperson

[1]Joseph Sobran, *The Charlotte Observer,* 18 May 1989 (syndicated column).

[2]*Campaign: The Primetime President,* copyright 1988, a coproduction of WETA and Public Affairs Television Inc., New York. Quotations taken from program transcript, pp. 3, 13-14, 22.

[3]Aristotle, *The Rhetoric,* trans. Hugh Lawson-Tancred (London: Penguin Books, 1990).

[4]Russell F. Weigley, "New York," *New York Times Book Review,* 20 December 1987, p.11.

[5]Quoted in Eugene H. Peterson, *A Long Obedience in the Same Direction* (Downers Grove, IL: InterVarsity Press, 1980), p. 143.

[6]Ralph Lewis, *Inductive Preaching* (Westchester, IL: Crossway Books, 1983), p. 74.

[7]Ibid., pp. 74-75.

[8]M. Scott Peck, *People of the Lie: The Hope for Healing Human Evil* (New York: Touchstone/Simon & Schuster, 1983).

[9]Lloyd John Ogilvie, *Loved and Forgiven* (Glendale, CA: Gospel Light Publications, 1977), pp. 57.

13 The Leader as Struggler

[1]John W. Gardner, *The Tasks of Leadership,* Leadership Papers 2 (Washington, DC: Leadership Studies Program, Independent Sector, 1986), p. 16.

[2]Gustav Aulen, quoted in Sherwood Wirt and Kersten Beckstrom, eds., *Living Quotations for Christians* (New York: Harper & Row, 1974), p. 39.

[3]Gardner, *The Tasks of Leadership,* p. 12.

[4]Garth Lean, *On the Tail of a Comet* (Colorado Springs: Helmars & Howard, 1988), p. 271.

[5]David Augsburger, *Caring Enough to Confront* (Glendale, CA: Regal Books, 1983), pp. 18-19.

[6]David McKenna, *Power to Follow, Grace to Lead* (Dallas, TX: Word, 1989), p. 134.

[7]Ibid., p. 130.

[8]Viktor E. Frankl, _Man's Search for Meaning_ (New York: Simon & Schuster, 1959), esp. pp. 74-75.

[9]William Barclay, _A New Testament Wordbook_ (London: SCM Press, 1955), p. 61.

[10]Eusebius, quoted in Ruth A. Tucker and Walter L. Liefeld, eds., _Daughters of the Church: Women and Ministry from New Testament Times to the Present_ (Grand Rapids, MI: Zondervan, 1987), p. 94.

[11]Stephen Neill, _A Genuinely Human Existence_ (London: Constable, 1959), p. 145.

[12]Ibid., ch. 6, esp. pp. 144-50.

[13]John R. W. Stott has discussed these and other controversies at some length in _Christ the Controversialist_ (Leicester: IVP, 1970).

[14]Bernard M. Bass, _Leadership and Performance beyond Expectations_ (New York: The Free Press, 1985), p. 4.

[15]McKenna, _Power to Follow, Grace to Lead,_ pp. 135.

[16]Ibid., p. 136.

[17]J. Wallace Hamilton, quoted in Wirt and Beckstrom, eds., _Living Quotations for Christians,_ p. 40.

14 The Leader as Sustainer

[1]This parable is not original to me. It is from an unknown author.

[2]Eugene Jennings.

[3]Timothy McCoy, in personal conversation. McCoy's doctoral research was on Spurgeon.

[4]Max DePree, _Leadership Is an Art_ (New York: Doubleday, 1989), pp. 98-99.

[5]John W, Gardner, _Renewing: The Leader's Creative Task,_ Leadership Papers 10 (Washington, DC: Leadership Studies Program, Independent Sector, 1987), p. 4.

[6]Robert H. Waterman, Jr., "The Renewal Factor,'" _Business Week_ 14 September 1987, p. 104.

[7]Benniss and Nanus, _Leaders: The Strategies for Taking Charge,_ pp. 69ff.

[8]DePree, _Leadership Is an Art,_ pp. 102-3.

[9]John W. Gardner, _The Tasks of Leadership,_ Leadership Papers 2 (Washington, DC: Leadership Studies Program, Independent Sector, 1986), p. 10.

[10]Michael Korda, _Power: How to Get It, How to Use It_ (New York: Ballantine Books, 1975), p. 219.

[11]John R. W. Stott, _The Cross of Christ_ (Downers Grove, IL/Leicester: 1986), p. 21.

[12]Kenneth Blanchard, _Leadership and the One Minute Manager._

[13]Waterman, "The Renewal Factor," p. 112.

[14]Gardner, _The Tasks of Leadership,_ pp. 10, 13.

[15]Ibid.

[16]See Paul Brand and Philip Yancey, _Fearfully and Wonderfully Made_ (Grand Rapids, MI: Zondervan, 1980), ch. 5.

Index of Names